The
Forgotten
Revolution

WHEN HISTORY FORGETS

Revisiting Critical Places of the
American Revolution
That Have Been Neglected
by History

Robert A. Mayers

HERITAGE BOOKS
2014

HERITAGE BOOKS

AN IMPRINT OF HERITAGE BOOKS, INC.

Books, CDs, and more—Worldwide

For our listing of thousands of titles see our website
at
www.HeritageBooks.com

Published 2014 by
HERITAGE BOOKS, INC.
Publishing Division
5810 Ruatan Street
Berwyn Heights, Md. 20740

International Standard Book Numbers
Paperbound: 978-0-7884-5559-9
Clothbound: 978-0-7884-9017-0

Dedicated to "My Witnesses"-- The local historians I met
in these fascinating places.

I salute their eagerness to share treasured and often previously uncovered
details, their reverence for these cherished sites and their passion to preserve
these locations for future generations. These are the people that keep the spirit
of the American Revolution alive.

Acknowledgements

At each of these fascinating places I sought out "witnesses," local historians with special knowledge. They were staff at national and state parks, reenactors, archeologists, members of historical societies, private owners who live on the land and descendants of original settlers whose ancestors are buried in local cemeteries. These caretakers of local history provided special insights and information that cannot be found in recorded history. They were eager to share treasured and often previously uncovered details and showed a reverence for these cherished places as well as a passion to preserve these locations for future generations. I want to publicly thank all of these individuals for their time and contributions to my appreciation and understanding of these important sites, and I salute their relentless dedication to carrying the torch of knowledge about our past.

At The Short Hills:

Walter R. Stockel, President, Metuchen-Edison Historic Society

George W. Stillman, Local Historian

Byron Miller, Historian, Plainfield Country Club

At Pompton and the Preakness Valley:

Paul Doll, Regional Historian and Reenactor

At Fort St. Johns:

Eric Ruel, Curator, Musee du Fort Saint-Jean

At Cooch's Bridge:

Wade P. Catts, Military Historian, Archeologist, Associate Director,

Milner Associates

At Head of Elk:

Mike Dixon, President, Cecil County, Delaware Historical Society

At Monmouth Courthouse:

Gary Stone, Senior Historic Preservationist, State of New Jersey

James Raleigh, President, Friends of Monmouth Battlefield

Thomas J. Hofmann, Park Ranger, Historian, Sandy Hook

At Newtown:

Rosamund Piatt, Proprietor, "The Outpost General Store"

Gary Ratchford, Metal Detector Expert

At Fishkill Supply Depot:

Lance Ashworth, President, Friends of Fishkill Supply Depot

Marty Byster, Trustee, Fishkill Historic Society

At Jockey Hollow:

Eric Olsen, Park Ranger, Historian, National Park Service

At The New Windsor Cantonment:

Michael McCready, Staff Director

Michael Diaz, Site Historian

At Fort Montgomery:

Grant E. Miller, Historic Site Manager

Richard McGuinness, Historian 5th New York Regiment – Reenactors

Contents

CHAPTER ONE

Fifty Days at Fort St. Johns-The War's Longest Siege
1775 Richelieu River, Quebec, Canada

CHAPTER TWO

Forgotten Fishkill- Military Nerve Center of the Continental Army
1776-1783 Fishkill, New York

CHAPTER THREE

*Head of Elk to Cooch's Bridge- Springboard to Victory for Redcoats and Rebels
1776-1781 Elkton, Maryland to Glasgow, Delaware.*

CHAPTER FOUR

*Where the War Almost Ended- The Battle of the Short Hills 1777
Central New Jersey*

CHAPTER FIVE
The Twin Forts, Montgomery and Clinton- Tragedy to Triumph 1777
Fort Montgomery, New York

CHAPTER SIX
An Unknown Dark Side of a Cruel Winter of 1779-1780
Jockey Hollow, Morristown, New Jersey

CHAPTER SEVEN
Lost Opportunities on the Highway to Hell- Monmouth Courthouse-1778
Freehold, New Jersey

CHAPTER EIGHT

The Last Stand of the Iroquois Nations - 1779
Newtown, New York

CHAPTER NINE

Cruel Mutinies but a Kind Winter. 1780 - 1783
Pompton and the Preakness Valley, New Jersey

CHAPTER TEN

The Last Cantonment- Forgotten Huts and Bad Memories. 1781-1783,
New Windsor, New York

APPENDICES

Introduction

Battlefields, encampments and sites of many critical events of the Revolutionary War have been lost or neglected by history. Places where patriots fought and died are unmarked, shrouded in mystery, distorted by mythology and unknown even to local people. After more than two centuries some of these sites have entirely disappeared while others have languished unnoticed. Some are on private property or have been built over by towns and highways.

Man made changes to terrain have been enormous since the time of the Revolution. The only way many places can be recognized is by historical markers. Fortunately, a few sites are in pristine condition and have been elevated to State or National Park status after being ignored for hundreds of years. My objective is to revive these forsaken locations with fresh research from original military records and onsite visits.

This quest took many unexpected turns. Analysis of obscure sources overlooked by earlier writers yielded many surprises and unknown details were revealed at well known sites. I often made detours outside of known boundaries and textbook timelines and found that myths were often created when the winner wrote the history. Familiar stories recounted about America's struggle for independence had other versions. Little known British, Hessian and Loyalist accounts often revealed more accurate details than those that we have traditionally accepted as authentic. Defeats received less acclaim regardless of the bloodshed and valor displayed. The pivotal battle at Fort Montgomery, New York and the hard winter at Jockey Hollow, Morristown, New Jersey were both overlooked for centuries because they evoked only painful memories.

At each place I sought out "witnesses," people with special local knowledge. They were staff at national and state parks, regimental re-enactors, members of historical societies, private owners who live on the land and descendants of original settlers whose ancestors are buried in local cemeteries. All have become caretakers of local history. They provided special insights and information that cannot be found in recorded history.

This book has been written so that it may be enjoyed by average readers and not just hard core fans of the era. Why were these places selected from among the many significant events in a war that lasted eight years and covered the original thirteen states and parts of Canada?

While researching for my biography of a revolutionary war soldier, *The War Man, The True Story of a Citizen —Soldier who Fought from Quebec to Yorktown*, I examined the details of the life of a real soldier whose army service in the Continental Army spanned the entire war. During this time he marched thousands of miles and was present at many of the most crucial and pivotal events of the conflict. While following in his footsteps many these forsaken places were revealed.

These locations extend from Canada to Virginia. Living in New Jersey, truly the crossroads of the American Revolution, I am geographically predisposed to many of them. Some are within 100 miles of my home or in nearby towns on ground that I have traversed all my life. I limited my selection to key events that could have changed the course of the war but the countless other fascinating and curious actions that occurred during the conflict were a tempting distraction. The chosen sites are viewed against an immense historical background. I have included only enough macro-history of the war to provide the context for each occurrence.

Some winter campgrounds of the war such as Jockey Hollow, New Windsor, New York and Valley Forge are better known to many people than battle grounds. The Continental army was modeled after European armies and for most of the eight years of the war, except for a few times, was immobilized from December to June. Nations were reluctant to finance armies that could wither from exposure and disease during the winter. The Patriots learned that Campaigns in the cold of winter were risky when they were tragically defeated trying to invade Canada early in the war. Vital transportation links such as Kings Ferry, New York or Head of Elk, (Elkton) Maryland are also included.

Geography was the pervading element that determined the location of all these places. Natural defenses were provided by mountains and waterways. Hills, rivers, cities, forests, and coastlines influenced troop movements, battle sites, supply routes and the flow of action during the entire war.

Reflecting on my own experiences, and those of many other veterans whom I have talked to over the years, I conclude that action during any war must have appeared much different to the participants at the time. The average soldier or small unit had little understanding of the overall campaign strategy, tactics or even why they are there. Reviewing the few extant accounts of common soldiers in the

Revolutionary War it appears that men of that era were no different. Dotted lines on campaign maps and historic accounts while adding to hindsight do little to reveal the frenzy, chaos and rush of adrenaline endured during the sting of battle.

Reviving these events, visiting them and relying on original documents provided an opportunity to view them through the eyes of those who took part. It creates a profound respect and empathy for the tenacity and stamina of the average soldier of the Continental Army. Many of these men endured for as long as the conflict lasted. These "War Men," serving because of zealous patriotism or vague enlistment terms, bravely accepted their fate and bonded together to achieve the final victory at Yorktown.

Muster Rolls, Orderly Books, other military records, diaries of officers and the few journals left by enlisted soldiers allow us to follow events often on a day to day or hour by hour basis. But no amount of archival research compares with actually visiting these places and visualizing how the appeared over two hundred years ago.

The American Revolution was an old war. It was a war fought with inaccurate muzzle loaded flintlock muskets and smooth bore cannons that were manhandled from place to place. The bayonet, the assault rifle of the time, was a more deadly weapon than the musket. Ineffective volley firing from lines of men responding to drum commands, standing as close as thirty yards apart, was a standard tactic but often was just the prelude to the bayonet charge. Senior officers personally led men in close combat.

When overcome, the entire Continental Army could disappear into the vast countryside and appear reinvigorated at a more advantageous time. It was a racially integrated army, not seen again until World War II. Threatening the enemy with a large army was often more effective than a battle itself. Soldiers marched thousands of miles and starved and froze in a bountiful country which failed to sustain them.

Not until this work was almost completed did I realize that I had followed the model of writer and historian Benson J. Lossing. He traveled to hundreds of the major historic sites in the early 1850s. It was only seventy years after the war but many had already been forgotten. His ambitious work is entitled *A Pictorial Field Book of the American Revolution.* He covered 8,000 miles to interview older people who remembered the war and created wood engravings of people, places and objects he found along the way. We visited the same places and it is interesting to compare our reactions and view the changes since then. He had the opportunity to speak to eyewitnesses and artistic talent to skillfully illustrate his work. I respect the many difficulties that he faced during his three year journey. He is often in my thoughts as I navigate superhighways with a digital camera. Sadly, his once popular classic has now been largely forgotten.

I hope this study provides as much thrill and comprehension of these places as I received from my research and seeing them as they are today. It was an enchanting experience to stand on a hill on unmarked private property in Newtown, New York, where a fierce battle raged in 1779. The place looked exactly as it did then. I rediscovered abandoned hut foundations at New Windsor, New York and walked the golf course of a posh country club in Plainfield, New Jersey where outnumbered Patriots held fast in 1777. The cruel wind stung my face on a winter day in deep snow at Jockey Hollow. Grasping a Brown Bess Musket and discovering documents that had not been read in hundreds of years made those intrepid soldiers come alive.

I often meet with many diverse groups having a common interest in the Revolutionary era. They are historically minded people who explore, discuss and share knowledge of this critical period. I am amazed that they are enthralled by my stories. Now, enthusiastic fans of history of this time, they regret that during their school days they tuned out history as distant and dull.

I hope that the description of these neglected sites will save the reader from traveling to each of these places or allow selective personal journeys to those found to be the most interesting.

> Robert A. Mayers
> Watchung, New Jersey

Chapter One

Fifty Days at Fort St. Johns -
The War's Longest Siege -1775

Richelieu River, Quebec, Canada

Our 14th Colony- Canada

1775 was a glorious year for the America. It was the year that a loose confederation of colonies, angered over the misguided and aggressive parliamentary actions of their mother country, turned fury and resentment into organized resistance. Thousands of Americans, mostly farm families, challenged Great Britain, the world's greatest superpower, to grant them independence. This bold approach, even before the colonies had officially become a nation, was sparked by a fortuitous chain of early military successes. These events provided enough hard evidence early in the year to convince a hesitant Continental Congress that independence could realistically be achieved.

In April, at Lexington and Concord, outnumbered citizen soldiers armed with their hunting muskets intercepted 1,700 seasoned British regulars. The courageous farmers drove them off and harassed the redcoat army with heavy gunfire as they retreated and fled 15 miles back to Boston. The British Army was the best fighting force in the world at that time.

In May, Fort Ticonderoga was the first American victory. A ragtag band of Green Mountain Boys surprised a sleeping garrison and captured the mightiest bastion on the critical waterway that stretched from New York to Canada. The victors then seized the fort's cannons and dragged them to Boston where they could be trained down on British ships from Dorchester Heights. Ticonderoga could serve as the staging area for an invasion of Canada.

The Battle of Bunker Hill in June 1775 was a Patriot loss but a pyrrhic victory for the hardened British army that took appalling losses by charging the American lines with undisciplined frontal assaults. A reluctant Virginia plantation owner, appointed Commander –in –chief of the armed forces, arrived in Boston two weeks after the battle

The increasing presence of Continental soldiers surrounding the British forces in Boston portended a British evacuation from the area where the captured cannon from Fort Ticonderoga could splinter any British ship in the harbor. The colonies reveled in these successes of its citizen soldiers.

Sir Guy Carleton the senior commander of British forces in North America was stationed in Quebec Canada. He was a brilliant general but made the mistake of sending many of his troops to Boston. Only two untested regiments were left in all of Canada. These regulars were joined by a unit of Royal Highlanders, Canadians of Scotch descent, and a few hundred Canadian volunteers. The total strength of British forces in Canada was estimated to be only 1,000 men. These forces were split between Quebec City and St Johns, a well armed fortress 20 miles south of Montreal.[1]

Other factors indicated that Canada was a realistic objective and could be in American hands by the end of the year. American troop strength was high from the wave of enlistments created by the patriotic fervor that was sweeping the colonies. There was no evidence that any reinforcements were on the way from England and several months of good weather lay ahead.

These propitious circumstances led the Continental Congress to boldly decide to take the initiative. The Americans decided to strike where the British were the most vulnerable-Canada. While the colonies were disorganized and unprepared with a fragmented army all conditions appeared to be perfect for embarking on this first major offensive of the war and adding Canada as the fourteenth colony. This invasion north would require trudging hundreds of miles through wilderness and getting past the fortress of St Johns a few miles south of Montreal. This vast country could be American land simply by taking the city of Quebec, Canada's lightly defended capital.

Timing was critical to the success of the invasion for two reasons. Quebec City had to be taken before the hard Canadian winter set in and fighting conditions became impossible. The American Army would be decimated in December by expiring enlistments. Most soldiers had joined up with the understanding that they would serve only until the end of the year. They would simply leave the field and return home at that time.

An invasion of Canada would accomplish many vital objectives that were necessary to win the war. Most importantly it would allow the American side to control the vital waterway which that divided the colonies. A 300 mile water highway ran all the way from New York City to Quebec. Starting with the Hudson River it flowed north through Lake George, Lake Champlain and the Richelieu River to join the St Lawrence River at Montreal. It then continued 150 miles northeast to Quebec City. British remained in control of this passage they would split New England from the rest of the colonies and win the war. Much of the strategy over the next eight years of the war would revolve around control of the corridor.

American leaders also believed that the 8,000 French settlers in Canada might be eager to join with them to escape from British tyranny. The French had been conquered only a few years before in the French and Indian War that ended in 1763. The people of Canada still considered France to be their mother country. Americans could offer them the opportunity to become part of a free society and restore their right to self government. The French should be eager to join the cause of freedom and rise up against their English conquerors.

Parliament enacted the Quebec Act in 1774. It placed all lands west of the Appalachians under Canada and at the same time granted official recognition of the Catholic Church and French civil law in the country. Patriot leaders and Protestants of all denominations in the colonies were alarmed and considered the law a direct threat to their philosophy of political and religious freedom. An expedition into Canada could rid them of two oppressive forces, the King of England and the Pope. These authoritarian powers that restricted the freedom of people to live and worship as they choose could be thwarted. [2]

John Adams appealed to Congress on June 7, 1775, "Whether we should march into Canada with an army sufficient to beat the power of the British, to overawe the Indians and to protect the French has been a great question. It seems to be the general conclusion that it is best to go. If we can be assured that the Canadians will be pleased with it, and join us." It was essential that the offensive be conducted diplomatically so as not to alienate the French Canadians.

Major General Philip Schuyler of New York was appointed senior commander of the mission. He was in poor health and lacked combat experience but was skillful in handling supply and support issues. Brigadier General Richard Montgomery was second in command. The charismatic Montgomery, age 39, was a vigorous and fearless field officer with combat experience gained during the French and

Indian war. These engagements took place in the same areas that he would pass through on the way to Canada. The combined talents of the two generals provided the perfect balance for the campaign leadership. By July a force of 3,000 scattered troops were available in Connecticut, Massachusetts and New York.

Campaign plans called for a two pronged attack. Schuyler and Montgomery would follow the waterway to Canada. From the staging center at Fort Ticonderoga bateaux sailing up the chain of lakes would carry troops and supplies 90 miles north to Canada.

A second prong of 1,000 men under Colonel Benedict Arnold, one of America's most brilliant young officers at the time, would move from New England up the Kennebec River through Maine. This daunting 250 mile trek through bogs and swamps would bring them to the St. Lawrence to join Montgomery's force at Quebec.

Great Britain had a major presence in the colonies in the spring of 1775 as these plans were being made. The Redcoat Army occupied New York City when Washington the newly appointed Commander-in Chief passed through the city traveling from Philadelphia to Boston to assume command. American delegation was justifiably apprehensive. There were British warships in the harbor and the streets were teeming with redcoat troops and militant Loyalists. Adding to the concern was that the royal governor, William Tyron, was returning from a trip to England on the same day. Protocol required welcoming receptions for both officials. The perplexed New York Congress, not having enough confidence to challenge the royal governor and wanting to avoid a serious incident, craftily arranged to receive the officials at events three blocks apart.

To prepare for the invasion the Continental Congress and state legislatures were appointing generals and other high ranking officers to staff the new Army. Determining seniority in the military was an issue of tremendous importance. Command position, advancement and pay all were decided by seniority.

The commissioning process was plagued by political maneuvering. Choices were often based on popularity, wealth and nepotism rather than superior leadership qualities and combat experience. Landed gentry usually became senior officers and those of the upwardly mobile merchant class were assigned to lower officer ranks. Sons of Liberty, the militant leaders of the insurgent patriots also became lower level officers. Their commissions were rewards for their zeal but they often became confrontational and challenged their senior officers. The common soldiers followed their example and the American Army would develop into an egalitarian legion that was unknown in the warfare of the time.[3]

Most of the troops were illiterate young men from the lowest economic classes. Two types of common soldiers made up the raw Canadian expeditionary force. There were those who were imbued with an intense spirit of patriotism and the fight for independence. Others joined the military to improve the quality of their lives. A new uniform and the promise of a regular income was often their incentive. Most had never been beyond the next village and sought adventure to replace the drudgery of farm labor. Enlistment times were short, typically until the end of the year, so joining the army was not viewed as a long term commitment. Military leaders hoped that their lack of training and military experience and would be outweighed by toughness, bravery and patriotism.

The first allegiance of both the officers and men heading for Canada was to their home colony. Most had a hostile attitude toward men from other areas. Connecticut troops regarded the Yorkers as wicked and irreverent. The New York men detested the devout and pious new Englanders. These soldiers, loosely disciplined and untrained had never served together. They were suspicious of strangers, their own officers and each other. Entire units were reluctant to take orders from officers who were not from their home province. This pervading distrust at all level was a formidable challenge for senior officers attempting to lead this diverse and disorderly rabble.

Most of the farm boys heading north were new recruits and lacked even rudimentary training. The 10th Company of the 3rd New York Regiment of Foot was typical infantry unit. The 73 recruits in the unit Commanded by Captain Robert Johnson came from the farm villages around Haverstraw, New York, in what today is Rockland County.[4]

Their training consisted of about two weeks of drilling on the town green. They did not have uniforms. Most did not have weapons. Those that did had brought their muskets from home or carried the few that were donated by civilians in the area Most were in their early 20s. Six were teenagers and the youngest was 10 years old. Most were farm laborers but about a third had trades or skills. Twelve were born in England Ireland and Germany.

Frantic calls for troops began coming from Schuyler and Montgomery at Fort Ticonderoga despite the army being fragmented, poorly equipped and without financial resources. In June Schuyler wrote "the troops are to be forwarded to Ticonderoga as fast as they arrive or as soon as those under your immediate command can be furnished with such articles as are absolutely necessary for them to take the field. The New York Provincial Congress replied. "Our troops can be of no services to you. They have no clothes, blankets or ammunition."

The men the 10ᵗʰ Company who had been in the army less than a month were ordered to move north on a 200 mile forced march to reach Ticonderoga. It was still another 100 miles from there to the Canadian border. Some supplies began to trickle in along the way on the first leg of the trip was to Albany but the men soon became sullen and homesick. They had been suddenly thrust into military life and were not accustomed to regimentation and discipline. Nights were spent in open camps and they were constantly prodded to move faster. Food became scarce and the new soldiers began raiding farms at night to supplement their meager rations.

By the time the 2nd Company had reached Ticonderoga on September 26, a third of its men had left to return home after only a few weeks in the army. Some of the deserters were simply insubordinate. For others it was the fall harvest season at home and the survival of their families over the winter depended on bringing in the crops.[5]

In July, the untried American forces began gathering at Fort Ticonderoga The invasion force was made up of Connecticut , Massachusetts and New York brigades, Rangers from New Hampshire and Green Mountain boys from Vermont. Artillery support was provided by Mott's Connecticut gunners and Lamb's New York Company.

Onward to St. Johns

Desertions had thinned out the ranks of the regiments arriving at Fort Ticonderoga in August 1775. Many of the new arrivals were sick. They came with light clothing that would not serve well as the colder weather approached. The scene at the fort was chaotic. The hastily cobbled together mob of new recruits was a challenge for inept officers to organize. The Connecticut volunteers were especially rebellious and insubordinate. Men disappeared into the night. When General Schuyler took command at the fort he immediately wrote to General Washington, *"You would expect that I would say something of this place and the troops here. Not one earthly thing for the offence or the defense has been done. This fort could be captured with a penknife!"*[6]

In the midst of all the turmoil the soldiers began an ambitious boat-building program. Bateaux would be used to carry most of the assault force northward down Lake Champlain. (Note Champlain actually flows north) These boats were about 30 feet long. Paddled by an eight man crew they could carry seven tons of supplies. When completed there would be a flotilla large enough to carry most of the assault force of 2,000 men the 120 miles to the objective, Fort St. Johns.

Informants to Sir Guy Tarleton, who was both Royal Governor and Commander of the British forces in Quebec, reported to him that American invasion preparations were underway. With fewer than 1,000 men he would have to go on the defensive. He moved to Montreal with all of his forces to be closer to the anticipated invasion route. Carleton had to confront the enemy before they could cross the Canadian border to threaten the key cities of Montreal and Quebec. He decided to make the stand at his strongest bastion, Fort St. Johns, 12 miles southeast of Montreal. The fort was at the entrance to the Richelieu River that flowed 50 miles north into the St. Lawrence River.

Fort St. Johns was an obstacle that would be difficult for the Americans to overcome. The fort had a heavy battery of 42 cannons and was well supplied with ammunition. Warships stationed there could sail out to intercept the invaders on Lake Champlain. Fort Chambly a few miles away could serve as a supply base.[7]

As the offensive began the unprepared American Army lacked inspiration but continued to be inspired by the confidence and professionalism shown by the dashing Montgomery. Schuyler's health had deteriorated and he began delegating command of the campaign to Montgomery. This was a fortunate combination of talents. Montgomery was a seasoned combat officer while Schuyler's military background was better suited for planning logistic support from behind the front lines. The two men had a good personal relationship and worked well together.

In mid- August the British were completing two gunboats at Fort St Johns. These vessels could gain control of the entrance to the Richelieu River and block the invasion. Montgomery decided he had to strike immediately. Troops massed for the invasion and reacted grudgingly to this sudden deployment.[8]

When the 10th Company left Fort Ticonderoga desertions had reduced the number of soldiers from 73 in June to 36 men. Men were staying on only because their enlistments were expiring. In a matter of weeks they would be heading home.[9]

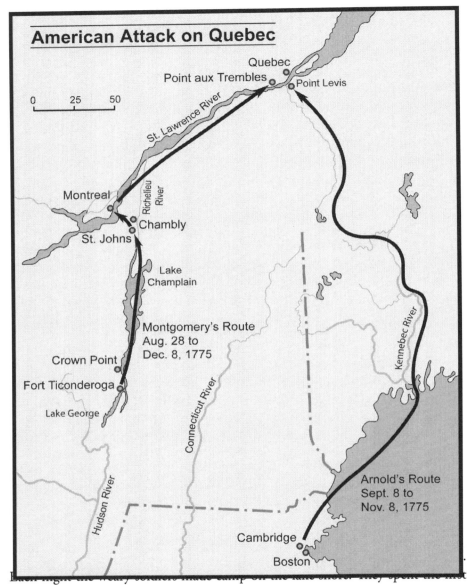

American Attack on Quebec

Quebec
Point aux Trembles
Point Levis
St. Lawrence River
0 25 50
Montreal
Richelieu River
Chambly
St. Johns
Lake Champlain
Montgomery's Route
Aug. 28 to
Dec. 8, 1775
Crown Point
Kennebec River
Fort Ticonderoga
Lake George
Connecticut River
Arnold's Route
Sept. 8 to
Nov. 8, 1775
Hudson River
Cambridge
Boston

night on Canadian soil at Isle aux Noix, a swampy island at the entrance to the Richelieu River at the northern end of Lake Champlain This place would serve as a base to launch an attack on Fort St. Johns, 12 miles down river.

Schuyler sent a proclamation from here to the French Canadian people in a desperate attempt to gain their support. It was delivered by a Canadian merchant who was an American sympathizer and in a position to disseminate the message and ensure that it reached the people of Montreal. Schuyler announced that he had been directed by America's Congress at Philadelphia to drive out the British conquerors enslaving them and he pledged to "cherish every Canadian" and to protect their property during the campaign.

American forces made their first attack on Fort St Johns the next day, September 6, 1775. Since Montgomery lacked fire power this thrust was a test of the fort's defenses. The reconnaissance in force of 1,000 men was led by two Connecticut officers, Major Thomas Hobby and Captain Matthew Mead.[10] The attackers landed in a swamp and moved up to within a half mile of the fort where they came within range of the fort's cannons. Enemy gunfire was inaccurate and the attackers continued to beat their way through the marsh and thick foliage that stretched all the way to the fort.

A hundred Indians led by a British officer ambushed an advanced party of the Americans in the thick woods. The Patriots took cover in the undergrowth and returned the gunfire. The skirmish lasted about half an hour with both sides losing about eight men. This was the first blood shed in the siege of Fort St. Johns. The Indians were driven off and retreated back behind the walls of the fort. Difficult terrain and darkness made it impossible for Montgomery to assess the size of the enemy force. He decided not to risk a further advance and fell back a mile to move out of the range of the fort's guns.

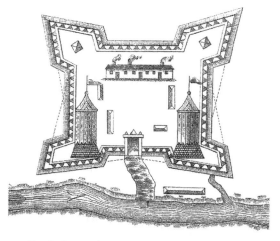

Fort St. Jean on the Richelieu River during the 1750s

This futile attack proved that the fort was well defended and that the French Canadians would not rise up suddenly to come to the assistance of the Americans. A 16 gun warship moored at the fort was ready to block any amphibious advance posed another threat.[11] Schuyler and Montgomery reviewed their strategy and decided that until the arrival of more artillery their force was too weak to sustain an assault on the fort.

The reconnaissance force pulled back to their base at Isle aux Noix where they fortified the island and built a boom across the river to prevent the enemy gunboats from entering the lake. As Schuyler's health deteriorated to the point that he was bedridden he must have reflected that there is no victory in defense. He wrote to Washington and the Continental Congress that he was officially turning over the command of the Canadian campaign to Montgomery and was sent back to Fort Ticonderoga in a covered boat.[12]

British Colonel Charles Preston was in command at Fort St. Johns. He was a capable and determined field officer and relied on the promise that Carleton would soon arrive with reinforcements.[13] Outnumbered by the Americans he had many artillery pieces and an open field of fire. From his strong defensive position behind the fort's walls he could inflict great losses on any attempted frontal infantry charges. Montgomery recognized this problem immediately. His raw, poorly disciplined troops would be slaughtered if they tried to storm the fort.

Over the next week conditions improved and the tide seemed to turn for the Americans. There was evidence that a large number of Canadians were ready to join them and reinforcements arrived. One hundred and seventy Green Mountain Boys appeared with another Connecticut company. Colonel James Easton arrived with a Massachusetts Regiment of 200 men. Two New York Regiments added another 425 troops. Even more significant was the arrival of Captain Lamb's capable artillery force from New York. The expeditionary force now on Isle aux Noix had increased to 1,700 men and had added seven more cannons and mortars.

The energized Patriots again headed back to Fort St. Johns on the morning of September 10, 1775 and landed three miles south of the bastion. Lieutenant Colonel Ritzema of New York was dispatched to attempt to encircle the fort.[14] Unfortunately, two of his columns met by accident in the thick woods as his regiment beat their way through the swamp. The tense soldiers, mistaking their own troops for the enemy and fearing another Indian ambush, broke ranks and fled before any shots were fired. The outraged Montgomery met the men as they stampeded and managed to turn them around. They moved forward again but came under fire from a British boat in the river. The uneasy attackers then became so confused and disorganized that they rushed back to the landing place. The New York boys from Rockland County, Johnston's New York 10th Company, were caught in this unfortunate incident.

The next morning Montgomery called all his senior officers together to plan a third attack on Fort St. Johns. He found that many of them had lost confidence in their men after the humiliating events of the previous day and were unsure they would continue to follow their orders. The general was astonished when his commanders recommended taking a vote among the men to gain their approval for continuing the invasion.

A report then came in that the British Warship, which had been christened the "Royal Savage," was approaching their position. The New England troops panicked as this alarm spread through the camp. Without waiting for orders and without their officers they ran to their boats and fled down the river to the safety of their base at Isle aux Noix. Montgomery was aghast but had no choice but to order the rest of the men back to the island.

At Isle aux Noix discouraged Montgomery appointed a court-martial board to single out those who were guilty of the most outrageous and mutinous behavior. He found that few men were willing to testify against their fellow soldiers. After three days of recurring acquittals there was only a single conviction punishable by flogging. The offense was threatening an officer with a loaded musket.

The General was now in the unenviable position of having all American hopes for conquering Canada entirely in his hands. He tried to console himself. In a letter to his wife Jane he explained that he believed the shameful behavior of his men was caused by their youth and that they would improve with "a little practice."[15]

Although Isle aux Noix was in a perfect position to defend the approach to Lake Champlain, it was a swampy tidal flat. It was an unhealthy place for a large encampment of men sheltered in tents. Heavy rains along with a lack of food and sanitation caused malarial fevers, colds, rheumatism and dysentery.[16] The men grumbled through these cold rainy days with nothing to eat except flour and pork. After eight straight days of rain Montgomery described his men as " half drowned rats crawling thru a swamp"[17] Everyone in the American camp was constantly haunted by the constant threat of the bitter Canadian winter. The unassailable Fort St. Johns still blocked the invasion.

The British ranks at Fort St. Johns had been strengthened in past weeks. Aggressive recruiting had enlisted the company of Maclean's Scottish warriors from Nova Scotia and about 100 French Canadian volunteers. Men willing to sign up were offered a generous bounty that must have been hard to resist. It included 200 acres in an American colony of their choice plus 40 acres for a wife and each child. With these new volunteers and Carleton's regiments with the Royal Artillery, the garrison at Fort St. Johns now had 750 troops. Another force of 90 men was posted at the supply depot at Chambly, the weaker fort, a few miles north.

Major John Brown of the Massachusetts was sent by Montgomery with 130 men to test the defenses of the British supply depot at Fort Chambly. Along the way they were able to capture a supply train on its way to the Fort. Brown was then attacked by troops sent out of Fort St Johns. Montgomery's main force soon joined the fray and the enemy was driven back into the Fort. The General then sent other forces to Longueuil and La Prairie. These towns were on the St Lawrence River directly across from Montreal.

The main force of Americans surrounding Fort St. Johns prepared for the siege by digging trenches and mounting artillery. Two batteries, each mounting only two guns, were built about 100 yards east and south of the fort. These positions were under constant cannon fire. The superior firepower of the fort continued to hold back the Americans with their superior numbers from making a frontal assault. No advance was possible until heavier guns arrived from Fort Ticonderoga. The siege was becoming a stalemate. The ominous colder weather with freezing rain was already making life in the trenches more distressing.[18]

Montgomery was almost killed while standing on the top of an emplacement supervising construction of the defenses. A cannon ball came so close that it spun him around, tore off his jacket and knocked him to the ground. This incident served to add to his glory and convinced the men of his invincibility.

More troops and cannons began to arrive from Fort Ticonderoga and by September 16 the American invasion force reached 2,000. That day Montgomery desperately launched another offensive. This assault struck from both sea and land. A fleet of 14 small warships with a cannon and 350 troops would block the river if the Royal Savage moved south. A landing force of 1,100 men would go ashore near the fort at the now familiar landing place.

The Siege at Fort St. Johns

The guns of Fort St. Johns pinned down the Americans for the first two weeks of the siege. The armament of the fort outnumbered their artillery ten to one. They might succeed in surrounding the stronghold but they could not compel its defenders to come out and fight. Any attempt to storm the ramparts would cost too many lives. One could sense the chill of the approaching Canadian winter in the wind and time was against them.

The Patriots began erecting gun emplacements and Captain Lamb's artillery company arrived on September 21, 1775. To the delight of the men huddled in the trenches the artillery company brought a sorely needed, heavy 13 inch mortar. It was soon grimly christened the "Old Sow." It did not have the range to reach the walls of the fort.

General Richard Montgomery, an expert in siege warfare, decided that his batteries would be more effective if the cannons were shifted to the northwest. This position was only 400 yards away from the ramparts of the fort and on the same side of the river. This move would put the Americans in a wall of enemy gunfire and expose them to a land attack. The general knew that this was the only way that the siege would succeed. He decided it was worth the risk.

Unbelievably, his officers reported that the men threatened mass desertion if ordered to the new northwest emplacement. Montgomery was appalled when the officers agreed with their men and now he was confronted with an insurrection that could cause the entire Canadian campaign to dissolve. Even worse, it would set a terrible example for future Continental Army campaigns. He felt a sense of helplessness and reluctantly agreed to continue concentrating operations on the east side of the fort.

Montgomery lamented the cowardice shown by officers and men as well as the secularism among the officers from different colonies. As a former British Officer, he was accustomed to strict discipline and was astounded by the insubordination of the troops. Montgomery wrote in a letter to Robert Livingston, "The New England troops are the worst stuff imaginable. There is such an equality among them that the officers have no authority ....The privates are all generals, but not soldiers."[19]

While the enlisted men adored their general, the officer corps continued to be unruly. They persistently requested furloughs despite the fact that Canadian campaign was at a critical stage. An artillery captain deserted his forward position and falsely reported that he had been overrun by the enemy. Ethan Allen, a founder of the state of Vermont and renowned for his leadership in the capture of Fort Ticonderoga, was among the worst offenders. He had spent the years before the war fighting New York settlers encroaching on Vermont territory.

On September 24, Montgomery sent the free spirited Allen north with Major John Brown to recruit Canadians who might be sympathetic to the Patriot cause. They were successful in finding about 300 men who were willing to join them.

The impetuous Allen decided to lead a spontaneous attack on the city of Montreal instead of returning to Fort St. Johns. Montreal, the largest Canadian city with its 9,000 inhabitants had only 60 British soldiers to protect it. Most of Montreal's defending troops had been sent to aid the besieged Fort St. Johns. Allen could not resist this tempting prize and led an attack across the St. Lawrence River during the night.

The plan was for Major Brown to meet him with the rest of his men a mile from the city. Brown's men failed to appear the next morning. Commander Carleton managed to gather 250 Canadian militia troops in the city while Allen anxiously waited for his main force to join him. Surrounded, Allen's outnumbered company surrendered after a single volley was fired into them. Ethan Allen and 35 of his troops were taken prisoner. His reckless behavior was unfortunate for the American cause. The debacle caused many sympathetic Canadians to lose confidence in the expedition.

Montgomery wrote to Schuyler, "I have to lament Mr. Allen's impudence and ambition, which urged him to this affair single handed." Despised by his captors for his role in their loss of Fort Ticonderoga earlier in 1775. Allen was clapped in heavy irons and imprisoned on a warship and not released until a prisoner exchange in 1778.[20]

The Campaign then was bogged down, and each morning brought hard frost. General Washington had become increasingly apprehensive as October began. He suggested bypassing Fort St. Johns and moving on to capture the lightly defended City of Montreal. However, Montgomery, convinced him to take the fort. If Fort St John's were not overtaken Montgomery's Troops could be attacked from the rear and trapped between two British forces.

Eight days of incessant rain and a lack of supplies once again began to crush the morale of the American troops. They continued to recognize only the authority of the officers of their home colony and refused to accept the commands of the unified Continental Army. A Connecticut Regiment of 250 men simply refused to join the attack when ordered to the front lines. Angered by the promotion of a younger, less senior officer, General David Wooster encouraged his men to disobey orders.[21]

Newly recruited Canadians from the surrounding area advised General Montgomery that Fort Chambly, the supply base north of St. Johns, might be easy to capture. Here was an opportunity for a victory that could inspire and unite the soldiers. It could also provide food, supplies, ammunition and weapons to continue the campaign. Montgomery sent an assault force of 50 Americans and 300 Canadians under Major John Brown and James Livingston to attack Fort Chambly on October 16, 1775.

Chambly was an antiquated stone fort on the Richelieu River. It was built in 1711 to protect Canada from British forces that could invade up the waterway and was located midway between Fort St. Johns and Montreal. Behind Chambly's thin walls was a garrison of only 90 British troops. The attackers met with little resistance. Maj. Joseph Stopford, of the 7th Regiment of Foot, the son of an earl, was the fort's commander but had little passion for taking a valiant stand. Despite having ample provisions, three mortars, muskets and ammunition, he made no effort to make a stand. Numerous women and children, the families of the garrison, lived in the fort. Perhaps, Major Stopford wanted to protect them from bloodshed that would result from the hand to hand fighting and the annihilation of the small number of defenders.

Brown and Livingston's guns blasted holes in the walls of the fort for two days but inflicted few casualties. Stopford unexpectedly surrendered and unwisely failed to destroy his supplies. Nineteen cannons and six tons of gunpowder were among the spoils taken. The capture of Chambly provided the Patriots with all the ammunition and weapons they would need to overpower Fort St. Johns and end the siege.

The victory at Fort Chambly was celebrated throughout the colonies. General Washington personally sent his congratulations but cynically commented that he hoped General Montgomery's next letter would be from Montreal. The American forces went on to occupy Longueuil and La Prairie on the St Lawrence River, 20 miles northwest of Chambly. These towns were across the river from Montreal and served as conduits to the city. Although his victory bolstered the confidence of the besieging American soldiers at Fort St. Johns the stalemate continued.

The 3rd New York Regiment, with Johnson's depleted 10th Company of Rockland County boys, was a late arrival to the deteriorating siege at Fort St. Johns. The desperate General Montgomery took advantage of their naiveté before they could assess the danger. He ordered the NewYorkers to the foreboding northwest battery where others had refused to go. Grape shot whined around Colonel James Clinton and his unusually courageous band of 200 men as they ascended to the exposed position. They built the emplacement under constant bombardment from the fort's heavy cannon and at night cut down a line of trees to open a field of fire. Their work was completed on October 14.[22]

The 3rd New York Regiment with Lamb's New York artillery men was able to mount two 12 pound cannons on the new position. Each weighed over a ton. These guns immediately began to have a devastating effect on the British fort and ships. The enemy countered by sending out the terrifying "Royal Savage" to silence the new position. The New Yorkers soon riddled the warship with cannon balls and it sank.

The American forces now flushed with success and numbering over 2,000 men began working on another new battery only 250 yards from the fort. Encouraged by the success of Clinton's men on the northwest battery this time the New Englanders did not object to occupying the perilous site. While the 3rd New York continued to hammer the fort, Montgomery began strengthening this new position. Over 500 men, including Wooster's unruly Connecticut troops, and New York 4th Regiment began the work. With the siege tightening, Montgomery, for the first time, believed the tide of battle was finally turning in his favor.

Senior British Commander Carleton received reports in Montreal that Fort St John was in peril and without reinforcements could be lost. At the end of October he began drafting all available men from as far away as Quebec City. He managed to recruit over 1,200 men.

His plan was to lead this relief force to Fort St. Johns to join Preston's struggling men and break the siege. Carleton's amphibious force crossed the St. Lawrence River from Montreal to Longueuil where he met unexpected and vigorous opposition. Hidden in the woods, along the river bank was a regiment of 350 fearless Green Mountain Boys from Vermont headed by Lieutenant Colonel Seth Warner. Many considered these men to be uncontrollable because of their cavalier attitude and their propensity to undertake independent and unauthorized missions. They served well at Longueuil.[23]

Warner pointed the cannons that had been captured a few days earlier from Fort Chambly at Carleton's 40 boats as they approached the shore. The Green Mountain Boys then opened up with devastating barrages of grape shot for five hours. Carleton's men made repeated attempts to land. He finally broke off the attack and retreated to Montreal. The besieged defenders of fort St. John would not receive the reinforcements they expected.

Major Preston's garrison stood alone but still held out hope that Carleton's men would soon arrive with the reinforcing force. A spy had attempted to smuggle a letter from Carleton to Preston. The message ordered him to hold out because help was on the way. This news would have inspired Preston to stiffen his resistance.

On November 1, the daunting new northwest battery was opened and mounted a mighty array of armament. Four twelve pounders, three nine pounders and five mortars were backed up by the huge cache of munitions that were captured at Fort Chambly. With the four cannons of the northwest battery the American guns then rained down an unceasing bombardment from their well placed vantage points.

The still heavily fortified British fortress persistently returned ineffective gunfire while the unrelenting American bombardment began to inflict heavy damage.

Defenders, huddled behind earthworks in the fort, agonized over the growing uncertainty that relief would reach them. Provisions were running low with only three days of rations were left. They knew that capitulation would open Canada to the American invaders. Preston's orders were to hold out at all costs and he was determined to withstand the onslaught until the reinforcements arrived with Carleton.

In the evening, Montgomery ordered a cease fire and sent a letter to Preston informing him that Carleton had been beaten at Longueuil. The American general offered, "to spare the lives of a brave garrison" if the British would surrender. Major Preston replied that he would surrender the fort if he did not receive reinforcements within four days. Montgomery replied that due to the approaching winter he could not agree to the time delay and demanded immediate surrender. The siege officially ended on November 2 when Montgomery and Preston agreed to the surrender terms. Fort St. Johns had fought valiantly and delayed the American invasion for two months.

British officers were allowed to keep their swords and soldiers kept their clothing and personal belongings. The next day Preston's valiant defenders marched out of the fort in full dress uniform and laid their arms down on the ground. Five hundred and thirty six British officers and soldiers, 79 Canadians and eight English volunteers surrendered. Forty two cannons and seven mortars were taken. Herded onto bateaux, the prisoners were remanded to a prison in Connecticut. Among the captives was a young lieutenant, John Andre who would achieve notoriety later in the war.

Carleton was aware that the fall of Fort St Johns made Montreal indefensible. As soon as he heard the painful news he decided to abandon the city and flee up the St Lawrence River to concentrate his remaining forces at the fortress of Quebec City. He immediately sent a request to England for reinforcements. Relief ships could land at Quebec in the spring of 1776 as soon as the ice broke on the river.

In December, the enlistments of most of the Connecticut soldiers expired. They disregarded the appeals of their officers and headed for home taking their muskets with them. Montgomery's pleas that the entire invasion would have to be abandoned without their support were ignored. He would have to move deeper into enemy land with a scaled down force. The patriotic fervor of the American Army earlier in the year had vanished. The farm boys from the colonies had not expected to freeze in a wintry land far from home.

With Montreal now defenseless Montgomery wasted no time pressing north. The lightly clad and poorly equipped patriots began to feel the sting of the Canadian winter. They slogged 18 miles through snow, ice and mud on a three day trek from Fort St. Johns to La Prairie, opposite the City of Montreal. The soldiers were enraged that the British prisoners taken at the fort were allowed to keep their uniforms while they froze in worn, tattered clothing.

American forces arrived in Montreal on November 11, 1775 and found that the British army was gone. The city fell with little resistance. They could now rest in warm quarters and enjoy the new scarlet uniforms and generous food supplies left behind by the vanquished Redcoats.

On to Quebec

The exhausted troops could not tarry long in the captured city. General Montgomery was under intense time pressure to meet with Benedict Arnold at Quebec. The time lost at Fort St. Johns had considerably slowed down the invasion. Time was against the Americans. The bitter Canadian winter had arrived and enlistments of most soldiers would expire in three weeks.

The expedition would reach Quebec in December, not mid October as planned. The founding fathers in the Continental Congress, in Philadelphia, expected the pattern of early victories at St. Johns and Montreal to continue. Hearing only vague reports from the front they unrealistically insisted on an early victory. General Richard Montgomery, commander of the American forces on the Canadian Campaign, summed up the situation in a letter to his brother-in law, "until Quebec is taken, Canada is unconquered."

The American army began to disintegrate. Men began to leave even before their enlistments were completed. Officers condoned the desertion and asserted that their men had fulfilled their military obligations since conditions had been so difficult. Entire New England regiments walked away. The Green Mountain boys and the Massachusetts men all departed. Only 200 men remained from the Connecticut Brigade. Another 200 men would have to remain in Montreal to occupy the city.

Montgomery became so disgruntled that only a personal letter from General Washington, pleading with him to stay on, prevented him from resigning his commission. Three thousand men had assembled at Fort Ticonderoga for the invasion. Two thousand troops had reached Fort St. Johns in September. At Montreal 300 only resolute New York men were able to continue to Quebec, the main objective of the entire campaign.

On November 28, 1775, Montgomery headed up the St. Lawrence River with his remnant army of "Yorkers." They departed for this final decisive battle in ships captured a few days earlier. The soldiers were clad in the new redcoat uniforms that were left behind when the British fled. They cast off for Quebec haunted by the fact that the size of their cannons and their undersized force might not be sufficient to capture the city.[24]

British Commander Guy Carleton had narrowly escaped from Montreal two days before the American occupation. He set sail up the St. Lawrence River with his garrison of 130 men and headed for Quebec. The voyage was harrowing. Shifting winds caused his ships to run aground and near Sorel the fleet was blocked by the American gun batteries and forced to surrender. Carleton avoided capture by escaping in a whaleboat disguised as a peasant

General Benedict Arnold's brigade was the first to reach Quebec City after completing a long and difficult 350- mile trek through the treacherous and frozen Maine wilderness. During the 45 day journey, 500 of his original 1,100 troops died or turned back. His soldiers endured incredible hardships. Food stores spoiled as boats were wrecked in the bad weather. Arnold's brigade went up the Kennebec River and down the Chaudière River. Six hundred starving survivors reached French settlements on the St Lawrence River opposite Quebec on November 9, 1775. This emaciated force did not bring sorely needed cannons. They immediately crossed the river to await the arrival of Montgomery on the Plains of Abraham, a plateau west of the city wall. Arnold's trek through Maine is regarded as one of the greatest military journeys in history.[25]

Montgomery joined Arnold at Quebec on December 5 and assumed command of the combined American Army. Montgomery arrived without heavy siege artillery. The frozen ground prevented the digging of trenches and earthworks to protect the gun crews from incoming cannon fire.

Quebec is on a hill overlooking the St. Lawrence River and is protected along the river by a 300- foot high cliff. On top of this ridge was a 30 foot high fortified wall that surrounded the city. The fortification bristled with heavy British fortress cannons. Along the base of the cliff was a lower town that served as the commercial center.

Carleton's defensive force at Quebec consisted of 1,800 British regulars, French Canadian militia and sailors. Montgomery and Arnold's combined force numbered 800 men. The city was well provisioned and, if besieged, could hold out for six months. This was adequate time for the ice to break up on the river and for the reinforcements to arrive from England

Montgomery assessed this predicament. He could not dig trenches in the frozen ground and his light artillery could not batter down the city's walls. The rest of his army would disappear when enlistments expired in 26 days. A British fleet with a large army of reinforcements would soon arrive and it was now certain that the Canadian people would not join the cause without first seeing their country in American hands.

The situation was clearly unsuitable for a time consuming, conventional siege. Storming the walls of the city at some vulnerable place with a frontal infantry assault was the only option. Montgomery and Arnold boldly deployed their thin ranks around the city. They appealed unsuccessfully to the inhabitants to join them then demanded that Carleton surrender. The British General burned the message and did not honor the threat with an answer.

The Americans began bombarding the city on December 9. Their light artillery lacked the range to have any effect. Gun crews attempted to build a wall of ice for cover but took severe losses from the heavy 32 pounders mounted on the city walls. After several day of constant firing there was little impact on the defenses of the city and the barrage failed.

Montgomery decided to gamble on an all out attack on December 31, the night before the army might dissolve with ending enlistments. Despite a terrible snowstorm on December 30, the decision was made to proceed with the attack.

Montgomery brought his 300 troops around to the west side of the city at 2:00 am. Arnold prepared his 600 soldiers to attack from the east side. They planned to charge into the lower area of the city and join forces. Then they would try to break into the city through a gate and fight through the streets into the upper town. This would force Carleton's army to withdraw from Quebec.

American signal rockets alerted the British to the impending attack and the entire city was alerted. British commander Carleton rushed his men down to the lower town and erected defensive barriers to meet Montgomery. On the east side of the city an ambush was set up to stop Arnold.

Montgomery's men began to move along the shore of the river toward the lower part of the city to link up with Arnold. They beat their way through a heavy blizzard with drifting snow and crawled two miles over ice packs thrown up on the frozen river bank. They were late for their linkup with Arnold, but he was also having difficulties. Blocked by a barricade, he led his men on a frontal assault and was hit in the leg by a musket ball. Arnold was carried away from the action and Captain Daniel Morgan of the Virginia riflemen assumed his command.

Captain Morgan's men continued to attack after Arnold was wounded. His troops rushed through the lower city and overcame all resistance. At this critical time the men refused to advance until Montgomery's contingent arrived. This delay cost the Americans an opportunity to enter the town. Carleton used the precious time to bring more men into the lower town. They built barriers as snipers hid in many buildings. The Redcoats then rushed out and surrounded the Americans.

Montgomery's column ran into the first resistance at a fortified stone house. Armed with muskets and four small cannons thirty Canadian militia defended the position. They were surprised by the sudden appearance of the Americans. Montgomery decided to assault the position before it had time to prepare defenses. Raising his sword, the valiant general called out for his men to follow him in a direct frontal charge to the blockhouse.

A first volley of grapeshot and musket fire hit the American column when it reached to within 50 yards of the fortification. Richard Montgomery was killed instantly as his men fell around him in the knee- deep snow. Survivors pressed forward until they reached a barricade and were hit with musket and cannon fire. With their respected leader down, the demoralized patriots fled the scene. They left their dead and wounded behind and Arnold's men had to fend for themselves. This skirmish effectively ended the American siege of Quebec.

General Montgomery's snow-covered body lay beside his fallen men for the rest of the day. On the morning of January 1, a British work party came into the lower town to survey the damage done to the fortifications and to remove the bodies of dead Americans from the deep snow. When they began pulling out the frozen corpses, they saw an arm protruding from a drift. Alongside the body was a general's sword that had been wrenched from the outstretched arm by the blast of gunfire.

Montgomery's body was recognized by the high quality of the uniform and a blood soaked fur hat with the initials R.M. American prisoners later confirmed the identification. Carleton ordered Montgomery's remains to be buried in Quebec with a simple ceremony to avoid inciting American sympathizers.

The general was deeply respected by both sides. A British major at his burial commented, "his death, though honorable is lamented, not only by the death of an amiable, worthy friend but as an experienced brave general, whose country suffers greatly by such a loss at this time." Congress had promoted him to Major General on December 9 in recognition of his victories at St. Johns and Montreal. He did not live to learn of this achievement.[26]

At Quebec, 385 Americans were captured, 30 Americans were killed and 42 Americans were wounded. They would not invade nor threaten Canada again during the war. The dream of the Continental Congress to add Canada as the fourteenth colony was gone forever. At the time, defeat had even worse consequences. The British army, 9,000 men strong was in the position to move from Canada down the lakes and into the Hudson valley. Dividing the colonies could end the rebellion.

The severely wounded Arnold managed to escape and collect the remains of the Patriot troops. The Americans, outnumbered four to one, made a futile attempt to continue the siege for the next four months and were eventually forced to retreat to Montreal. Carleton, safely ensconced behind the walls of Quebec did not risk further combat and patiently waited for the spring fleet to arrive from England.

British General John Burgoyne reached Quebec in May 1776. His fleet had 40 ships an army of 5,000 British regulars and 4,000 Hessian mercenaries. This strengthened British forces in America which with the loss of Montgomery's leadership, doomed the American invasion of Canada.

Patriot forces focused on making a safe retreat without being surrounded by the superior enemy force. In the spring, the Americans fell back and burnt all of the forts they had captured north of Lake Champlain, including Fort St. Johns. Soon, all the lands conquered by the American forces from Fort Ticonderoga north to Quebec were back in British hands. British and Hessian forces massed at Fort St. Johns prepared a counter offensive to strike south down the lakes

The Canadian Campaign was the first American defeat of the Revolutionary War. It was a devastating loss for the colonies and the assault on Quebec was a complete fiasco. However, it did have a profoundly positive effect on the next seven years of the war. The invasion distracted the British forces in Canada from marching south for almost a year. This made the successful siege of Boston possible by preventing Carleton from adding his forces in New England.

The victory at Fort St. Johns was the high point of the campaign for the American side. Few other encouraging events occurred on this ill-fated adventure. Montgomery's superior strategy and courage in the field could not overcome the adversity he encountered. The siege was the great victory but it cost the Americans the campaign. Major Preston had stopped their advance for two months. If the encounter had been brief, the outcome of the campaign and the future course of the war could have changed, though it is unlikely that the new nation could have held onto Canada during the next dark year of 1776.

St. Johns in History

Today, Saint-Jean-Sur Richelieu is a bustling Canadian city of 90,000 people 10 miles east of Route I. 87/C. 15 on the Richelieu River in the province of Quebec. The Marchand Bridge built in 1966 spans the river here. The narrow streets in the older part of town emanate out from the fort site on the river bank and give the visitor a sense of earlier times. Early English settlers knew the place as St. Johns and Americans have always used its anglicized name.

The city is a manufacturing center for textiles as well as food and wood products and is in an ideal location for all water sports and activities offering a marina, popular restaurants, concert halls, museums and a public market. Each August the city is host to the prestigious International Balloon Festival. Until 1995 it was the location of Le College Militaire Royal de Saint Jean.

American historians remember St. Johns only for the 50 day siege during the Canadian Campaign of 1775 when the 200 British regulars along with a small band of Indians delayed the patriot forces until the hard winter had set in and caused their defeat two months later. The old garrison town has a vibrant history and a military tradition that stretches back to the original Fort Saint-Jean built in 1666-1667. It was a main bastion in the chain of military posts built along the Richelieu River to protect the early French settlers from the frequent raids by the Iroquois Indians.

The Early French Forts

The first fort was erected after the French King Louis XIV decided to establish control over his North American Colony New France. These lands were previously colonized and managed by trade associations. The King directed the construction of forts along the Richelieu River and Lake Champlain and ordered a punitive expedition against the Iroquois who were raiding French settlements and attempting to gain control over the bountiful hunting ground.[27]

The original Fort St. Johns is believed to have been a small square-shaped structure with four redoubts surrounded by wooden palisades. It was located on the river at the end the Chambly rapids. This strategic site provided the French with control of a vital portage location where an enemy advance up the waterway could be blocked.

The French offensive into Indian Territory was successful and a peace treaty was signed with the Native Americans in 1667. In 1672, after five peaceful years, the French Governor of the colony decided that the fort was no longer required so it was abandoned. The site vacant under French rule languished or the next 76 years but did not disappear.

St. Johns under the British

In 1748, a second French fort was built at St. Johns because of the growing hostility between France and England that led to the French and Indian War in 1753. This fort was two hundred feet by two hundred feet and had four bastions, two of which were stone. It was an important stopover between Montreal and Fort St. Frederic or Crown Point as the British later named it. Crown Point, 100 miles south of Fort St. Johns was the strongest French installation in North America except for Quebec. It was located in New York State on the west bank of Lake Champlain ten miles north of Fort Ticonderoga. The lake was the water highway to St. Johns and a road linked it to La Prairie the town across from Montreal on the St. Lawrence River. This direct and accessible route facilitated travel and communications over the 120 miles between Crown Point and Montreal.

The second fort Saint-Jean was remembered as "Fort aux Maringouins" (Fort of Mosquitoes) because of its location in a swampy area. In 1760 an outnumbered French garrison was forced to evacuate the fort as a British assault force of 5,000 men moved up the Richelieu River to take Montreal. Before the French retreated they burned the fort. The two stone bastions of the fort that survived the fire were afterward used as signal towers by the British troops.

American Occupation

At the start of the American Revolution in 1775 St John's served as the main defense for the protection of Montreal. Two redoubts connected by a trench were added by the English for defense against an American invasion The English garrison at Fort St. Johns fought valiantly against the American troops during the long siege and slowed down their offensive. Because of this delay, the winter weather and the weakened state of their remaining troops they failed to take over Quebec City on December 31, 1775. The Americans abandoned and burned the fort as they retreated south after British reinforcements arrived from England in the spring of 1776.

Fearing that the Americans would return, the British reconstructed the fort in 1776. New ramparts were added and the shipyard was revived to build the shallow draft boats needed to oppose the Patriots on Lake Champlain. These vessels took part of the Battle of Valcour Island where a small American fleet under Benedict Arnold was destroyed on October 11, 1776. This was the first naval battle of the Revolutionary War and the first engagement in the history of the U.S. Navy.

Fort St. Johns was used as a supply base by the British Army and lost its importance after the end of the revolution in 1783. It was used as a stopover and supply base during the War of 1812 when the Americans tried again to take conquer Britain's Canadian colony. In the years that followed the fort's condition deteriorated and some of its structures disappeared.

19th Century Fortifications

The Patriot Revolt of 1837-1838 was caused by Canadians and Americans attempting to overthrow British rule of Canada. This uprising convinced the British of the need to again strengthen the fortifications at St. Johns and new buildings were added. Many of the brick structures built during this time by the Royal Engineers are still in use today.

Benson Lossing the American historian who traveled to many Revolutionary War sites visited the fort in 1851. He drew a sketch of the bastion and provided this colorful and detailed description of the site at that time.

> *"St Johns is pleasantly situated on the western side of the Sorel (Richelieu River) at the termination of steamboat navigation on Lake Champlain and near the head of Chambly Rapids. It has always been a place of considerable importance as a frontier town since the Revolution, although its growth has been slow, the population amounting to not quite four*

thousand. The country on both sides of the river is perfectly flat, and there is no place where the tow may be seen to advantage. A little south of the village, and directly upon the shore is a military establishment, garrisoned, when we visited it by three companies of highland infantry. We crossed the deep sluggish river in a light zinc shallop, and from the middle of the stream we obtained a fine view of the long bridge which connects St Johns with St Athenaise on the opposite shore, where the steep roof and lofty glittering spire of the French church towered above the trees. After visiting the remains of Montgomery's blockhouse, we recrossed the river and rambled among the high mounds which compose the ruins of old Fort St Johns. They occupy a broad area in the open fields behind the present military works. The embankments, covered with a rich green sward averaged twelve feet in height, and the whole were surrounded by a ditch with considerable water in it. We lingered half an hour to view a drill of the garrison, and then returned to the village to prepare for a pleasant ride to Chambly, twelve miles distant."

Lossing sketched the fort from the east side of the river near the remains of a blockhouse erected by General Montgomery when his troops besieged the fort in 1775. His drawing shows the fort on the right that encloses the magazine. In the center are the officer's quarters with soldier's barracks on each side. The large building on the left is a hospital, and a smaller one further to the left is a "deadhouse," that was probably a morgue. He reported that the river there was about a quarter of a mile wide.

Finally, a Multipurpose Facility

At the end of the 19th and beginning of the 20th century, the fort was used as a training school for several civilian groups and army regiments. Troops were trained at the fort before being sent to Europe during the World War I. After that war the first French-speaking Canadian regiment, the Royal 22nd was stationed at the fort.

In 1952 the Collage Militaire Royal of St.-Jean the first bilingual military college in Canada was opened to train French- speaking Canadians to become officers. The School occupied some of the buildings built in 1839 by the Royal Engineers and closed in 1995.

In order to preserve the site and its buildings a non-profit body, the

Corporation du fort Saint-Jean was created and has leased some of its facilities to institutions such as the University of Quebec. However, the place continued its military function by reopening in 2008 as a college for cadets. The museum and a multisport complex are also located here.

In the early 1980s, Parks Canada led archaeological digs at Fort Saint John's and discovered on that occasion the foundations of the 1748 French fort and many artifacts of both the French and British occupation. In collaboration with Fort Saint Jean Museum, the Royal Military College of Saint-Jean and Laval University began a five-year digging project in 2009. Excavations by archaeology students during summers focused on discovering the remnants of the early French, British and Canadian forts and the shipyards.

The Scene Today: A Pleasant Park on the Riverbank

In the Summer of 2011, the site of the fort at Saint Jean-Sur-Richelieu was easily reached by following the Rue Champlain along the river bank. Eric Ruel, Curator of the Musee du Fort Saint-Jean greeted me. As we entered the museum Eric reviewed the history of the site over the past three centuries. Each exhibit was an era in history of the fort. These fascinating and well designed displays start with Paleo history go on to show the fort under French and British rule and finally portray the events of the Canadian era.

The military history of the fort from 1666 is depicted with maps, models, uniforms, weapons and artifacts found on the site. Of special interest is a plan of the galley Royal Savage, the ship that was built at St. Johns and played such a prominent role in the siege of 1775. A comprehensive video covering the entire history of the place can also be viewed.

During my research of the 1775 siege at St. Johns I had difficulty visualizing the exact positions of American gun batteries, front lines and campsites. Understanding their locations was critical to following the flow of the battle. The entire scene was instantly apparent when I saw a rendering of the original British mural "Plan of St John's as blockaded and besieged anno 1775." It showed the American batteries including the critical east battery that led to the breaking of the siege, the location of the American camp and the landing place and the locations of the September Indian attack.

Fort Saint-Jean Museum traces the history of the only site in Canada that has known continuous military occupation since the French rule. Over the 340 years the place has witnessed the struggles of the Native American warriors, French and British troops, American Patriots and of Canadian regiments. The museum is housed in the former protestant chapel.

On outside guided tour of the grounds one is reminded that the Revolutionary War siege was only one of many episodes in the history of the Fort. Trenches and elevated mounds of redoubt and rampart positions cover the grounds. A team of archeologists from Laval University was busy at work in an excavation.

A detailed plan of the fort, drawn by the British in the summer of 1775, shows the north and south ramparts and the trenches that connect the 1200- foot installation. Each building is identified with its purpose described. On our tour of the grounds we were introduced to author Andrew Beaupre. He is a PhD. Candidate from the College of William and Mary in Virginia preparing his dissertation on Fort St. Johns.

After leaving the fort complex we followed Eric Ruel along the river on the Rue Jacques Cartier. We passed the unmarked area where the American front lines stretched out several hundred yards from the walls of the fort. About a half mile from the fort is the site of the American Camp. General Montgomery and the Continental Army were camped here A stone obelisk marks the location but the commemorative plate has been removed. Eric observed that the captured supplies were brought here from Chambly and revitalized stalled Americans.

Follow Route 223 south along the scenic Richelieu River to reach Ile-Aux-Noix the American base for the Assualt on St. Johns. Signs for Fort Lennox, the name given to the place in 1819, lead to a small visitors exhibit and a water taxi to the Island. The "island of nuts," named by the French for the walnut trees that once covered the 210 acre isle, was built to guard against the Iroquois and later the British.[28]

A sign warned "Closed Flooded." served as a reminder of the unwholesome conditions on the low swampy ground in 1775 when the island was taken by American forces and used as a base for attacks on St John's. After being defeated at Quebec and abandoning Montreal the Continental Army regrouped at the island in its retreat south from Canada in 1776. During the months of occupation more than 900 American soldiers died from smallpox. They were cared for and buried on Hospital Island further downstream and were buried in two mass graves on the island. The British then built a new fort at Ile - Aux-Noix in 1778 and used it to supply their operations against the American fleet on Lake Champlain during the War of 1812.

The present Fort Lennox was built from 1819 to 1829, when the old fortifications were completely demolished. Fort Lennox is built of stone and surrounded by earthworks and a 60-foot-wide moat that is filled with water during the summer months. It remained a military post until 1870. A museum on the site contains 17th century Indian relics and old French and British military equipment.

The seige at St. Johns was an important American victory but the critical holdup there led to their ultimate defeat at Quebec City. Colonel Charles Preston's remarkable resistance held up the Americans for two months. General Richard Montgomery should be credited with holding together his disorganized and rebellious army leading them against a heavily armed and well entrenched force of British regulars. The fall of St. Johns opened the way for the capture of Montreal the most valuable prize on the route to Quebec.

Chapter Two

Forgotten Fishkill- Military Nerve Center of the Continental Army 1776-1783.

Fishkill, New York

A Revered Place Threatened by Development

Revolutionary War history is typically focused on heroic battles. The thunder of musket fire and the snap of fixed bayonets usually veil the many remarkable places not caught up in combat. The supply depot and encampment at Fishkill, New York served as the nerve center for the Continental Army and state militia forces in the north for almost the entire eight years of the Revolution. George Washington stated that the war could not have been won without the food, shelter and supplies that the depot consistently provided. The hallowed location was partly covered by a shopping mall three decades ago and more recently by a gas station. Even then it was recognized as the last major site of the Revolutionary War in the northeast that was never properly explored

This armed camp was larger and operated longer than Valley Forge, in Pennsylvania or Jockey Hollow in Morristown, New Jersey, but is one of the least understood and most threatened historical sites in the nation. With its official state historic marker ten miles away on a busy parkway, it remains unknown even to New Yorkers.[1]

The supply depot at Fishkill made a tremendous contribution the American war effort. Excavations unearthed cannon balls, muskets, utensils, and uniform buttons during the construction of the mall in 1974. The Fishkill Historical Society now holds about 10,000 artifacts collected there over the years.[2] The partially built over site today covers more than 70 acres on both sides of a heavily trafficked highway. What remains of the supply depot is threatened by more commercial development. Residual open space is currently for sale and seems ready for a new round of construction.

At its peak, the center was the principal depository for stores and provisions and at various times served as the headquarters for most of America's top military leaders. Fishkill was also the seat of government for the New York Provincial Congress, the equivalent of today's state legislature.

At the junction of major roads, the place was accessible and safe. The village of Fishkill provided a rallying place and gathering point for both Continental troops and militia before campaigns and served as headquarters for the Commissary and Quartermaster corps. It was the site of a major hospital facility for the armed forces from 1776 to late 1778 and provided a barracks for more than 2,000 soldiers. Upward of 6,000 men encamped here at one time and several regiments wintered here in the war years. The complex had hundreds of single huts as well as barracks, prisons, hospitals, an artillery park, powder magazines, a print shop as well as guard houses, a sawmill, an armory and a paymaster's and post offices. A blacksmith shop is shown also directly across the Post Road from the Van Wyck home on the Erskine's 1778 map.

In unmarked graves, hundreds of soldiers lie. Many of the wounded and smallpox victims were brought here and those who died were buried on the site. There is no other place in New York State that has as many buried soldiers of the revolution as Fishkill.

Placed on the National Register of Historic places in 1974, Fishkill was proposed as a national park but never achieved that status. Surprisingly, there was no attempt to reveal the story and importance of the encampment or to locate and preserve its remains. It was forgotten for 200 years. No interest was shown until the bulldozers arrived and amateur volunteers began archeology projects. The location of the blacksmith's shop was excavated for the gas station and the location of the barracks is the site of the shopping center. The Van Wyck House is the last remaining building. Because of its many uses and the fact that the most important Revolutionary War leaders stayed there the site has not been entirely built over and still provides a unique opportunity for research and archeology

It wasn't until the 1970s that serious consideration for preserving the Fishkill encampment began. Richard Goring of the New York State Parks and Recreation and Stephan Bielinski, a community historian summarized Fishkill's history and reviewed its condition. They found that nothing had been published and the little information that existed was not readily available. There had never been any sustained effort toward researching documents relating to the Revolutionary history of Fishkill and few records of the meager archeological efforts undertaken when sites were faced with imminent development.

An Ideal Location for an Armed Camp

The Village of Fishkill is at the northern part of the Hudson Highlands, 45 miles north of New York City. A distance of five miles from the Hudson River made it less vulnerable to attack from the waterway. By chance, the town occupied a critically strategic place. It was far enough from the river that it could not be attacked by surprise by a British amphibious force and supplies could be either removed or destroyed if its fall was looming. It had access to the river where supplies and men could move in and out by water, the fastest method of transportation of the day. It was between New York and Albany and the main roads from New England and Ticonderoga passed through it. Ferries connected these rustic highways to New Jersey and the southern colonies.

Fishkill had a natural defensive barrier to the south formed by 20 miles of craggy mountains that formed the Hudson Highlands. Only one easily defended passage led through these hills to check any British invasion north from their bastion in New York City. This gap, now Route 9, would have been the road taken by the Redcoat army to attack Albany or to move into New England. The defenses of the depot guarded the corridor.

The town was well positioned as a hub of transportation and communications and provided a collection place for agricultural products. Tory prisoners captured in the so -called neutral ground in nearby Westchester County were confined there. In the years before the people of this small bucolic hamlet never suspected the astonishing role that their town would play in gaining independence for the new nation.

History of the Fishkill Site

The most heavily traveled road in early American passed through Fishkill. It followed an animal path and later and Indian trading trail that ran from the Great lakes to Georgia. A village existed on the site of Fishkill as early as 1716. The area was known as Fishkill during the eighteenth century because of the many fish filled "kills" the Dutch word for creeks.[3]

Fishkill Landing, now the town of Beacon, New York, five miles away on the river, served as the port for the village. Cornelius Van Wyck the first settler migrated north 50 miles from Hempstead Long Island with his family in 1732 to purchase 900 acres of the fertile bottom land and build a cabin. By the time of the revolution the simple farm had evolved into a large homestead. A simple path with the pretentious name of "Kings Highway" bisected the Van Wyck property. It would eventually become the Albany Post Road, part of the main north-south road that linked the colonies. Today the Taconic State Parkway and Interstate 84 have replaced this ancient route.

The Van Wyck homestead was wooded and populated by deer and other wildlife and fish filled the nearby creeks. British soldiers passed down the King's Highway in 1757during the French and Indian War. Although the Van Wycks were British subjects the Redcoats pillaged and foraged the farm and the family was forced to flee. Isaac Van Wyck the grandson of Cornelius inherited the dwelling and a part of the property when the Revolution began. He became a Captain in the Dutchess County Militia and continued to occupy the house.

In August, 1776, the New York Provincial Congress decided to convert the village of Fishkill into the main base for the state's military activities. Their plan was to station troops, store provisions and establish a hospital there. The Van Wyck house was requisitioned along with the entire farm. The next month the Army began to arrive and Washington ordered construction of a barracks for 2,000 men. Later that year when British forces occupied New York City all public stores were removed to Fishkill.[4]

Washington followed the advice of New York leaders Governor George Clinton and Major General Alexander Mc Dougall in selecting the location but soon feared that this decision was a poor choice. In 1777, there was considerable action in the Hudson River valley The Hudson River when linked with Lake George, Lake Champlain, the Richelieu River and the St Lawrence formed a natural water highway from New York to Quebec. Control of the waterway became the major British objective. Occupation of it would divide New England from the other colonies and could end the war.

In October of 1777 Sir Henry Clinton's Army would pass Fishkill as he sailed north up the Hudson River from New York City. The strategy was for him to meet General John Burgoyne who was moving down the lakes from Canada with another large force. If the plan succeeded, the vital waterway would be in British hands.

On his way north up the Hudson, Sir Henry's first stop was at Peekskill where he landed a detachment of his amphibious force. The Americans anticipated that the invaders would continue to the Fishkill Depot 30 miles away. This was a feint attack and the British turned around and did not move inland. Their real objective was a surprise attack on the Twin Forts, Montgomery and Clinton, on the west side of the River. The forts were valiantly defended by the vastly outnumbered 5th New York Regiment. After defeating the Patriots, Sir Henry Clinton continued sailing on up the river. He passed Fishkill on the way to burn Kingston, New York's capitol city at the time. Had the Redcoats attacked Fishkill they could have been annihilated by a superior force of Patriots.[5]

"General McDougall wrote to General Washington from Fishkill during a Court of Inquiry convened there three months after the fall of the Twin Forts. *That by the 9th of October there were 4000 militia in Fishkill from Connecticut which with Continental troops and Militia from the State of new York, on the east of the river, amounted to at least five thousand 500 men.*"

Clinton abandoned the attempt to join Burgoyne after the British Army was defeated at Saratoga and returned back down the river to New York City again bypassing Fishkill. Washington reprimanded General Putnam for not removing the stores during this critical period. These narrow escapes caused the Commander -In-Chief to remain apprehensive about the security of his major supply base for the rest of the war.

Most historians have regarded the defeat of the British defeat at the battle of Saratoga as the turning point of the Revolution. The depot soon experienced the consequences of the vanquished enemy. Between November 28 and December 1, 1778, 4,000 captured British and Hessian troops guarded by 1,000 Connecticut soldiers passed through the Fishkill. The gloomy procession ambled down King's Highway, then the main street of the village and were herded on to Fishkill Landing and ferried across to the west side of the river on the way to prison at Charlottesville, Virginia over 600 miles away.

By 1778, the small, quiet pastoral hamlet of Fishkill became a hectic hub of military activities. The rustic charm town before the war dramatically changed; immersed for the remainder of the war in the flow of action of the American and British Armies.

Eye Witnesses Describe the Fishkill Depot

Lieutenant Thomas Auburey was a British officer who had been captured at Saratoga and with thousands of other British and Hessian prisoners he was driven through Fishkill in 1778.[6] He provided a detailed description of the depot on his brief visit. Auburey reported that the place was the center of communication for the American Army, linking north, south and east and that it was the principal depot of the American army. He saw a great number of huts and believed the place could accommodate the entire army for the winter. Auburey saw a powder magazine. Near it were some well constructed barracks and a prison surrounded by tall palisades. He claimed that the prison held arrested Loyalists who had refused to take the oath of allegiance to the United States.

That same year the Marquis de Chastellux visited Fishkill. He was one of the three major generals who accompanied Rochembeau and the French expeditionary forces to America. The account of his visit provides an intriguing glimpse of the armed camp during the war. He reported that the location was ideal for "a place of deposit." It was on the main road to Connecticut, near the Hudson and protected from the South by an inaccessible chain of mountains. "*I reached Fishkill at four o'clock. This town in which there are not more than fifty houses in the space of two miles, has long been the principal depot of the American Army: it is there they have placed their magazines, their hospitals, their workshops etc. but all of these form a town in themselves, composed of handsome large barracks built in wood at the foot of the mountains; for the Americans, like the Romans in many respects, have for winter quarters only wood, or camps composed of barracks, which may be compared to the hiernalia of Romans. …..It was necessary to procure a place on this river; West Point was chosen as the most important point to fortify, and Fishkill as the place bear adapted to the establishment of the principal depot for provisions, ammunition etc. These two positions are connected with each other."*[7]

Chastellux also saw a sawmill, and furnaces. Workshops scattered throughout the depot included a bakery, a tent shop a chandlers for candles and soap, a wheelwright, and a blacksmith shop. He also observed a prison surrounded by palisades and saw a number of men in British uniforms and Tories captured when they invaded the Mohawk River are with the Indians.

A map drawn by Washington's cartographer Robert Erskine in 1778 shows a cluster of 10 buildings in the center of the village of Fishkill.

In 1777, redoubts were constructed, on a sand hill five miles south of the town where the valley narrows, to protect the southern approach to the depot. These defenses held three batteries of cannons and protected the only pass through the mountains. There were 2,400 soldiers guarding the depot in 1780.

Fishkill as a Supply Depot

The most vital function of the Fishkill facility was its use as the main supply base for the Northern Department of the Continental Army. This command directed all military action north of the Hudson Highlands to Canada. The American Army, during most of the war, was hungry and ragged in a bountiful land with abundant food and other natural resources. Merchants refusing to accept the near worthless Continental Dollar, poor communications, transportation and other logistic problems exacerbated the difficult problem of supplying the troops. However, no army could fight very effectively for eight years without some centrally located facility that could attempt to provide resources efficiently and consistently.

American stockpiles of arms and provisions were scattered before 1777. That year as supplies began to be assembled at Fishkill since the waterway from the Hudson River, up the lakes to Canada, was threatened by the British Army. Loss of this water highway would divide the colonies. The Patriots had to establish a store of supplies in the central Hudson region near where the American Army would have would have to fight in what could be a decisive battle of the war.

The destruction of Patriot supply bases bracketed Fishkill. British raiders burned stockpiles of supplies at the river ports of Peekskill to the south and at Kingston in the north. General Washington followed the recommendation of New York's Governor George Clinton and decided to concentrate supplies at Fishkill. Although most people who lived in the surrounding area were Patriots, New York's Governor George Clinton remained concerned about the security of the new base. The front lines of the enemy were only 30 miles south in Westchester County.

Despite the fact that American soldiers were often hungry and ill clad despite the great quantities of provisions that were kept at Fishkill. The Commissary Division of the army was headquartered there and maintained a great variety of stores. Food provisions included flour and bread, vegetables, rye, corn oats, buckwheat, salt, salt pork, rum and hay and other forage. Essential raw material for the war such as iron, lead and lumber were also stockpiled at Fishkill. The Van Wyck farm in the village served as the center of military activity but the storage of supplies was not all centered there. Available buildings as far as five miles away, at Fishkill landing (Beacon, New York), were used for storehouses.

Clothing, shoes, stockings and blankets were all issued to the Continental Army from Fishkill during the war. Philip Livingston a New York member of the Continental Congress sent 11,000 pounds of clothing there in 1777.[8] The impoverished army stored and refurbished used clothing there and Orderly books are replete with instructions. When the New York Brigade was issued new uniforms at Continental Village, 15 miles from Fishkill, on November 4, 1778, General Orders called for *"Old cloaths, coats, Jacketts and briches fit for service are to be deposited in the hands of the Clothyer at Fishkill. Old Cloaths are to be well aired and packed in secure casks. Old cloaths are to be returned in the casks which carry the new."*

Boats were stored at Fishkill Landing and horses, teams and wagons were stored at the depot to provide rapid transport in times of emergency. Draft animals were often kept on private farms where they could be well tended and yet be available. Farmers were allowed to work the animals.[9]

The depot was also the major repository for muskets, gunpowder, shot and other weapons. Facilities included an artillery park where heavy ordinance was stored including an assortment of cannons ranging from three to eighteen pounders. An armory to repair guns was built in 1781and 1782.[10]

Churches Became Hospitals and Prisons

Fishkill's three churches were used for unusual purposes during the war. The Presbyterian and the Trinity Episcopal Church, built in 1760, became hospitals. The Dutch Reformed Church, organized in 1716 by descendants of the original settlers, was a meeting place for the New York Provincial Congress and later was a prison.

After the Battle of White Plains in October 1776, the wounded were sent to Fishkill and overflowed from the barracks hospitals into the Episcopal and Dutch churches. An elderly lady reported in the 1850s that as a child she remembered dead bodies of American soldiers piled between the Dutch and Episcopal churches in stacks as high as a cord of wood after the Battle of White Plains.[10]

In December of 1778, General McDougall ordered the Presbyterian Church occupied as a hospital because facilities at the barracks and the Episcopal Church were so crowded with the wounded and sick that conditions were dreadful. Later that year a larger medical facility in a barracks was established about five miles south of the town. This facility also served as the main depository for all medical supplies for the northern army.

Thousands died at Fishkill from wounds, smallpox, dysentery, malnutrition and hyperthermia. During the Revolution disease was more dangerous than the enemy and incredibly for every soldier killed in battle nine died from illness. Hospitals were abodes of infectious diseases and were regarded as one of the main sources of sickness and death in the Continental Army. Contagion was the result of overcrowding. Sick and dying men were packed into cold rooms with open fires and dirt floors. Men were placed head to foot on straw that was rarely changed. Filthy clothing, dampness and typhus carrying lice spread germs rapidly. Men contracted new illnesses after being admitted and many soldiers did not leave alive. Medical practices were very crude for the wounded and amputation was the chosen treatment for even minor wounds and old tent cloth was often used for bandages.

Smallpox was a constant problem. About 200 soldiers consistently had the illness at Fishkill. The 5th New York Regiment at Fishkill and in nearby Continental Village reported in 1778 that almost half of the unit had smallpox. Washington who had battled the disease in his youth ordered all troops at the depot vaccinated. Surviving smallpox conferred a lifetime of immunity and inoculation resulted in immediate but temporary sickness. The troops were suspicious of the treatments and resisted vaccination. It was not until 1781 that all men stationed there had finally been vaccinated.

The first prison in Fishkill was the Dutch Church which became so overcrowded that some of the prisoners were kept in the balcony. A nearby hat shop served as the guardhouse. Prisons also served as the point of exchange for prisoners. Tories captured in the unrest along the Mohawk River were kept here after having their land and property confiscated. Many were driven south to the British lines above New York City.

Traveling from the north, Fishkill was the final American camp before crossing the Hudson. It was the logical place to hold the British and Hessian troops of Burgoyne's army that had been defeated at Saratoga. Four thousand of these prisoners, guarded by almost 1,000 Connecticut men, marched into Fishkill. After being incarcerated in Boston after the battle they were being herded to internment at their final destination at Charlottesville, Virginia, 623 miles away. Governor Clinton feared there might be a rescue attempt by the British Army from New York City. After four days at the depot they were marched to Fishkill Landing and then ferried across the river to a more secure out of the way location at Newburgh, New York. [11]

Fishkill as a Seat of Government and Military Tribunals

Fishkill, a focal point of transportation and communications, served as a governmental center and often as the place for important military tribunals. A Committee of Observation was set up there when the war began in 1775. Its purpose was to identify loyalists and confiscate their weapons.

The New York Provincial Congress fled north when the British invaded New York City in 1776. Fishkill became the state capitol in September of that year. The Congress met first at the Episcopal Church but soon left because of the filth. "It was very foul with the dung of doves and fowls and without benches" The governing body then reconvened at the Dutch Reformed Church and wrote the state constitution there. The original document was also printed at Fishkill.

The New York Congress provided clothing for the state troops and coordinated the movements of the militia regiments. A Committee of Safety was established to meet when the state congress was not in session. The groups departed for Kingston, New York, in April 1777. Since this city was thirty miles up the Hudson River they assumed that it would be more secure, but a British fleet burned the town to the ground after the fall of the Twin Forts later that year.

So much time and effort was expended to root out citizens who were suspected of being Loyalists that a Conspiracy Committee was set up in September of 1776 specifically for this purpose. They captured loyalists by using spies to lure them into ambushes. The Conspiracy Committee moved out of Fishkill to Kingston with the New York Congress during a smallpox epidemic in April 1777. The group continued to meet at Kingston.[12]

The depot also served as a center for military justice. Tribunals and court martial hearings were held at the home of Abraham Brinkerhoff. George Washington ordered a court of inquiry at Fishkill in February 1778 to determine the causes of the appalling loss of the Twin Forts, Montgomery and Clinton. General Alexander McDougall conducted the hearing three months after the defeat. Fifteen officers who were at the battle gave eyewitness accounts.

"Fish Kills Monday the 30th March 1778-the Court met at the home of Col Brinkerhoff's and having published their commission proceeded to Business."

After the hearing Washington concluded, *It appears that those posts were lost, not from any fault, misconduct or negligence, of the commanding officers, but soley through the want of an adequate force under their command to maintain and defend them.*[13]

Winter Hardships, Punishments and a Mutiny

As with all other major encampments during the war civilians complained about the freezing soldiers plundering their gardens, cutting their timber and robbing fence rails for firewood. The villagers grumbled that there was a plentiful supply of kindling in the forests near the barracks but the men found it easier to pillage their stocks.

The suffering endured by the soldiers during the winters at Fishkill equaled the chilling winters at Valley Forge and Morristown. It is hard to imagine that a supply depot could not provide for its own soldiers. General Putnam reported, in the winter of 1777-1778, several hundred men unfit for duty because they did not have sufficient clothing. *"There was not one blanket in the regiment and very few soldiers have a shirt, and most of them have neither stockings, breeches or overalls."* the hard winter of 1780 the soldiers had patched their clothes until patches and clothing both gave out and their garments dropped from their bodies.

The 5th New York Regiment spent most of the winter of 1778 in the barracks at Fishkill and suffered from lack of clothing. Their number had fallen from 300 men to 160 men from sickness, desertion and their massive losses suffered at the Battle of the Twin Forts. [14]

Many soldiers were housed in barracks although General McDougall stated that in December 1778, two entire regiments lived in tents. Construction on barracks began in at least two sites in October 1776. Complaints by civilian residents about the theft of firewood were directed at this complex. This indicates that it was close to town. The "lower barracks" were located three miles south of the village and may have had accommodations for as many as 2,000 men. Barracks housed prisoners, the sick and those wounded. A regiment of "invalids," disabled officers and men, occupied the lower barracks at Fishkill during most of the war. [15]

The term "barracks" and "huts" were used interchangeably, which caused confusion as to the details of their construction. The descriptions of the buildings varied greatly depending on the site observed and the observer. Lieutenant Auburey the captive British officer wrote *"the soldier quarters were miserable shelters with huts consisting of only little walls made with uneven stones, and the intervals filled up with mud and straw, a few planks forming the roof."* Chastellux described them as *"handsome large barracks in which is found the comfortable places were troops could pass an entire winter without suffering or sickness."*

Food supplies dwindled at the depot during the winters. General Washington wrote in December 1778 that the troops ate every kind of horse food including hay. There was a complete lack of vegetables. The desperate men fought over animal food while cattle starved to death.

In November 1777 Enoch Poor's brigade of New England troops arrived at Fishkill after fighting valiantly in the thick of the action at the battle of Saratoga. After marching south 100 miles the weary and disgruntled soldiers, not paid in eight months refused to continue across the Hudson and mutinied. Officers tried to restore order for five days but the situation deteriorated. A captain bayoneted one of the mutineers. Before the man died he fatally shot the officer. Several of the protesters were put in a stockade. Twenty of the prisoners escaped and left for home. General Putnam frantically tried to borrow 1,500 pounds to provide the men with a month's pay without success. After order was restored these unfortunate men marched south to an even worse fate-- the winter at Valley Forge. In May 1778, two regiments of New England troops were paid with worthless Continental currency. They laid their muskets on the ground and refused to work on building construction.

The Van Wyck Homestead

Van Wyck house has been completely restored and now contains an interesting museum.

The Van Wyck House the last remaining structure of the supply depot and only one that has been maintained stands on the northern edge of the encampment. The white frame house was built in 1731 by Cornelius VanWyck and the main section was added before 1756. Cornelius died before the war and the farmhouse was occupied by his son, Isaac Van Wyck during the conflict. Now owned by the Fishkill Historic Society, the Van Wyck house has been completely restored and now contains an interesting museum.[16]

Major General Israel Putnam, affectionately called "Ole Put" by the troops was the Commander of the Continental Army in the Hudson Highlands. The home served as his headquarters. Revolutionary leaders such as George Washington, The Marquis de Lafayette, Friedrich Wilhelm von Steuben, General Alexander McDougall, Colonel Alexander Hamilton, and John Jay Washington, all visited there for dinner there during1778. This was the one visit that can be verified. Although it was believed that the home served as the residence for these top Army commanders it is unlikely that any of them stayed there with the Van Wyck family still in residence. The house was not a living quarters but a headquarters office for the depot. Clerks and paymasters worked from there, and court martials and other military tribunals were held in the room's large parlor.

The mock trial of Enoch Crosby, the first secret agent of the United States was held in the building. Crosby, a Danbury, Connecticut shoemaker, went to White Plains, New York to enlist in the Continental Army. On the way he fell in with a group of Loyalists who mistakenly believed he was one of their number and invited him to their meeting. He reported their plans and identities back to the Americans. This valuable intelligence led to his being chosen by General Washington to be a spy. Masquerading as a Tory he served as a spy for British General Howe and was able to infiltrate loyalist groups. He was captured and tried by the American side to maintain the hoax but was allowed to escape from confinement in the Dutch Church at Fishkill. The Van Wyck house is the likely setting for James Fenimore Cooper's novel, "The Spy" which was based on Enoch Crosby's story. [17]

The Van Wyck House also served as the headquarters for the Quartermaster Department which was in charge of clothing the troops. In addition to its military functions, it also housed the printing press for the newspaper "New York Packet," which was relocated to the Van Wyck homestead from British-occupied New York City. The paper was printed here from January 1777 until the end of the war in 1783 when it was relocated to New York City. The newspaper's publisher, Samuel Louden, was appointed Postmaster for the State of New York with Fishkill becoming the official New York State Post Office. Orders for the Army were also printed here. After the Revolutionary war, the house was given back to the Van Wyck family and remained the family's home until the suicide of Sidney Van Wyck in 1882

Just beyond the Dutch Church a yellow house overlooks the highway. It was owned by the staunch Patriot Dirk Brikerhoff. Washington stayed here during his visits to Fishkill and Lafayette spent six weeks here recovering from pneumonia. A Prussian officer captured at Saratoga reported that Washington stood in front of the house reviewing the prisoners as they passed by. The house is now privately owned. [18]

The Depot at Fishkill served as a rendezvous place for large units defending the state of New York. Major General William Heath in command of the forces of the Hudson River Highlands was here with a large part of the army, division of with 5,400 men, in 1776. The 2nd and 4th New York Regiments spent the winter here in 1777 along with major General Israel Putnam's 600 Hudson Highlands defenders. The 5th New York Regiment led by Colonel Lewis Dubois wintered in Fishkill in 1778. Major General Putnam's division was also here with 1500 men in the summer of that year. Baron Dekalb a Bavarian officer who fought in the French Army, before coming to America with Lafayette in 1777, was at Fishkill with Delaware and Maryland troops. De Kalb was killed soon after at the battle of Camden, South Carolina where he was hit 11 times by musket fire.

Thousands of British loyalist prisoners at Fishkill suffered overcrowding, disease, hunger and abuse by their guards. In October, 1775 the Continental Congress ordered the arrest of any people who might pose a threat to the American cause. After only two weeks 96 Tories had been apprehended and incarcerated in the gallery of the Old Dutch Church. They were an eclectic group of local citizens, wealthy and poor, educated and illiterate. Their occupations included merchants, a judge, an attorney, an innkeeper, farmers, a potash maker, a doctor, a sheriff and a cordwainer. Most were being punished for refusing to take the Oath of Allegiance to the new country.[19]

Among the unfortunate groups were the Loyalist leaders. Beverly Robinson was an affluent landowner from Garrison, New York 10 miles south of Fishkill. He had a palatial mansion on an immense plantation along the Hudson River. Robinson had refused to take the Oath of Allegiance but was granted a month to reconsider. During this time he fled to the British held New York City. In the months that followed he joined the British Army as a colonel and organized a regiment of loyalist Americans. His unit led an attack on Fort Montgomery, which resulted in the horrific defeat of the Twin Forts in October of 1777. He was a participant in the Major Andre-Benedict Arnold plot and was exiled to England after the war. Abraham Cutler, the former mayor of Albany was another Tory organizer. He managed to escape from the church prison. The enraged patriots forced the Lieutenant who was his guard to take his place.

The Lost Cemetery

Deaths at Fishkill were frequent and due mostly to small pox and battle injuries. Beginning in 1776 wounded and sick soldiers were brought to medical facilities at the depot after the battle of White Plains and from all over the north east during the war years. For many years the location of the burial place of the soldiers who did not survive was unknown. The earliest accounts reported it to be at the foot of the mountains. In 1897 a monument was placed by the Daughters of the American Revolution (D.A.R.) on present Route 9, between Snook and Van Wyck Lake roads but did not state the location of the cemetery. This site was probably selected based on Lossing's 1850 report that placed it between the foot of the mountains and a road that branches eastward from the turnpike.

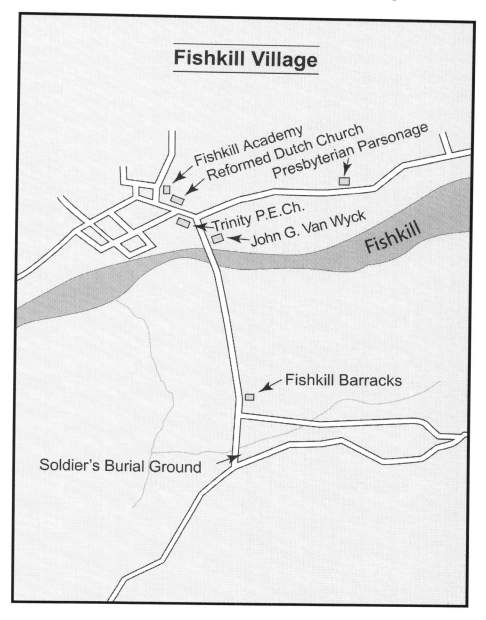

Archeological efforts at the Fishkill Depot in the 1960s did not reveal any evidence of a cemetery and in 1977 the D.A.R. monument was struck by a truck and moved to the grounds of the Van Wyck House. In the years that followed this American military burial place was lost in local mythology and the depot area was built over. Mention of Fishkill Depot was relegated to a few old history books.

One of the greatest archeological discoveries in United States military history was made on the grounds of the depot in 2007. Archeologists of the New York State Office of Historic Preservation dug a shallow trench in a plot that was marked for development and found seven outlines. Each was the size of an adult grave. One was examined and proved to be the coffin burial of an adult male.

At this site another breakthrough was made later that year on one of the remaining open lots. Using ground-penetrating radar scans archeologists from John Milner Associates located hundreds of graves and estimated that the number of graves on the site could be more than 1,000. This would make Fishkill the site of one of the nation's first and largest identified military cemeteries known to exist and the largest Continental Army Burial Complex identified in our country's history.[20]

A more thorough investigation is necessary to assess the true value of the site, but only two remaining open space parcels are currently slated for development. A thorough inventory of the Fishkill Supply Depot cemetery should be undertaken to determine how many American soldiers were laid to rest on the grounds.

Most American Military Leaders Visited Fishkill during the War

A remarkable array of top military leaders visited the Fishkill Depot during the Revolutionary War. George Washington inspected the facility and stayed at the John Brinkerhoff house. From this residence he observed the passage of the prisoners from the battle of Saratoga. Lafayette recuperated from an illness in this same house in 1778. Alexander Hamilton while serving on Washington's staff boarded at the inn in the center of the village across the road from the old Dutch Church. Hamilton issued troop movement orders from there and witnessed the mutiny in 1778.

Area commanders of the Fishkill-Peekskill Highlands were headquartered at the depot throughout the war. General Israel Putnam was in charge after withdrawing American defenders from Peekskill to Fishkill in the summer of 1777. At that time the British were preparing for their October amphibious invasion up the

Hudson River from New York City. General Alexander McDougall commanded the Highlands in 1778. He strengthened the river defenses and set up a line of communications between New York and New England

Activity at the Fishkill crossroads decreased in 1782, as the fighting in the north wound down. By the end of that year the Quartermaster Department removed all supplies to other sites although thousands of Continental troops, many with families, resided there until April 1783, Quartermaster General Timothy Pickering described the place in May 1783, three months before the treaty of Paris was signed ending the war. "At Fishkill there are many public buildings, some valuable, others of little worth-Large arrears for rent and damages done to his plantation are due the owner"(Van Wyck). Soon local residents tore down the abandoned buildings and used the lumber for their own purposes.

Archeology at Fishkill

Archeologists William Calver and Reginald Bolton from the Field Exploration Committee of the New York Historical Society visited Fishkill early in the 20th century. They only saw open fields. The only visible reminders of the war years were the Van Wyck House and the DAR marker.[21]

While surveying along a stretch of the Old Albany Post Road in1914 the remains of more than two dozen horseshoe shaped stone dry walled stuctures were unearthed. They may have been built by the soldiers for added shelter or were cannon enclosures.The contractor used them for material for the road bed under construction for the present Post Road.

In 1968, Paul Huey a New York State Historical archeologist investigated the site. He wrote a a plan for developing the area into a cultural heritage park. His plan was never implemented. Huey drew an exellent map showing the locations of the depot facilities.[22] Marty Byster of the Fishkill Historic Society updated the map in 2006 to include later discoveries. From1971 to 1973 Temple University students and professors, working with the Historical Society tested and documented several sites. These diggers unearthed the ruins of a camp building and a ditch filled with animal bones, which appeared to be the remnants the soldier's food.

When I-84 was built in the 1960s, and the Dutchess Mall was completed in the 1970s foundations of structures ranging from officers' quarters to a blacksmith's shop were uncovered. Bulldozers stood by poised to excavate as local, often amateur, volunteers worked hastily to document the many traces of depot activities. These surveys prompted the restoration of the officer's headquarters and the Van Wyck Homestead by the Fishkill Historical Society. The efforts produced some tantalizing possibilities considering that the depot stretched three miles south of Fishkill.

In 1974 the Fishkill Supply Depot and Encampment, consisting of more than 70 acres along Route 9, was placed on the National Register for Historic Places. Plans were made to open it up to serious archaeological investigation and to create a national park. This did not transpire and the land, never properly assessed by experts in the field of military archaeology, once more became seriously threatened by a new round of commercial development.

Preservation Efforts

In 2006, plans for extensive commercial development of the depot area were being finalized. That year local historians and activists united to advocate permanent protection of the properties within the Depot historic district. The group which became known as "Friends of the Fishkill Supply Depot," lobbied for further archaeological review of the endangered area.[23] Their objectives were to hold off further disturbance and development of the properties within the 70 acre site and to encourage private organizations, the town, and the state and federal government, to purchase properties within the site that were under the imminent threat of development. Petitions were circulated by the group calling for action and signed by archaeologists, historians, environmentalists and concerned citizens throughout the country. Their efforts resulted in an archeological survey of the site lands slated for development. The momentous the discovery of evidence indicating the presence of hundreds of soldier's graves was made on a site being readied for commercial retail development during the final archeological effort.

In November 2009, Mara Farrell, co-founder of the Friends of the Fishkill Supply Depot, testified on behalf of the site before a Senate subcommittee. As a result of this attention U.S. Senator Charles Schumer introduced legislation to make the site eligible for federal preservation funds. Schumer urged the National Parks Service to conduct a thorough inventory of the Fishkill Supply Depot to determine how many American soldiers were buried on the grounds and what items of cultural significance still remain. The Fishkill Supply Depot may soon become eligible for federal preservation funds. The 20 acres of remaining open space that still remain within the 70 acre National Register-designated site is currently on sale and proposed for a shopping center. The loss of this open space will destroy most archaeological features and artifacts.

In April 2011, U.S. Senator Charles Schumer announced plans to propose legislation that could help municipalities gain funds through the National Park Service and the American Battlefield Protection Program. This program would buy and preserve Revolutionary War sites, such as the Fishkill Supply Depot. Currently, only Civil War battlefields qualify for the program. The following month the National Park Service gave its support to the bill that would make the Fishkill Supply Depot eligible for federal preservation funds. The bill, S. 779, cleared committee in November and was submitted to the Senate floor for debate.

Farrell dreams of building an interpretive center on the site and incorporating public art and trails: "Perhaps some of the features could be excavated and stabilized. We foresee a partnership with a university to have on-site archeologists and a learning center." She envisions the day when chemical and DNA testing can be used to determine the identities of the soldiers buried at the site. Schumer said preserving the local treasure would honor the memory of Revolutionary War soldiers and could become a tourist destination, which in turn could help the local economy.

Fishkill Today:
A Courageous Defense Against Continued Development

Fishkill today is a growing town of 2,000 residents and remains a busy crossroads that can be easily reached from all directions. The major east-west highway I- 84 intersects with Routes 9 and 52 at the town. Route 9, also known in the past as the King's Highway and the Albany Post Road, starts 50 miles south at Broadway in Manhattan and runs through Times Square. It uses portions of the old Post Road as it runs through the Hudson Highlands to the state capitol. Route 52 a major route between Boston and Philadelphia is Main Street in Fishkill.

Evidence of the role the town played in the War for Independence is still apparent despite disregard over two centuries. Wicccopee pass the critical single gap through the mountain to the south looms in the distance as a constant reminder that Fishkill was selected for the depot because of its natural defenses. The Van Wyck House owned and operated by the Fishkill Historic Society still stands in an impressively restored state. The Dutch Church occupies a prominent place on the main street. It is still active and its adjacent cemetery contains graves that date to the colonial period. Several colonial homes, still occupied by private owners, are in pristine condition.

The location of this critical nerve center of the Continental Army is a classic case of the desecration and neglect of a historic site. Over the past fifty years, the lands have been

defiled and disjointed by commercial development. The abandoned Dutchess Mall covers the site of the barracks. A gas station was built directly across from the Van Wyck House on the site of the depot's blacksmith shop The Van Wyck House narrowly escaped being torn down in the1960s to make room for a cloverleaf for I- 84. The site of Moog's farmhouse a colonial era home and a confirmed soldier's burial site is occupied by a café.

I met with Lance Ashworth, President of the Friends of the Fishkill Supply Depot in July, 2011. Before we started out to explore the Fishkill area he gave me a preview using a Power Point presentation that summarized the history of the depot, preservation attempts through the years and the present threat of development. It focused on the opportunity that still remains for reverent preservation and archeology on remaining open space that could begin with the acquisition of available properties.

Our first stop was at the Van Wyck House where we met Marty Byster, a trustee of the Historical Society. The original section was begun in 1732 and has the original wide plank floors and hand hewn beams. The larger part of the home, built in the 1750s, contains an interesting collection of artifacts found on the site including the iron claw from the walnut tree whipping post or tollgate. During the construction of the Duchess Mall many artifacts, such as cannon balls, muskets, utensils, and uniform buttons were unearthed. The Fishkill Historical Society holds about 10,000 pieces collected in the depot area. The relocated D.A. R. monument is found on the house grounds along with a pyramid assembled with stones donated by other historical sites throughout the northeast during the nation's bicentennial. Remains of foundations, a cistern and an old well also surround the homestead.

We drove south on Route 9 for three miles to the "lower barracks" where as many as 2,000 men were billeted. In addition to regular troops these barracks housed prisoners, the sick and wounded and a regiment disabled officers and enlisted men.

In this area were the defensive positions that guarded the vital Wiccopee Pass. On the roadside were two markers that read "on the hills back of this stone stood three batteries guarding this pass. Another marker a few feet away read, "On this hill during the American Revolution was a battery for the defense of Fishkill Clove."

The 2007 re-discovery of the burial ground spurred great interest and additional historical research about the site. By August 2010, Hudson Valley residents Lisa Bruck and Liz Kurtlik had developed a preliminary list of 25 Revolutionary War officers and soldiers who either died or were buried in Fishkill.

The Fishkill Supply Depot was critical to the success of the Continental Army during the American Revolution and was central to the founding of the United States. Its importance to the Continental Army as an essential military facility cannot be overestimated. The Depot played a vital role in the victory over British forces, which have earned it a place on the National Register of Historic Places. The last 20 acres of open space within the National Register-designated site are proposed for development that would destroy its archaeological features and artifacts. The opportunity to achieve preservation it is not likely to ever come again. The two remaining large open space parcels, currently for sale, represent the only remaining intact vestiges of an important part of the nation's founding.

There has been recent good news on the congressional front for preservation of the Fishkill Supply Depot. H.R. 2489: American Battlefield Protection Program Amendments Act of 2011, has passed the House's Natural Resources Subcommittee on National Parks, Forests and Public Lands – and will go to the full Natural Resources committee, where it is expected to be sent to the floor of the full House. Meanwhile a similar bill is going before the full Senate. Legislation that could save Depot is making progress in Congress.

Chapter Three

Head of Elk to Cooch's Bridge-Springboard to Victory for Redcoats and Rebels, 1776-1781.

Elkton Maryland to Glascow Delaware.

Today and in Times Past— A Heavily Trafficked Route

Every day thousands of cars rush along Interstate 95, America's major north-south route from Maine to Florida. For a short stretch in Delaware and Maryland of about 10 miles, people travel beside a long forgotten old road that witnessed two crucial actions of the Revolutionary War. There are no historical markers along here. The high land of Iron Hill, a promontory a few 100 yards away, is the only remnant of the era visible from the superhighway.

In 1777, this pathway served as the springboard for British invaders advancing north to their crucial victory at Brandywine and the capture of Philadelphia the capitol city of the new nation. Four years later the Continental Army and its French allies marched south to embark on ships to sail down Chesapeake Bay to Yorktown, Virginia where they would win the final decisive victory of the war. The old road and its adjacent modern counterpart span the Maryland - Delaware border and run between Elkton, Maryland, and Newark, Delaware.

During 1777, the third year of the war, the area known as Head of Elk encompassed the town of Elkton and a landing place 10 miles south. After a century the town became known as Elkton and the port was referred to as Elk Landing. The place was strategically located at the head of navigation of the Elk River that led north from Chesapeake Bay. Ships coming in from the ocean could enter the bay at Cape Charles and sail 200 miles north to Head of Elk. This was the start of the road to Brandywine Valley and Philadelphia and from here the heartland of the new nation would be penetrated.[1]

Along this route a massive Anglo-German assault force would be surprised by stiff resistance at Cooch's Bridge, now Glasgow, five miles from Newark, Delaware. This event was the only battle of the American Revolutionary War fought on Delaware soil. Many historians claim that it was here the Stars and Stripes were flown in battle for the first time.[2] The British invasion pushed north 25 miles to defeat the unseasoned Patriot forces at Brandywine. The Redcoats went on to capture Philadelphia and force Washington's untrained and poorly equipped farm boys to Valley Forge, Pennsylvania, a barren plain 16 miles north of the city, where the desperate men would starve, freeze and die from illness during the bitter winter of 1777-1778.

Four years later in March, 1781, the Marquis de Lafayette passed down the old road with 1,200 men from New England and New Jersey to assist in the defense of Virginia after Benedict Arnold, with a British force, invaded that state. Later that year when the tide turned in favor of the cause for independence, the entire Continental Army and its French allies, a force of about 15,000 men, marched down the same old pathway to Head of Elk and set sail down Chesapeake Bay to land at Williamsburg and Yorktown. This march is an epic in the military history of the world and was the longest and largest troop movement in the Revolutionary War. These hallowed events, unknown to most people today, all happened along this obscure thoroughfare.

The year of 1776 was a disaster for Americans. After being driven from New York, Washington's diminished and demoralized troops were pursued across New Jersey to the Pennsylvania side of the Delaware River. A miraculous year end victory at Trenton followed up a week later with more success at Princeton saved the war for the Patriots.

Not expecting further action, both armies followed the usual martial practice of the time and withdrew to winter quarters in secure areas. The Continental Army found a safe haven in Morristown, New Jersey, where they were protected by the natural defenses of the Watchung Mountains and the Great Swamp. His majesty's troops and Hessian mercenaries moved to the security of occupied New York City and the hospitality of its many Loyalist residents.

Capture the Rebel Capitol and the Rebellion Will End

During the following summer of 1777, Washington tried to anticipate the strategy of the two main British forces in America. General Howe, the supreme commander of the British occupation forces in America remained in New York City with the main part of the British army and was gathering a large fleet in the harbor. Major General John Burgoyne, second in command in America landed in Quebec in May and had assembled an army of 8,000 British, Hessian, Canadians and Indians. Burgoyne's next move was apparent. He prepared to divide the states by occupying the vital waterway that ran from the St. Lawrence River down to Lake Champlain and Lake George to New York.

It seemed logical that Howe would sail up the Hudson River with his fleet and meet Burgoyne in the Albany, New York area. Linking the two armies would ensure the separation of New England from the other states and crush the American rebellion. Washington began moving regiments toward the Hudson Highlands to place them between the two British Forces. General Howe, however, had other options which puzzled the American side. He could march across New Jersey or sail south with his fleet and capture the American capitol of Philadelphia or he could continue south on the sea route to capture Charlestown, South Carolina and invade the southern states.

Washington guessed wrong when he began reinforcing the Hudson Highlands. Howe unpredictably decided that he would leave Burgoyne to fend for himself at Saratoga, New York. He would try to break the back of the rebellion by capturing Philadelphia, the Patriot capitol. When Washington learned that the entire British fleet, last seen off Sandy Hook, with many troop ships, had sailed south he was sure their objective was Philadelphia. They would round Cape May, New Jersey and sail up the Delaware River to make an amphibious landing at the city. This assumption was confirmed when the huge armada was spotted at the mouth of Delaware Bay on July 30.

The American Commander -In- Chief was mistaken again. The fleet suddenly turned around and was next spotted 30 miles below the entrance to Delaware Bay, off the Maryland coast. Washington, now in a complete quandary, had erroneously concluded that this maneuvering was a feint and the wily Howe might be heading back north to sail up the Hudson to meet Burgoyne after all. He was wrong again.

Howe elected to take a sea route from New York City down the New Jersey coast. When the ships reached Delaware Bay the scouting frigate Roebuck met the fleet and reported that the Delaware River was heavily defended by fire ships. These vessels were filled with combustibles and set afire. They could be steered or allowed to drift into an enemy fleet to destroy it or break up its formation. Patriot shore batteries were also believed to block the way. This artillery could demolish cumbersome men-of-war trying to maneuver in confined areas. Moreover, navigation up the Delaware was hazardous for the large warships.[3]

Actually, the intelligence from the Roebuck was greatly exaggerated. The river was defended only by a small American fleet. To avoid these formidable but mostly imagined obstacles Howe decided to continue following the coastline 140 miles south to the Virginia Capes, as far as Chesapeake Bay, the next estuary. Here he could enter the long navigable Chesapeake Bay and sail north into the heartland of the rebellion. His army could land at Head of Elk, Delaware, 50 miles south of Philadelphia, where legions of Loyalists were reported to be ready to join him.[4]

The Fleet had left New York to begin the 200 mile voyage on July 23, 1777. Bad weather delayed caused the 265 ships carrying 18,000 British and Hessians soldiers to flounder off the Delaware Capes for three weeks. Rough seas as well as lack of provisions and water made for an arduous passage. Twenty seven men died and 170 horses perished, Another 150 animals, so critical to the mobility of the campaign, were too emaciated for further duty. The debilitated British assault force spent five weeks on a voyage that took eight days in normal weather.[5]

The fleet, commanded by Admiral Richard Howe, General William Howe's brother, reached Cape Charles and entered the mouth of the Chesapeake Bay. It took the flotilla 11 days to sail up the bay. The river shoaled up at the mouth of the Elk River and required skilled seamanship to maneuver the heavy warships. General William Howe bragged, "*The shoalness of the Elk convinced the Rebels that our fleet would never navigate it but through the great abilities of our naval officers it was happily affected, although the bottom was muddy and the ships were cutting channels for those that followed.*" The flagship Eagle finally anchored at Turkey Point at the mouth of the Elk River on August 25.[6]

Head of Elk is located in Cecil County, Maryland. The property was purchased by Zebulon Hollingsworth an original settler in 1735. Its location at the source of the Elk River made it the northernmost inland water route on the mid Atlantic coast. During colonial times it was an ideal place from which to ship the products of the surrounding countryside. Cargoes included flour, lumber and bar iron, bags of nails, apples and pork. Arriving ships from other colonies and Europe brought coffee, whiskey, clothing and furniture. Farmers on the bountiful eastern shore of the Chesapeake fed both friend and foe during the war and their produce was shipped from Elk Landing south major markets from Baltimore to the West Indies.[7]

In 1776, residents of the area surmised that their location was the perfect place for an invasion from the sea. They formed a local militia and began hiding their horses, cattle, and valuables in the woods.

Washington Reconnoiters

The vast armada, the largest ever launched in America by the British, disappeared off the Delaware coast for three weeks due to the bad weather. Where it would land along the coastline remained unknown. Washington agonized over where he should position the Continental Army to best defend the country. He did not know that the flotilla had turned around at the mouth of the Delaware Bay and headed south. He still assumed that the most logical route for the invaders would be to sail up the Delaware River Bay. The river port of Chester, Pennsylvania, only 10 miles south of the city, was the most likely landing place for the invaders. The suspense ended when innkeeper Jacob Hollingsworth, sighted the flotilla off Turkey Point at Head of Elk on August 23.

While the enemy had arrived 35 miles away from where they were expected, Washington recognized that their objective was the same, the nation's capitol city, Philadelphia. Its fall would be a disaster. He had to rapidly move his troops between Howe's army and a nervous Continental Congress and commit all his military resources. It would mean confronting the seasoned British Regulars, with their superior numbers and firepower, in a major pitched battle.

Earlier in the year he had avoided a major head- to- head fight by resisting the attempt of the British to lure him down to the central plains of New Jersey.[8] Prudently he kept his army secure at Middlebrook in the Watchung Mountains. Now, he would be coerced into confronting the professional Redcoat Army, the most effective fighting force in the world, with his untrained regiments of farmers.

At this time Washington was camped at Neshaminy, a few miles north of Philadelphia on the Delaware River. Now certain of the enemy's strategy, he responded instantly. His first move was to add strength by calling in the militias of Pennsylvania, Delaware and Maryland. He then ordered all his scattered brigades to march south so the Continental Army would be between the landing place at Head of Elk and Philadelphia. The pathetic army of 16,000 marched through the capitol to the cadence of fifes and drums. This was a show of force designed to impress the large Loyalist population. Washington headed the procession followed by the eager young volunteer from France, the 20 year old Marquis de Lafayette.

John Adams stepped out of a meeting of the Continental Congress to witness the two hour procession. The founding father observed that the men "did not have quite the air of soldiers," marched out of step and did not stand erect. The Americans reached Darby, Pennsylvania by the end of the day and continued on to Wilmington, Delaware. Now it was essential to ascertain the strength of the British invasion.

The history of the war could have been very different if the Americans had learned earlier that the British fleet would end up at Head of Elk. An amphibious campaign is at its most vulnerable stage during landing, the time when it is moving men ashore and unloading equipment and supplies. The Continental Army, though raw, had grown. If it could be on site awaiting fleet's arrival in Maryland, the assault could be disrupted. With Burgoyne beaten three weeks later at Saratoga the war would have ended with an American triumph. With only a two days notice it was impossible to move the Patriot forces into the advantageous position and the opportunity was missed. The war dragged on for another five years.

On August 25, the Commander-In -Chief rushed from the camp at Wilmington through a torrential rainstorm toward the anticipated British landing place at Head of Elk. He wanted to personally assess the state of affairs. This perilous scouting mission would take him to within a few miles of the enemy. Washington took with him two of his most trusted subordinates, General Nathaniel Green and Marquis de Lafayette. From Grey's Hill near the village he was able to get his first look at the vast enemy force and observe the first large scale amphibious landing in American history.

Usually the size of the enemy force could be estimated by counting their tents. But since the invaders had not set up an encampment the American officers learned little about the strength of the task force. Washington wrote to Congress, "*They remain where they had debarked at first. I could not find out from inquiry what number is landed or form an estimate of it from the distant view I had of their encampment.*"

The scouting party dined and spent the night at the hotel in the town owned by patriot Jacob Hollingsworth who had first reported sighting the fleet. Two nights later General Howe slept in the same room and was waited on by the same servant.

During the day the severe thunderstorms continued and the roads became impassible. Rather than attempt to struggle back to Wilmington through the mud, Washington insisted on spending the night at a farmhouse along the way near Cooch's Bridge. It was the home of Seth James, a Tory, where he and his party could have been easily surrounded by Loyalists and captured. Lafayette later admitted to having been apprehensive about sleeping "very close to the enemy" on this night. Washington confessed that at the time a single traitor could have betrayed him. The three American generals arose at dawn and hurried back to Wilmington to await the onslaught of a relentless, destructive and ruthless enemy.

A Massive Redcoat Invasion Comes Ashore in Maryland

On, August 25th 1777, a mighty flotilla of 265 warships and troop vessels began the first large scale amphibious landing on the west side of the Elk River in Maryland. The armada carried 18,000 of His Majesty's troops along with General William Howe the commander of all of these royal forces in America, Their objective was to capture Philadelphia the capitol of the American Patriots. George Washington and the fledgling Continental Army, a few miles away, stood between them and this city. In only two weeks these adversaries would clash at Brandywine in one of the largest and bloodiest battles of the Revolutionary War.

This awesome British offensive was more vulnerable than it appeared. Unlike D Day at Normandy, a century and a half later, nobody, including Howe, had any idea what to expect and feared the "blind landing." His most vulnerable time was when troops disembarked and supplies were unloaded. Attempting to reach shore in bateaux, the fragile landing craft of the day, they could be pounded by American artillery or trapped on the beach and annihilated. The landing, however, was unopposed. The Continental Army 20 miles north learned of the approach too late to reach Head of Elk to repel the assault or take any defensive action. Philadelphia, the seat of the Continental Congress was the pivot of the American rebellion. Its loss would be devastating to the cause for independence.

The closest any Americans approached the landing place that day was a nearby hill where George Washington along with Generals Lafayette and Greene observed the landing activity. So much time had been lost at sea that Howe ordered his men not to set up camp on arrival but to be prepared to move out. Counting tents was the best way to judge the size of an army, but the absence of these shelters puzzled the American generals. They left without an accurate estimate of enemy strength. The day of the landing was sweltering. The same thunderstorms that had delayed Washington on his return to Wilmington prevented the British from starting their advance north. Dressed in sodden wool clothing, exhausted from being so long at sea His Majesty's troops were wretched suffering from the night chill and the oppressive humidity of the day. Several Hessians died from exposure that week.

The Landing Place at Head of Elk

No plans were in place for supplying the troops with fresh provisions after they landed. Most of the local residents had fled, and the few who remained did not wish to trade with the enemy. The famished soldiers immediately began to scavenge for food at nearby farms and slaughter cattle that had been left behind. Many horses had died during the long voyage and those that survived were too weak and sick to haul cannon and supplies. It would take time for the task force to recover and find food. These difficulties allowed time for the Americans to add to their numbers by assembling area militia forces and making other preparations to stop the invasion. The British remained at the Head of Elk landing area for two days, planning strategy, stocking up on supplies and waiting for the storm to pass.[9]

Mud Slows Both Redcoats and Rebels

Both armies spent Wednesday, August 26, recovering from the storm's damage and the loss of critical stocks of ammunition. Gunpowder and paper cartridges for muskets and canon were useless when they were wet. That morning Washington arrived back at his Wilmington headquarters after stumbling over the soggy and almost impassible roads. These conditions stopped him from immediately sending out part of the Continental army to confront the invaders. The weather and mired roads also plagued Howe. He was impatient to start the campaign but canceled all troop movements on his second day ashore.

That same morning Cornwallis went north to scout the route of the assault that led to the town of Elkton eight miles away. He reported that the roads were still of no use. Howe later wrote, *"Since the heavy rain continues and the roads are bottomless, and since the horses are sick and stiff, we had to countermand the order to march."* Both armies spent the day drying out equipment and replenishing their ammunition supplies.[10]

Cornwallis also was on the alert to detect the presence of Loyalist support. Howe had been convinced by Tory leaders in Philadelphia that an enthusiastic greeting and a groundswell of assistance awaited him from the many civilians in Maryland who remained loyal to King George III. He fully expected that legions of loyalists, eagerly expecting his arrival, would take control of the local government, provide supplies and form regiments to join his forces. The disappointed general saw no evidence of these reinforcements on the first days of the landing. The countryside was eerily deserted. Abandoned farms and fields where cattle and horses had recently grazed were desolate.

Howe had close ties with prominent Loyalists from the Maryland area and three Tory military units were in his invasion force. While support failed to appear, there was one notable exception. Robert Alexander, a prominent Maryland politician, owned the large tract of land that encompassed the town of Elkton. He was a militia lieutenant and served as a delegate to the Continental Congress. Washington knew Alexander as a Patriot and visited him at his mansion, "The Hermitage" while on the scouting expedition to observe the British landing. Washington assumed that the wealthy land owner would flee from the enemy occupation but Alexander curiously said that he preferred to stay.

Washington did not know that Alexander had resigned from the Maryland Militia after the signing of the Declaration of Independence the previous year and had been meeting with the state's Tory underground. Howe visited Robert Alexander's Hermitage two days after Washington, he was warmly welcomed. Alexander sold livestock and grain to the invaders and went along with the Howe when they moved north. He never returned to Maryland. Judged guilty of high treason in 1780, his property was confiscated and he later died in London, England, in 1805. His estate became the town of Elkton, and the superbly restored Hermitage still stands. [11]

Howe made a desperate attempt to gain the support of the local population. He ordered a proclamation in the form of a broadside poster to be printed on a press aboard one of the ships. A broadside was a large sheet of paper, printed on one side that announced events, public statements, or advertisements. It was posted in public places or distributed and was the common form of a news bulletin in that era.

The document was addressed, *By His Excellency Sir William Howe, A declaration to the inhabitants of Pennsylvania, the lower counties on Delaware and the counties on the eastern shore of Maryland.* Howe promised the local population that any British troops caught plundering or molesting civilians would be severely punished. He guaranteed that anyone who had opposed his forces would be pardoned and allowing to return peacefully to their homes. Any militia officers or men could surrender and also be fully pardoned.[12]

Maryland Militia leaders were apprehensive and feared that many people would take advantage of the benevolent terms of the amnesty. Disregarded, the defection did not happen. Local Patriots and those already in the militia remained true to the cause for Independence. Most of Head of Elk's inhabitants were farm families who had been on their lands for generations and had little interest in fervently supporting either side of the conflict. Howe would have to push on without the local Loyalist support he anticipated.

The Red Tide Rises

By August 28, four days after the landing, the roads had dried. The first wave of troops, led by Cornwallis, left the landing place at 6:00 AM and headed for the village of Elkton. They marched in formations wider than the road and tore down fences and cleared other obstacles to clean up the path for the thousands of troops who would follow. Despite the proclamation there was torching of farmhouses and homes were looted along the way. The few livestock found were routinely slaughtered. Bateaux, carrying supplies, accompanied the troops up Little Elk Creek toward the town. Progress was slow due to the hauling of heavy cannon over the rutted road. One eyewitness in the town could not help but be impressed as the columns pressed forward, *"they came in sight of the river west of town, with their scarlet coats, their bright coats and bayonets gleaming in the rays of an early August sun."* As the formations advanced, the day warmed and the skies finally cleared.

There was no resistance when the first Redcoat regiments arrived at Elkton at 9:00 AM. The town of 40 brick and stone houses was deserted. Minutes before residents and the Delaware Militia removed most supplies from town. The 1,000 Delaware troops fell back to nearby Gray's Hill but burned the bridge on their way out of town to slow down the British invaders. The waves of Redcoats easily forded the shallow creek where the bridge had been destroyed and entered the town. They set up camp northeast of the town where the Delaware Militia had camped. Officers lodged in the deserted houses. The invaders were pleased to find that left behind stocks of molasses, Indian corn, tobacco and flour.

General Howe arrived at the end of the day and set up his Headquarters at the Elk Tavern. That evening he dined in the same room and was waited on by the same servant who served Washington at the inn two days before. From here he maintained communication with his two divisions. Cornwallis was with Howe in the town while General Knyphausen, commanding the Hessians, was still back at the landing with the rest of the army unloading the ships.

At Elkton scavenging parties immediately began searching the surrounding countryside for food and fodder for the horses. The ravenous soldiers continued to violate the proclamation. The following week two soldiers were hung and five others flogged for looting.

On the morning of September 3, Cornwallis and Howe left Grey's Hill near Elkton and headed north to Aiken's Tavern, now Glasgow Delaware. Howe's inaccurate maps of the area and scanty intelligence were a problem, and he knew he had to make up for the time lost at sea. Hurrying along what is today Route 40, they reached at Aiken's Tavern at 9:00 A.M.[13]

General Knyphausen after completing the unloading of the ships, did not head for Elton to join the main force. On August 30, Howe ordered him to march five miles east to meet up with the brigades of Cornwallis at Aikin's Tavern. Knyphausen's units crossed the Elk River at Cecil Courthouse and then turned north at Lums Pond and camped the first night of the march at Carson's Tavern. The Hessians collected many cattle, sheep and horses along the way. They reached Aiken's Tavern about an hour after Cornwallis arrived. Now the entire invasion force was together and massed for the Philadelphia Campaign. But a nasty surprise awaited them as their forward columns neared Cooch's Bridge over the Christine Creek.

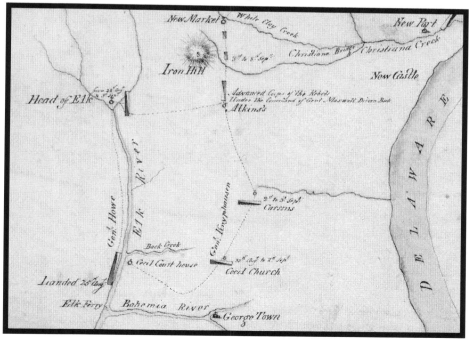

Detail of a 1777 military map. Cooch's Bridge is just to the right of Iron Hill; Philadelphia is off to the northeast.

Scotch Willy's Commandos Check Redcoat Advance

In the Continental Army most infantry regiments had an elite "light company." Its mission and men were comparable to today's Navy Seals, Green Berets, Ranger battalions and other special forces. Its members were handpicked for physical size, agility, shooting ability and boldness. They did not fight in disciplined ranks as regular soldiers. In combat they were widely dispersed to be effective in fast moving skirmishes. Their tactic was to surprise and harass the enemy, then fall back. They fought in front of the lines of the main army and avoided hand-to-hand combat. Light infantry companies were often temporary in organization, created for a single critical strike. At Cooch's Bridge both sides used their choice light infantry units.

Washington was still puzzled as to where Howe's fleet headed after it left New York in August 1777. It appeared most likely that the huge task force would head up the Hudson River campaign to link up with Burgoyne forces coming down from Canada. The American defenders caught between the two halves of the British Army in the Hudson River Valley needed reinforcement. Reluctantly the American commander sent Colonel Daniel Morgan's Riflemen, his top light infantry corps, to that area. It soon became apparent the British would not follow that strategy but instead would sail south to attempt an amphibious landing with the objective of capturing Philadelphia, the capitol of the young republic. Morgan's men were in the wrong place and he would have to move fast to replace them.

Washington ordered a hundred of the best soldiers to be selected from his six brigades. Those selected were placed under the command of Brigadier General William Maxwell of New Jersey. Affectionately known as "Scotch Willie" to his men, the seasoned officer was a veteran of the French and Indian War and the ill-fated Canadian Campaign of 1775. Maxwell had distinguished himself two months earlier in The Battle of the Short Hills in central New Jersey. Greatly outnumbered, he led a light infantry brigade against British and Hessian troops and held them off long enough for Washington to withdraw the Continental Army to the safety of the Watchung Mountains. This action was believed to be critical in keeping the new nation in the war.

Maxwell's new company numbered 720 men. They would be fighting together for the first time yet the Commander-In-Chief expected much from them. Their mission was not to stop the advance of the entire invasion but "to be constantly near the enemy and to give them every possible annoyance." They were to delay the advance and make an estimate of enemy strength.

On September 2, Maxwell was ordered to position his corps along the road on the Christiana Creek that led three miles from Aiken's Tavern in what is today Glasgow, Delaware to Cooch's Bridge. The British Army assembled at Aikin's Tavern was expected to attack the next morning. The Americans set up defensive positions in the creek beds and woods along the little road that today parallels Route 896, from Glasgow to Newark, Delaware and runs behind Glasgow High School.

On September 3, Scotch Willie deployed his men, hidden by the verdant September foliage, along two miles on both sides of this road. They were told to fire volleys from their ambush and then fall back a short distance, reload and fire again. This repetitive tactic would give him time to decide on an advantageous place to make a stand.

Cornwallis left Aiken's Tavern and headed toward the bridge with a forward column of 4,000 British light infantry and Hessian Jaegers. Jaegers were the equivalent of American light infantry. In the van of the column were 300 Anspach chasseurs, a unit of Jaegers from the province of Anspach, Germany, who were specifically selected to lead the advance. define These crack Hessian troops were specially trained to excel in marksmanship, could deploy rapidly and execute maneuvers at high speed. British light infantry who dragged along two amusettes were backed up by chasseurs. Three men or one horse could haul these light cannons.[14]

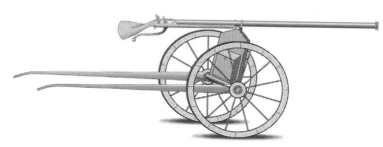

Hessian Amusette

Lieutenant Colonel Ludwig Johann Adoph von Wurmb led the chasseurs. He ran forward with a patrol of six men to scout the road ahead. As they reached what is now the site of Du Pont's Glasgow Plant, a sudden barrage of musket fire from the concealed patriots felled all six men. The confused German troops at first did could not detect where to return the gunfire. Von Wurmb, writing to a friend after the battle, reported that, *"about a mile beyond [Aikin's Tavern] the country was close — the woods within shot of the road frequently in front and flank and in*

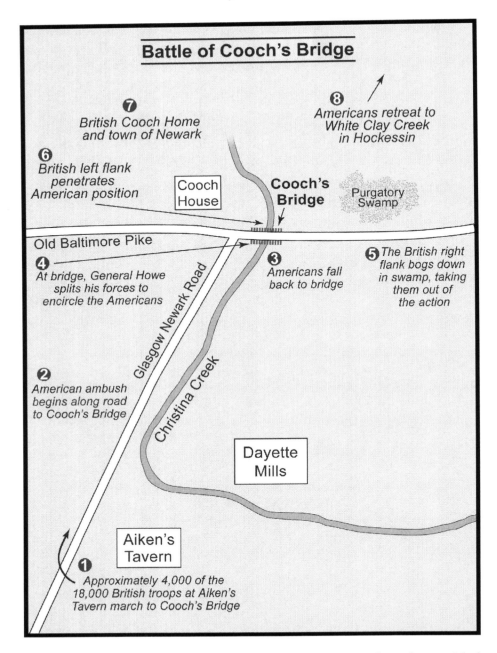

Battle of Cooch's Bridge

❼
British Cooch Home
and town of Newark

❽
Americans retreat to
White Clay Creek
in Hockessin

❻
British left flank
penetrates
American position

Cooch
House

**Cooch's
Bridge**

Purgatory
Swamp

Old Baltimore Pike

❹
At bridge, General Howe
splits his forces to
encircle the Americans

Glasgow Newark Road

❸
Americans fall
back to bridge

❺ The British right
flank bogs down
in swamp, taking
them out of
the action

❷
American ambush
begins along road
to Cooch's Bridge

Christina Creek

Dayette
Mills

Aiken's
Tavern

❶
Approximately 4,000 of the
18,000 British troops at Aiken's
Tavern march to Cooch's Bridge

*projecting point towards the road. Here the rebels began to attack us about 9 o'clock
with continued irregular fire for nearly two miles.*[15]

The nimble chasseurs quickly formed up and returned the fire wheeling the amusettes into the firefight. Some of the Hessians left the road and ran into the woods to attack the American's right flank. Von Wurmb's men then fixed bayonets and charged forward. This onslaught caused the Americans to fall back in a series of 20- yard intervals to take up new concealed positions and reload. The courageous Von Wurmb remained directly in front of his men and rallied them on. The Americans were slowly driven back up the road. They formed a defensive line at the bridge and poured well directed volleys into the advancing enemy until their ammunition began to run out.[16]

Jaeger Captain Johann Ewald gave this eye witness account of the action at Cooch's Bridge. *"I…had not gone a hundred paces from the advance guard, when I received fire from a hedge, through which these six men [the dragoons] were all either killed or wounded. My horse, which normally was well used to fire, reared so high several times that I expected it would throw me. I cried out, "Foot jaegers forward!" and advanced with them to the area from which the fire was coming…At this moment I ran into another enemy party with which I became heavily engaged. Lieutenant Colonel von Wurmb, who came with the entire Corps assisted by the light infantry, ordered the advance guard to be supported…The charge was sounded, and the enemy was attacked so severely and with such spirit by the jaegers that we became masters of the mountain after a seven hour engagement … The majority of the jaegers came to close quarters with the enemy, and the hunting sword was used as much as the rifle … The jaegers alone enjoyed the honor of driving the enemy out of his advantageous position.*[17]

The British light infantry then joined the fray. The Americans gave ground again but fired as they fell back. Maxwell's men, outnumbered four to one, now faced point blank- fire from the amusettes and vigorous bayonet charges. The battle turned into a hand- to- hand mêlée with bayonets and swords. Unfortunately, the patriot had a serious disadvantage. Their muskets, many brought from home, were originally hunting rifles and did not have bayonets. The Americans were forced back beyond Cooch's Bridge where the road leads to the Welsh Tract Church that was damaged when a cannon ball passed through it. The battle

Johann von Ewald (1744-1813) Jaeger Captain a German from Hesse-Kassel commanded infantry regiment attached to British forces.

lasted most of the day. Maxwell's warriors, their mission accomplished, rejoined the main army five miles away at White Clay Creek.

Early in the engagement, the British 2nd Grenadier battalion was sent to the right across Christiana Creek to surround Maxwell's men. They went too far from the action and became entangled in the woods and bogged down in what was known at that time as Purgatory Swamp.[18] Blocked from returning to the fight, they gave up and retraced their way back to the bridge and rejoined the other attackers. When they returned Maxwell's corps were disorganized and hastily retreating while still returning sustained musket fire. Major John Andre reported that the Americans left hastily throwing down their arms and blankets.

The Americans reported 20 men dead and 20 men wounded at Cooch's Bridge. A camp follower who deserted from the British reported that nine wagon loads of wounded men were sent back to Head of Elk. The British consistently gave low numbers during the war to minimize their losses. Howe only admitted to losing a number equal to the Americans. The Pencader Presbyterian Church in Glasgow was used as a British hospital after the battle. Considering that Maxwell's men were skilled marksmen and ambushed their enemy, British losses must have been greater. [19]

General George Washington made this comment in the evening after the battle. *"September 3: "This morning the Enemy came out with considerable force and three pieces of Artillery, against our Light advanced Corps, and after some pretty smart skirmishing obliged them to retreat, being far inferior to them in number and without Cannon. The loss on either side is not yet ascertain'd. Ours, tho' not exactly known is not very considerable; Their's, we have reason to believe, was much greater, as some of our parties composed of expert Marksmen, had opportunities of giving them several close, well directed Fires, more particularly in one instance, when a body of Riflemen formed a kind of Ambuscade. They advanced about two Miles this side of Iron Hill, and then withdrew to that place, leaving a Picket at Couch's Mill about a Mile in front. Our parties now lie at White Clay Creek, except the advanced Pickets, which are at Christiana Bridge."* [20]

For the next week the British and Hessian forces occupied the area around Iron Hill from Glasgow to Newark. Howe set up headquarters at Aikins tavern which stood across the road from the Pencader Presbyterian Church. Knyphausen occupied the Andrew Fisher house between Iron Hill and Newark near Silverbrook. Cornwallis stayed at the Cooch House near the battlefield. The home's owner, Thomas Cooch, had fled with his family to Pennsylvania. Cooch's mill and several other buildings on the property were burned. Howe's forces used this break to regroup, strengthen their horses and finalize their strategy for the drive north.

Supplies were still arriving and were being unloaded from the fleet back at the Head of Elk Landing.

Maxwell had achieved his objective. He successfully delayed the invasion force before withdrawing to join the main army. His light infantry proved that the Patriots would be a tenacious adversary. Moreover, the stand at Cooch's Bridge caused Howe to halt the entire Philadelphia campaign for a week.

The Redcoats Surge North

Howe prepared to resume the invasion on September 4th. The gravely sick and wounded were evacuated to the ships. Tents and dispensable baggage were left at Iron Hill with those less sick or injured and all available wagons were loaded with ammunitions and provisions.

Washington learned that the British fleet was leaving. The ships were heading south down the Elk River and out into Chesapeake Bay. A British prisoner admitted that he knew the flotilla intended to go around to Delaware Bay and head up to Philadelphia. The fleet's departure confirmed that a large scale decisive land battle was close at hand.

On September 6, 1777, three days after the Battle of Cooch's Bridge, the American army was camped less than five miles north of the British lines at White Clay Creek just south of Stanton, Delaware. The invaders had not made a move since the Battle at Cooch's Bridge and Washington speculated about their next move. What would be their route of advance? Would they attempt a flanking movement from another direction?

He decided to hold a war council with his top commanders. He invited the Marquis de Lafayette and Generals Anthony Wayne and Nathaniel Greene and other top Continental Army officers. They met at the Hale-Byrnes House on old Route 7 close to Stanton, Delaware, near the intersection of today's Routes 4 and 7.[21] These were the two most likely routes of British advance.

Over the years much has been written about this old house and the conference there. This collective account by local authors is based on recollections that were passed down orally by members of the Byrnes family, the occupants of the house at that time.

"The well-to do Quaker miller Daniel Byrnes and his wife Dinah with their three young children watched in awe as Continental soldiers marched in front on their substantial brick house at the intersection of Ogletown Road from Newark and the King's Highway from Christiana. They knew that the British army was only a few miles down the road and would soon be there. General Washington had ordered cannons to be placed directly in front of the house so that his gunners could cover both roads. Should the enemy appear, Dinah Byrnes was ready to take the children to the cellar where they could hide under the huge arch beneath the fireplace.

The generals rode up to the house with Captain Robert Kirkwood a Delaware officer who was familiar with the countryside and had arranged the meeting at the house. It was a warm day and they sat briefly under a sycamore tree near the front door. The enthralled children brought them glasses of water from their nearby spring. At the meeting Washington concluded that he would move his frontlines a few miles closer to the enemy.

As the officers rode off the Marquis de Lafayette tousled the hair of eight year old Caleb Byrnes as he mounted his horse. For the next 24 hours troops marched by the front of the house and the children gave them cool water from the spring. The family awoke the next morning to find the cannon gone and only a few soldiers straggling north toward Stanton enroute to Chadds Ford. This was the last time the Byrnes would see American soldiers, but on September 11 they heard the distant sound of gunfire. It was from the battle of Brandywine where the outnumbered and out gunned raw army of American farmers was tragically defeated as the massive British invasion moved on to capture Philadelphia."

On September 8 the British invasion forces decamped and headed north to resume the Philadelphia campaign. The British Army left Iron Hill and swung around the American right flank. They marched over Mill Creek through Newark and Hockessin, Delaware, and looted houses along the way. The regiments converged at New Garden, Pennsylvania and then moved on to Chadds Ford and the Battle of Brandywine. This clash on September 11, 1777 was the largest battle of the American Revolution. An estimated 26,000 soldiers engaged in desperate combat 20 miles south of Philadelphia in the rolling hills of Chester County, Pennsylvania. Washington positioned his army there on the north banks of the Brandywine River to block Howe's path to the city. The untried army of Patriots lost 1,300 men out of their force of 11,000 in what was a disastrous American defeat. Fifteen days later the victorious Cornwallis entered Philadelphia and the British invaders settled in for a nine month occupation of the rebel capitol. Washington and his crushed army began a new fight- a battle against nature during the bitter winter at Valley Forge.

The pillaging Redcoat aggressors would never return to the 10 mile stretch of road between Head of Elk, Maryland and Newark, Delaware. Four years of war would pass before another massed troop movement moved through the corridor. This time it was the Americans and their French allies heading south to Yorktown. During that interim the patriot residents of the area provided assistance to passing friendly troops and provided officers and men to the armed forces of the new nation. Local people actively apprehended profiteers who sent food supplies to the British in the occupied city of Philadelphia and punished Quakers who because of their beliefs remained neutral.

General Washington regarded the Delaware and Maryland Brigades as some of his finest soldiers and referred to them as the "Old Line." They fought valiantly during the entire war on many battlefields in both the northern and southern states.

Tragedy to Triumph- Patriots Return to Head of Elk-1781

In August 1781, the American Army, emboldened by the added military power of its French allies, returned to the stretch of road between Cooch's Bridge and Head of Elk. This time the raw army of Patriots was not being pushed north by a superior British task force. They were heading south to what would be the final decisive battle of the war. The pastoral countryside on the Delaware-Maryland border again became the artery for another critical advance of an entire army.

Fighting had shifted to the southern states in the summer of 1781. At that time the Continental Army was stalemated for two years encircling the main British Army with 14,000 troops in New York City. They were commanded by Sir Henry Clinton, his Majesty's forces and had occupied the city for the past five years. North of the city, the Americans dominated the area in and around Westchester County. They believed that from there they could keep the enemy penned up and would be able to counter a British invasion up the Hudson River. If there was an opportunity the Patriots might even be able to attack and trap the British in water-bound New York City. The Redcoats forces were comfortably entrenched in Manhattan where they savored the news of a string of victories in the south that they believed portended the end of the rebellion.

In reality, neither side had the confidence or strength to attack the other. In the spring of 1780, the most encouraging event of the entire War for Independence occurred when a French expeditionary force of more than 8,000 men, supported at times by a huge fleet of warships, joined the American side. In July, the French moved down from New England to join General Washington and the Continental Army around New York. The obvious plan was for the combined force to attack the fortifications at Kingsbridge and push down Manhattan Island. The Franco – American army would suffer appalling losses in assaulting the well dug in Redcoats defenses, but a victory there could end the war. Ultimately, the attack would not be here but at Yorktown, Virginia, 500 miles south

American troops marched down the old road to Head of Elk twice in early 1781. These lesser deployments were fortuitous harbingers of the great troop movement that would occur six months later. In March, Washington entrusted Lafayette, "the boy general," to take a small army to Virginia to stop British raids. He faced a formidable adversary, the traitor and former American General Benedict Arnold. Lafayette arrived in Elton, along with 1,200 troops and was then transported to Annapolis. Expected French reinforcements failed to arrive and Lafayette returned to the Elkton the next month on his way north to rejoin the main army. When he reached the town, Washington ordered him to turn around and return to Virginia to join forces with General Nathaniel Greene. Their defensive tactics resulted in Cornwallis making the fateful decision to move to Yorktown, a place that he believed was strategically safe.[22]

On August 14, 1781, the allies received astonishing news. The French fleet was on its way from the West Indies to Chesapeake Bay. The port of Yorktown was only 30 miles from the bay entrance. Lafayette in Virginia also confirmed the news. The eager young Marquis reported with some hesitation, *"should a French fleet come to Hampton Roads [the entrance to Chesapeake bay], the British army would be ours, I think."*

Washington and the top French commander, Rochambeau, immediately changed their plans to attack New York City and made a brash decision to move all their forces south to Virginia where they might be able to trap Cornwallis, with his 11,000 men, a third of the entire British Army. The move would require the entire allied army to travel as much as 600 miles and across nine states in a race against time. It appeared to be an impossible achievement. But, if this audacious strategy succeeded the enemy could be surrounded and cut off at the small port city of Yorktown. The French fleet could block an evacuation by sea and the allied armies could overwhelm the town by land. This abrupt and precarious shift in strategy would require secrecy.

Many things could go wrong. A small force of 2,500 remained at West Point, New York to protect the water corridor to Canada. The British Army could easily overrun them from New York City. Washington's and Rochambeau's vulnerable split columns, moving down through New Jersey, could be attacked from the rear. The French ships had to reach Chesapeake Bay before the British fleet could come to the rescue of Cornwallis. The French fleet was scheduled to return to the Caribbean and might not be able to wait for the allied army to arrive. Sir Henry Clinton could send a rescue fleet from New York for an evacuation and the town would be deserted when the allies arrived. Cornwallis could break out of the trap and head back to the Carolinas. The French fleet could be beaten off by the British Navy or could run out of time and sail away.

The exodus began on August 20. American and French forces started moving south from as far away as New England. Their journeys were as long as 600 miles. There were great efforts made to make it appear that there would be an amphibious assault on New York from Staten Island. Most of the army, including some generals, were not told that the destination was Virginia until they reached the Raritan River at New Brunswick, New Jersey.

This march south, in 1781, is an epic in the military history of the world. This astonishing feat was the longest and largest troop movement in the entire Revolutionary War. It all had to come together at Head of Elk where the Continental Army and its French allies would board sloops and sail 200 miles down Chesapeake Bay to Williamsburg and Yorktown. No contemporary itineraries exist for the Americans but their path was well defined by eye witnesses and military records. The French expeditionary force carefully documented and mapped their routes and campgrounds along the entire way.[23]

The armies crossed the Hudson River at Kings Ferry to Stony Point, New York and gathered at nearby Haverstraw. [24] From there the American and French columns split to move through New Jersey and covered 15 miles a day in the good weather. It was not until September 1, when the army reached Philadelphia that Sir Henry Clinton realized what had happened. The British commander was disturbed but did not panic. He was convinced that the strength of the British fleet could protect or evacuate Cornwallis.

The armies crossed the Delaware River at Trenton on September 6 and continued 25 miles to Philadelphia. The American capitol prepared an enormous welcome for their soldiers and French comrades. The two mile long American column of ragtag, barefooted, war weary veterans proudly paraded with fifes and drums past cheering throngs that lined the crowded streets and filled windows. The French regiments caused a great sensation. By contrast, they wore elegant uniforms, their aristocratic officers were mounted on noble steeds and regimental bands accompanied their columns. The crowds lining the streets were transfixed by this display of splendor and the exotic sound of a foreign language.[25]

The allied forces still had 260 miles to go and could not tarry long to enjoy the celebrations given in their honor. It was an apprehensive time. Many generals began to have strong doubts that they would arrive at their objective on time. There had not been any news of the arrival of the French fleet in Chesapeake Bay. Were the support ships delayed or stopped by the British Navy?

Washington had severe problems at Elkton. The most vexing was back pay for the troops. Many men had not received any pay in over a year and that had been in devalued Continental dollars Most of the soldiers were now far from home and refused to continue without receiving back pay. Between Philadelphia and Head of Elk some regiments lost ten percent of their strength due to desertions. When the war weary men from New York, New Jersey and Pennsylvania reached Elkton they refused to go further. The grumbling over pay that began in Philadelphia had escalated into rumors of mutiny which were not empty threats. Both the New Jersey and Pennsylvania lines had mutinied earlier in the year near Morristown, New Jersey.

Washington wrote to Robert Morris, Superintendant of Finance for Congress from Elkton imploring him to send at least one month's pay to the army or risk massive desertions. He warned that the Yorktown campaign might have to be abandoned. Congress simply did not have the funds. Morris then made a bold move that may have saved the cause for independence. He asked Rochambeau for a loan. The benevolent French General agreed to advance $20,000 in pieces of eight. This was enough to provide all American soldiers with a month's pay. The money had an immediate effect. Some of the delighted soldiers had never been paid "real money" since enlisting five years before. For a few soldiers it was the only remuneration they received during the entire war. The grateful veterans remembered the occasion for the rest of their lives and referred to the joyful event in pension applications they filed 40 years later.

The Commander-in -Chief's problems still were not over. He expected that a sufficient number of ships would be waiting at Head of Elk to transport the armies down the bay to Yorktown. Since only small craft could navigate the head waters of Elk River, he found only 80 undersized vessels This diminutive fleet was not nearly enough to carry even half of the men. About 3,000 American and French troops were able to board but most of the allied forces marched the 50 miles south to Baltimore and Annapolis and picked up by larger French frigates to complete the voyage. By September 18 the entire Franco-American assault force was sailing 150 miles down Chesapeake Bay to Williamsburg and Yorktown, Virginia.

General Washington left his home in Virginia to command the Continental Army when the war began in 1775. He had not returned for six years. He took the opportunity of being close to Mount Vernon to make a quick stopover at his beloved plantation where his devoted wife Martha would be waiting. He left Elkton for a two day visit and invited General Rochambeau to come along. There is little recorded about the visit of the top commanders on September 10 and 11, 1781. The event suggests a warm friendship and trust had developed between the men that would serve them well in the challenging days ahead. They faced an enormous test. There were great differences between the armies and it would be difficult to coordinate their tactics in combat. Timing remained critical and much depended on naval actions that were beyond their control. Weighty military matters must have been the main topics of their discussions as they prepared to embark on this high risk operation.[26]

Those troops that had boarded vessels at the Head of Elk had a dreadful trip down the bay. It took eighteen days to travel the 200 miles. Their vessels were so small there were no facilities for cooking and the men lived on cheese and biscuits. Troops that had marched to Annapolis or Baltimore and boarded larger ships to complete the 200 mile trip to the Yorktown peninsula made the trip in five days and enjoyed a relaxing cruise. On September 26, 1781 almost three months after they left from as far away as Providence, Rhode Island, the allied armies landed at their destination on the shore of the James River.

The allied armies and navies besieged Yorktown and isolated Cornwallis from supplies or military support. The surrender was unconditional. A total of 7,000 British and Hessian soldiers became prisoners. They turned over 244 cannons, thousands of small arms and tons of supplies and equipment. Yorktown was the last major battle of the Revolutionary War but it did not end the conflict. The British side still had two-thirds of its army intact and was firmly in control of New York, Charlestown and much of the south. However, the American victory destroyed political support for the war in London although hostilities continued for another year and a half. Following the news from Yorktown a national holiday was declared and the entire country celebrated the final decisive victory together

The Scene Today, Bucolic Beauty

Exploring the area between Cooch's Bridge and Elkton is an enthralling excursion.

The area lies along the upper banks of the Chesapeake Bay, halfway between Philadelphia and Baltimore. It is a place of shimmering harbors, rolling hillsides, horse country, antiques and charming inns. This 10 mile stretch of road teems with reminders of Revolutionary War events. Following this path of both the British invaders in 1777 and the Yorktown bound Franco-American forces in 1781 is a pleasant and fascinating digression that is easily accessible from Interstate 95. At the northern end, Route 896 from Newark, Delaware, runs directly into Glasgow and the vicinity of Cooch's Bridge. Route 273 in Maryland, the next exit south, leads to Elkton. Both places are only about two miles from the superhighway and are connected by Route 40, the Old Baltimore Pike. This is the road along which all the action occurred.

Head of Elk

Elkton, Maryland, the county seat of Cecil County has 15,000 residents. Lining Main Street is an eclectic mix of structures that back to the 19th century. Buildings housing small retail stores and modern public buildings share the thoroughfare with historically significant colonial era buildings.

Most people remember the town as a "quickie marriage" mecca. An operating wedding chapel near the town's center is a reminder of that colorful era. Maryland did not pass restrictive marriage laws as other northern states did in the early 20th century. The towns near borders with other states became known as places to get married fast without a waiting period. Elkton, the county seat in Maryland closest to Philadelphia, New York and New England, was especially popular. In the 1920s and 1930s it was "the elopement capital of the East Coast." Thousands of marriages were performed there each year. National celebrities chose the town for their weddings. People in the town and throughout the state became uncomfortable with the lurid image projected by these activities and imposed a 48-hour waiting period in 1938. Although hundreds of people are still married in Elkton each year Las Vegas soon replaces it as the wedding capitol.[27]

Mike Dixon, Historian of the Cecil County Historical Society, has a prolific knowledge of the history of Head of Elk. He kindly offered to give me a tour of the area. The Society is housed in an elegant building on Main Street that was constructed as a bank in 1830.[28] They have an outstanding collection of local genealogies, church records, maps, court reports, military records, newspapers and books on the history of Cecil County. A collection of artifacts is displayed in an 18th century log cabin on the grounds. It was the home of Reverend William Duke, the first Episcopal clergyman in Elkton who started a private school for boys in 1799 in the building. The parsonage was moved here when a nearby street was being widened.

Mike commented on the fact that numerous cannon balls have been found in excavations around town yet no fighting took place here. He believes that artifacts were jettisoned by the massive British invasion force that camped here in 1777 before they pushed on to Philadelphia in 1777. The Hollingsworths, always were devoted Patriots, and the Livingstons, who were ardent Loyalists, were the pioneer families who owned most of the land at head of Elk in the colonial days and during the war. Their homes in town have been restored are still in use today.

The Hollingsworth House on Main Street was built by Colonel Henry Hollingsworth in 1750. It stands on Partridge Hill on high ground above the Big Elk Creek which runs through the town. The wealthy merchant owner could walk down to the creek as merchandise arrived and left by boat. Hollingsworth played a prominent role in the Revolutionary War, donating money and recruiting men for the Elk Battalion in 1775. The armies of Washington, Rochambeau and Lafayette were with supplied cattle, flour and boats by Hollingsworth and other patriots. Currently, the building serves as the home of the Elkton American Legion. A marker there reads,

> *"Henry Hollingsworth, merchant legislator and Colonel of the Elk Battalion of militia in the Revolutionary War. As commissary for the eastern shire he obtained supplies for the American and their French allies embarking near here on their way down the Elk river to Yorktown, Virginia.*

"The Hermitage," the home Robert Alexander built in1735, is close to Main Street. During the same week in 1777, the Loyalist first welcomed Washington and then Howe to his home. Howe used the home as his headquarters before heading north with his assault force. Alexander left his wife and moved to London to escape the wrath of the Patriots when the war ended. His estate, which included most of the Town of Elkton, was confiscated, but his wife was allowed to keep the house.

The Mitchell House also stands on Main Street. Dr. Abraham Mitchell, a well-known physician, arrived in Elkton from Lancaster County, Pennsylvania, in 1750. He built the brick house in1769. This devoted Patriot converted his home into a hospital to personally care for the wounded soldiers of the Continental army.

Elk Landing, less than a mile from the center of town, lies on the confluence of Little Elk and Big Elk Creeks. This is where the Yorktown bound soldiers boarded small boats in 1781. A Swedish trading post stood here as early as 1690. The land, acquired by the pioneer Hollingsworth family in 1735, is now a well tended 42 acre park area. Two early houses stand a few yards apart at the site. An old stone house was built by Zebulon Hollingsworth in 1783, the year the war ended. A log structure attached to it was used as a store house by the Delaware Militia in 1775. There is evidence of a redoubt a few yards from the house which was erected in 1813 to repel British raiders attempting to capture Elkton. The frame building nearby, known as "The Hollingsworth House," was also built in 1783.

The landing was abandoned for several years, and both structures fell into disrepair. The Historic Elk Landing Foundation, created in 2000, signed a lease with the town to operate the site as a living history museum. Since then the Foundation has restored most of the Hollingsworth House and stabilized the Old Stone House. Seven archeological studies have been conducted here since 2002.

The place where Howe landed with his massive invasion force is six miles south of Elkton. The region is sparsely developed and looks much the same as it did in 1777. Mike and I passed through the quaint village of Northeast with its pretty shops, antique stores and restaurants offering the ubiquitous Maryland crab cakes. The pleasant little town is the gateway to Elk Neck State Park on the 12 mile long peninsula that extends into Chesapeake Bay. At its tip is Turkey Point, the vantage point where Jacob Hollingsworth first sighted the vast British armada and flashed the ominous news to the Patriot defenders.

The landing place of the British Invasion is known today as Oldfields Point.[28] The terrain here appears much the same as it did during the war. The surrounding hills offer a panoramic view of an expanse of open fields that slope up from the broad Elk River. The fields, fringed by woods along the river bank, stretch out for more than a mile. The vast open area provided the space for the thousands of Redcoats and Hessians with their supply trains after they landed. British Major John Andre in his diary mentioned a ferry at the landing place. Remains of an old ferry wharf were still visible in 1937. The Elk Ferry crossed the river from Oldfields Point to Courthouse Point on the eastern shore.

Cooch's Bridge

The area surrounding the Cooch's Bridge battleground was originally known as the Pencader Hundred or the Welsh Tract. This fertile flat land south and west of the Christiana River was granted to Welsh settlers by William Penn in 1701. Churches, early houses and place names provide abundant evidence of their presence.

My tour here began at Glasgow at the northern end of the historic stretch of road. Wade P. Catts, a nationally known professional archeologist, was my guide. Wade is Associate Director of Cultural Resources for John Milner Associates, a historic preservation firm. One of his specialties is military site archeology. He lives in nearby Newark, Delaware and has spent many years exploring and researching the area of the battle and is regarded in Delaware as the expert on the combat here in 1777.

Wade Catts is concerned that most people have the impression that the engagement at Cooch's Bridge on September 3, 1777, was a minor action fought at the bridge and the adjacent field by the Cooch House. He claims that physical evidence proves that the battle was much more widespread. Fired lead musket and rifle balls were uncovered by a metal detector study in2008 on the parcels of land covering. The archeology on 148 acres along Rt. 896 and Old Cooch's Bridge Road indicates that the fighting covered an area that fans out three miles from Glasgow to Iron Hill. Eyewitness accounts of the participants in the battle match these findings. The digs were prompted by approval of a proposal for the development of the land by the City Council in 2008. The plan proposes the development of 1.6 million square feet for office, warehouse and manufacturing space. The endorsement remains in effect but construction has not begun.

The parking lot of Glasgow High School on Route 896 is only about 100 yards away from the hub of the hotly contested battlefield. Knyphausen's Hessians camped here after the battle. Iron Hill, the 120 foot high mount, located a mile to the north, overlooks the area.

We followed the corridor of the battle down Route 896 to Glasgow. The town's center is at the junction of Route 40, the old Pulaski Highway. Aiken's Tavern is at this crossroads. The inn served as Howe's headquarters for five days in September 1777. Knyphausen's Hessians came up Route 40 from Elkton and camped here before the battle. Some traces of the old road still exist along the shoulders. John Aiken operated the tavern in 1777. The single street village was called Aikentown in that era. The tavern was well situated in that roads from here led north to Cooch's Bridge, south to Middletown, west to Elkton and east to New Castle.

The Pencader Presbyterian Church stands directly across the road from Aiken's Tavern. The first meeting house was built there in 1706 by Welsh settlers. It was a small frame building and was used by the British as a hospital after the battle at Cooch's Bridge. Pencader, a Welsh term meaning "chief chair or seat," was the name of this modest building that lasted until 1913 when it burned down. A second church was built on the site in 1782, and the present building was erected in 1852.

Maxwell's men fell back to the bridge as the battle raged along Old Cooch's Bridge Road. The patriots ambushed the Von Wurmb's Chasseurs here as Cornwallis began to advance north from Aiken's Tavern. Cornfields now share this hallowed ground with a sizeable power station. Eggerts Lane traverses the site. The Eggert Family witnessed the battle from this modest farmhouse. The house is still occupied by family members. Wade commented that nothing along these obscure side roads has changed since 1777.

We continued north on Route 896 for about a mile into Newark to visit the Welsh Tract Baptist Church. A log meeting house was first built here in 1703 by a congregation that had been organized in Southern Wales. The present structure, with a distinctive half-hipped roof, was built in 1746. A conspicuous bricked in patch on the west wall is often described as the result of a cannonball passing through the church during the action at Cooch's Bridge. The oldest tombstone in the walled cemetery is dated 1707 and inscribed in Welsh. Legend also places unmarked graves of Revolutionary War soldiers somewhere in the churchyard.

Old maps show a schoolhouse behind the church located next to a few small houses across the street. One of these was a tavern owned by the James family. Generals Washington, Greene and Lafayette took shelter there as they attempted to return to Wilmington. A fierce thunderstorm drove them off Iron Hill where they were spying on the British.

Most drivers speeding along Interstate 95 do not notice Iron Hill as the scene of countless Revolutionary War events. George Washington spied down on the British from here, and the clashing armies swarmed around its base. Its slopes served as the campgrounds for both sides several times. Native American tribes came to the hill in the 1600s. Archaeologists believe they quarried jasper, a sharp-edged variety of quartz, and made it into tools on-site. Thousands of jasper chips were left by the ancient toolmakers. Iron Hill derives its name from the iron ore mined there starting in the early 1700s. Several abandoned pit mines still dot the hill.

Iron Hill Museum and Iron Hill Park are the principal attractions here. The Museum is housed in a one-room schoolhouse and focuses on natural history.

Exhibits include rocks, minerals fossils and wildlife displays. The park that surrounds the museum is a favorite of mountain bikers. An old schoolhouse that is listed on the National Register of Historic Places is found in the park.

The Pencader Heritage Museum can be reached by continuing north on the Old Baltimore Pike, crossing over Cooch's bridge and turning onto Route 72. This fascinating collection displays artifacts that reflect life in the surrounding area from the Colonial era to the Vietnam War. Cannonballs found in local backyards from the battle of Cooch's bridge, a replica of a Delaware regiment flag and statues of revolutionary war soldiers can be seen here. [29]

The Cooch House is the centerpiece of this historic area. the Thomas Cooch arrived here from England in 1746 and built the first two stories of the house in 1760. The Cooch family has occupied the gracious home for seven generations. Thomas organized a militia regiment when the war began in 1775 and served as its Colonel. The current inhabitant is Edward W. Cooch Jr., who has been practicing law for 50 years. His son, Richard Rodney Cooch, is currently a Delaware Superior Court Judge.[30]

The venerable house is safely situated on a rise a few feet away from the bank of the Christiana River. A mill stood here in 1777. Nearby are a smokehouse and a springhouse built of stone in the late 1700s. Washington ordered the mill stone removed to prevent the British from making flour. Cornwallis burned the mill down when he arrived. The Redcoat general made the Cooch house his headquarters until the army resumed its advance toward Philadelphia. His horse occupied the parlor according to the oral history passed down in the Cooch family. [31]

A Revolutionary War monument on Old Baltimore Pike stands at the entrance to the drive leading to the house. It consists of a granite marker surrounded by four cannon and was erected in 1901 by the Patriotic Societies and Citizens of Delaware to commemorate the battle.

Just a few feet to the east of the monument is the bridge over the Christiana River that carries the name of the battle. The current bridge was built in 1922. How many bridges preceded it is unknown. The site of the battle has been preserved as the Cooch's Bridge Historic District and is listed on the National Register of Historic Places. In 2003, the Cooch family sold the state some land as well as development rights for an additional 200 acres of land in the area of the battlefield.

The historic stretch of road between Head of Elk and Cooch's Bridge remained an active military transport corridor for the remaining years of the war. The Continental Army returned north on the route after the battle of Yorktown, the French came north nine months later and followed the same path. The Duc Lauzun's French Legion of Hussars returned to Wilmington and stayed for five months until May 1783 to help guard the approaches to Philadelphia and Baltimore.

The Philadelphia campaign achieved its objective with the capture of the patriot capitol. But strategically it portended the downfall of His Majesty's forces in America. Howe missed an opportunity in 1777 to destroy the military and political forces that drove the American Revolution. Parliament was very disappointed that he did not annihilate Washington's fledgling army at the Battle of Brandywine. Howe, the Commander -in- Chief of the British forces in America, resigned soon after. After enduring a hard winter at Valley Forge where the Patriots survived and were molded into a disciplined force by Baron Von Steuben, the soldiers emerged eight months later to confront the elite troops of the British Empire at Monmouth Courthouse and beat them at their own game.

Chapter Four

Where the War Almost Ended
The Battle of the Short Hills

Central New Jersey, 1777

Confusion over the Place Name Obscures this Location

Few people have heard of this incredible Revolutionary War battle in central New Jersey. The engagement should have been called The Battle of Edison, Scotch Plains or Plainfield, but it has come down in history as the Battle of The Short Hills. This label causes confusion since it is assumed that the combat occurred in another New Jersey town, Short Hills, ten miles away, in adjoining Essex County. Many people who drive every day over the heavily trafficked streets of these New Jersey towns and even hit golf balls from the site of Patriot defense positions on the grounds of the Plainfield Country Club are completely unaware of the amazing display of patriotism and the fierce struggle that raged here in June of 1777.

This historic event in America's struggle for independence was a defeat. Losses, regardless of the bloodshed and valor displayed, usually receive less acclaim from the vanquished than victories. Most of the details of this significant event are found in the little known accounts of British and Hessian officers and not American sources. The British side also gave the event little publicity since it failed to accomplish its objective of luring Washington out of the mountains and wiping out the Continental Army with superior numbers and weaponry. [1]

At the Short Hills the Patriots, outnumbered six to one, were driven back, but in reality they achieved a crucial strategic American success. This pivotal engagement delayed the entire British Army which enabled George Washington to save the Continental Army by pulling it back to a safe haven in the Watchung Mountains. Encirclement and defeat on the Plains below at that time could have ended the war. [2]

What is astonishing is that the clash involved more than 16,000 British and Hessian troops and the top military leaders on both sides of the war. The entire strength of Washington's poorly equipped Continental Army at the time was about 10,000 soldiers, but allowing for sickness only 5,700 of them were effective fighting men.

Washington directed the action of his forces in the lowland below with semaphore flags. He signaled from a rocky promontory on the first ridge of the Watchung Mountains in what today is Green Brook Township. In later years the site became known as Washington Rock.[3] The action covered a ten mile area and the fighting encompassed the towns of Plainfield, Scotch Plains, Edison, Woodbridge, Westfield and Rahway, New Jersey.

Brigadier General William Alexander-Lord Stirling (1726-1783)

The American detachment at Plainfield was commanded by Brigadier General William Alexander, a wealthy gentleman farmer and soldier from nearby Basking Ridge, better known as Lord Stirling. The British were led by Major General William Howe, commander of all British forces in North America. Major General Charles Cornwallis was second in command of the Redcoat Army. The infamous spy Major John Andre and the most vilified British Commander of the war, Banastre Tarleton, were both present.

Many Fascinating Firsts

Aside from preventing a final British victory many of the most fascinating and significant events of the entire Revolutionary War occurred during this two day engagement. The flag of the new nation, the stars and stripes, may have been flown in combat for the first time during the engagement. [4] Congress adopted the banner on June 14, 1777, only twelve days before the battle. The British first used repeating rifles here. Primitive chemical warfare was used for the first time by both sides. Musket balls were dipped in toxic fungus.

The event also marked the first time that French command and arms came to the aid of the American cause. France did not officially enter the war for another seven months. The British planned to introduce an innovative pontoon bridge to cross to Staten Island from Perth Amboy. Non-English-speaking Pennsylvania German Regiments played a major role in the fighting. The British plunder of the countryside during the campaign produced detailed claims for damages of property looted from the farmhouses and shops of the time. Many of these documents have survived and provide historians with clues of troop movements.[5]

In 1776, the previous year, the war had gone badly for the Patriots. Washington lost Manhattan and Long Island and was chased across New Jersey with his fledgling Continental Army and into Pennsylvania. The horror of this humiliating retreat turned to joy when his beleaguered troops managed a surprise turnaround at the end of the year. They crossed back over the ice choked Delaware River on Christmas night to defeat a Hessian garrison in a surprise attack in Trenton, New Jersey. A week later, twelve miles away, the Patriots were victorious again at Princeton. These triumphs electrified the new nation and gave hope that it could survive to celebrate its first anniversary.

Redcoats Pillage New Jersey

After these back to back victories the Continental Army withdrew to Morristown, New Jersey for the winter. Most of the military action during the ensuing winter and spring was a foraging war. To sustain itself, the British Army, headquartered at New Brunswick, constantly plundered local farmers and merchants. The area from Sandy Hook north to New York State along the Hudson River was regarded as a no man's land, not controlled by the Americans and susceptible to frequent attacks by British forces which were based in New Jersey and New York. The New Jersey Militia, the citizen soldiers of the state, clashed with Loyalists and British regulars and Hessians who robbed and burned civilian homes. During this time prosperous farmers in Somerset County along the Raritan River had their property ransacked by British foraging parties.

In March, Washington sent General Benjamin Lincoln with a force of 500 soldiers to Bound Brook in the center of the devastation. From here Washington could protect area farms from further deprivation and send an early warning if the enemy began an advance inland through the Watchung Mountains known then as the Blue Hills.

On April 12, 1777, Cornwallis with a force of 2,000 men started out from New Brunswick to attack Bound Brook. His plan was to surround General Benjamin Lincoln and prevent his escape into the mountains. In the surprise pre dawn attack Benjamin Lincoln narrowly escaped but managed to make a stand when he reached higher ground. The Americans, greatly outnumbered, fell back after losing 36 men and three cannon in this stinging setback.[6]

In late May, 1777, Washington moved the entire Continental Army to Middlebrook on the heights above Bound Brook. This prime location was near major roads, villages and streams and 20 miles closer to the enemy in New Brunswick. The Middlebrook encampment was on the south slopes of the first ridge of the Watchung Mountains. Today the site is on the high ground just west of the junction of Routes 22 and 287. This strategically placed position allowed the American Army to defend the mountain passes at Westfield, Scotch Plains, Watchung and Bound Brook. These were entrances into the interior of the state that could lead to an overland attack on the capitol at Philadelphia.

From Middlebrook the Continental Army could threaten British-held New York and Staten Island and could rapidly move north to defend the Hudson Highlands. This river valley was the entrance to a waterway that extended all the way up the New York Lake to the St. Lawrence River. British control of this water highway could split the new nation by separating New England from the other states. The high ground at Middlebrook also provided an observation post from which General Washington could watch British troop movements over the 30 miles of flatland that stretched east to Staten Island.

Meanwhile, Lord Howe encamped in New Brunswick with the main body of the British Army continued to raid and forage eastern New Jersey and prepared to open a campaign in the state. His master strategy was to crush the American Army by drawing Washington out into the open flat land where the Continentals would be at a disadvantage in numbers and arms. A decisive victory would enable the British forces to march unopposed directly across New Jersey, cross the Delaware River and capture Philadelphia. If Washington's Army was annihilated on the plains of New Jersey in 1777, the American rebellion would be over.

From the Middlebrook encampment Washington often walked two miles north along the crest of the ridge to a natural outcropping of rock. From here he had which he had a thirty mile panoramic view of the eastern plains of New Jersey stretching out to Staten Island. The rock could be reached from the plain below, now Plainfield, where a militia post was established on the farm of Cornelius and Frederick Vermuele. This post protected the mountain passes and guarded the main road from Scotch Plains to Bound Brook (which is present day Front Street in the town of Plainfield).[7] From here, Brigadier General William Winds gathered the Militia of Somerset and Essex Counties, New Jersey.

In June 1777, Howe attempted to lure Washington into a battle on terrain where he would have no advantages. Howe has assembled his main army in the Raritan Valley in central New Jersey. His forces totaled 17,000 and his plan was to draw Washington down from the security of the Watchung Hills and into the open ground near Somerset Courthouse. Initially he tried to feign an overland march back toward the Delaware River. When this failed his pulled his troops back to New Brunswick and planned his next move. He appeared to be preparing to leave the state. He then advanced his forces from New Brunswick to Somerset Courthouse on the Millstone River. This eight-mile distance was half-way to the American Lines at Middlebrook. Washington wisely remained in his secure mountain stronghold. When Howe saw that his plan was futile he withdrew all his troops from New Brunswick to nearby Perth Amboy. Patriot homes were plundered and burned along the ten- mile route in the present day towns of Highland Park and Edison.

Perth Amboy was a Tory stronghold and the home of Loyalist Governor William Franklin. Ironically he was the son of the great Patriot Benjamin Franklin. The town also had barracks built during the French and Indian war in the 1750s. But these buildings were inadequate for the size of the army and most troops were quartered in tents set up along the streets of the town. Despite these benefits Perth Amboy was bordered on all side by populations of ardent Patriot sympathizers and Howe believed that he was at a strategically disadvantage here.

The New Jersey Militia interrupted the British on the march to Perth Amboy. Re-enforced with some Continental soldiers they attacked the rear of the Redcoat column with a force of 1,200 soldiers and two cannon in the town of Piscataway. By June 22, 1777, it appeared that this show of strength by the Patriots had caused Howe to give up on a New Jersey Campaign. He then moved his army from Perth Amboy across the Arthur Kill to Staten Island. This was a sign that the British were abandoning New Jersey and would instead attack the nation's capitol, Philadelphia, by a sea route. While British sources of the time deny it, this withdrawal from New Jersey may have been a move to deceive the Americans. By feigning a major retreat Howe again hoped to tempt Washington out of his mountain stronghold at Middlebrook. While his motive is uncertain, the plan worked.

Washington remained steadfast with his strategy of avoiding any major engagement and continued to prefer the smaller scale surprise offensives that had been so successful at Trenton and Princeton. His style of warfare was son recognized both in America and England. In 1777 the London annual Register commented, "*These actions and the sudden recovery from the lowest state of weakness and distress, to become a formidable enemy in the field, raised the character of General Washington as a commander both in Europe and America and with his preceding and subsequent conduct serve to give a sanction to that appellation which is now pretty w2ell applied to him, of the American Fabius.*"

This reference was to the Roman General Quitus Fabius Maximus. He was known as "The Great Delayer" for not attacking the superior Chartheginian forces of Hannibal. His plan proved to be the correct approach that led to victory. Even the ill tempered John Adams began to realize the value of this tactic. He wrote to he wrote wife Abigail "Our Fabius will be slow but sure." [8]

The Americans were thrilled to see the withdrawal of the British and were eager to pursue the retreating army. Washington observing the evacuation from his perch on the rock above was so confident that the enemy was permanently withdrawing from the state that he allowed the New Jersey Militia to return to their homes on June 23. Moving his entire army down to the plains at Samptown (South Plainfield) and Quibbletown (Piscataway) he then fanned out his regiments in a ten-mile arc to defend New Jersey from what seemed to be an unlikely counter attack.

He remained apprehensive over this move but yielded to the criticism for lack of aggressiveness and pressure from his zealous officers. On the day before he moved down from the hills he wrote to Joseph Reed, Adjutant-General of the Continental Army

People seem disposed to think of him[General Howe] as capable but that his army has absolutely gone off panic struck; but I cannot persuade myself into a belief of the latter, notwithstanding it is the prevailing opinion of my officers, I cannot say that the move I am about to make towards Amboy accords altogether with my opinion, not that I am under any other apprehension than that of being obliged to lose ground again, which would indeed be no small misfortune as the spirit of our troops and the county is greatly revived (and I presume) the enemys not a little depressed, by their late retrograde motions."

The American lines on the plains of central New Jersey extended from Quibbletown, north to The Short Hills and Ash Swamp (Plainfield and Scotch Plains). The Short Hills name also referred to a hamlet on the site. It was a well defined Patriot neighborhood with its own tavern on the junction of today's Inman Avenue and Old Raritan Road in Plainfield.

General Stirling Confronts the Entire British Army

American Major General Lord Stirling was assigned to the critical Short Hills-Ash Swamp location to protect the northern flank of the American forces. With the British departure to Staten Island he could also try to reoccupy the Tory infested area down to Perth Amboy. Stirling's force included the divisions of Brigadier Generals Thomas Conway and General William, (Scotch Willie) Maxwell. They were joined by Morgan's Rifles and four New Jersey Regiments commanded by Colonels Matthias Ogden, Elias Dayton, Israel Shreve and Ephraim Martin. On June 24, Stirling left the post at Vermuele's farm below Washington Rock and moved his force of 1,798 soldiers to the Short Hills and Ash Swamp. He set up his headquarters at a central location along Inman Avenue.

An American deserter alerted the British commanders that Washington had descended with his army down from the hills to the vulnerable position on the flatland. This was the opportunity that Howe had been awaiting. He immediately began ferrying his troops back from Staten Island and at 6 PM on June 25, 1777. He ordered that tents be taken down and to move rapidly, yet still preserve the element of surprise supplies and other baggage would be left behind. The men were order to sleep on their weapons and to be prepared to march toward The Short Hills.

The British and Hessian troops massed at Perth Amboy then began their assault inland. Howe planned a fast surprise attack that would first wipe out Stirling, then encircle the main American Army in a pincer movement to crush it with his superior numbers and artillery.

Expecting an easy victory, supply wagons carried only three days rations and two day's rum. They had planned to start out at 1:00 AM but due to problems in transporting troops from Staten Island and handling the Hessian artillery they were delayed five hours.

The right wing of 5,000 soldiers under Cornwallis left Perth Amboy and started out on the twelve mile march to the Short Hills. They moved west through Woodbridge on a course which followed present day Amboy Avenue, Green Street and Oak Tree Road. Minor British units had plundered and foraged in the bountiful countryside many times in the months before. The Americans sensed that this major troop movement was far different from these raids and skirmishes.

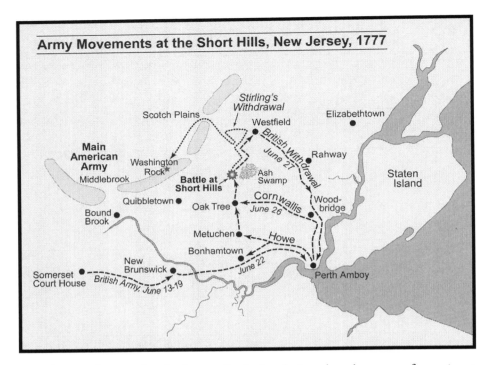

Army Movements at the Short Hills, New Jersey, 1777

The assault moved only three miles before losing the advantage of surprise at sunrise. At 6:00 AM the Redcoats clashed with a detachment of 150 troops from Morgan's Riflemen. This elite corps was an advance patrol of the Continental Army that was heading toward Perth Amboy. The Riflemen were selected from Virginia Regiments and were commanded by Captain James Dark. This skirmish occurred at a place called Strawberry Hill the junction of present day Green Street and Route 1 in Woodbridge. Here Dark's smaller patrol clashed with British Captain Patrick Ferguson's 250 riflemen using innovative repeating rifles. These guns could be loaded at the breech and fired up to six shots a minute. [9] Despite this superior weaponry and being outnumbered, Dark's patrol held off the entire advance of Cornwallis for about a half hour before being forced back up Oak Tree Road by a massed bayonet charge.

As Dark's pickets fell back the sound of the gunfire alerted the American camp and Stirling sent out Brigadier General Thomas Conway's Brigade to support them with about 700 Pennsylvania German volunteers. This front line detachment commanded by General Maxwell and French Colonel Armand-Tuffin was known as Ottendorff's Corps. [10]

Moving along Oak Tree Road the Cornwallis column encountered its first major resistance when they met the Ottendorf's Corps, who had been joined by Dark's retreating riflemen and a large number of local militia. They were supported by three new French brass cannon. The clash occurred at about 8:30 AM along the high ground where Oak Tree Road intersects with Plainfield Road and New Dover Road. After heavy hand-to-hand combat the vastly outnumbered Patriot defenders were forced back up Oak Tree Road to New Dover Road and Woodland Avenue. They withdrew up the rising ground through Martin's Woods a mile toward The Short Hills. The valiant Pennsylvania troops took heavy losses. Thirty two men out of eighty fell but they saved the cannon and slowed the British advance.

Cornwallis continued his advance west along Oak tree Road to link up with the left wing force of 12,000 British regulars and Hessians and to close the pincer. General John Vaughan accompanied by Howe had left Perth Amboy at 3:00 A.M. and headed up New Brunswick Avenue to the town of Metuchen. From there the left wing continued over Plainfield Road in Edison to approach The Short Hills from the south. The two prongs of the British attack force merged at Oak Tree Junction. [11]

The sounds of gunfire from the skirmish at Strawberry Hill first alerted Washington. At 7:00 AM a scout reported that the invaders were only two and a half miles away. The Commander-In-Chief ordered alarm guns to be fired. Lacking both arms and enough fighting men, a brash counter attack could have led to a decisive battle. He began rapidly withdrawing his army back to the high ground at Middlebrook relying on Stirling's troops at The Short Hills to stall the entire British advance.

Lord Stirling had his command post at the rising ground nearer Ash Swamp at the junction of Inman and Old Raritan Roads, the site of the Short Hills Tavern. He gathered 1,000 men of the New Jersey Brigade and formed a defensive line along Tingley Lane and Rahway Avenue. Here the battle raged for two hours. At first the Continental troops had a brief advantage. As the British advanced along Tingley Lane on the east side of the Short Hills. they took heavy fire from American artillery concealed behind trees and in the foliage of the higher ground which is now occupied by the Plainfield Country Club.

Von Minningerode's Hessian Grenadier battalion attacked positions from Inman Avenue and attempted to block the Americans from retreating toward Westfield by circling north around Ash Swamp. Curiously they came face to face with Pennsylvania German troops, so shouts of German expletives must have come from both sides during the fray. The Hessians were repulsed by grapeshot from the American cannon. A single discharge of canister killed six of the advancing Hessians.

The British assault was supported by at least fifteen cannons and intense musket fire. The fighting was extremely severe with much of the hand to hand combat around four French three pounders that were slowing the enemy bayonet charges with blasts of grapeshot. Captain John Finch, a courageous but reckless British officer, charged up to a Rebel cannon alone and with his pistols forced the crew to abandon it. He spotted Lord Stirling nearby and shouted "Come here you damned rebel and I will do for you." Stirling directed the fire of four marksmen on him and he fell instantly.

The cannon were lost, then retaken, but three were lost again. French Colonel Armand saved the remaining gun as the defenders fell back. Lord Stirling's horse was shot from under him and General Maxwell was almost captured by Hessian Grenadiers during the fray.

House of Gershom and Elizabeth Frazee c. 1760 near the intersection of Raritan and Terrill Roads, Scotch Plains, New Jersey

About noon, the fighting broke off at the house of a carpenter Gershon Frasee on Raritan Road in Scotch Plains. As an advanced patrol of famished Redcoats, led by Lord Cornwallis himself, fought their way along Raritan Road toward the concealed American positions in Ash Swamp they approached the house. Frazee was a staunch Patriot, whose family provided bread to the embattled American soldiers as they fell back along the road to Westfield. The mouth-watering aroma of fresh baked bread wafted through the Redcoat ranks. The general himself approached the modest farmhouse and was met by Frazee's 61 year old wife Elizabeth. Cornwallis asked her for her newly baked bread. Aunt Betty Frazee replied, "Sir I give you this bread in fear and not in love." Cornwallis admired her audacity and said to his troops, "Not a man of my command shall touch a single loaf." The Frazee house still stands near the corner of Terrill and Raritan Roads in Scotch Plains. Aunt Betty died in 1792. She rests in the old cemetery at the Westfield Presbyterian Church.[12]

The Redcoat Evacuation Left a Path of Destruction

Another local legend tells of the weary British soldiers ending their offensive that day when they reached a cider mill, brew house and distillery owned by James Lambert at 2011 Raritan Road and captured three barrels of applejack. It was a hot day and the well water at the Jonathan Terry house on Rahway and Cooper Roads was drunk dry by the British troops.

Massed volleys of cannon fire from guns as large as twelve pounders forced the outnumbered Americans, now in danger of being surrounded, to fall back into Ash Swamp where they continued to stubbornly resist. With a group of volunteers Maxwell stopped the plundering invaders for a short time at Little's Tavern between present-day Martine and Lake Avenues in Scotch Plains. Stirling's main force, hidden in the woods, continued to harass the enemy along the way. As they pushed on toward Westfield the British forces began plundering and burning homes along the way.

At Westfield the pursuit ended. As the day came to a close the Americans retreated toward the mountains with wounded soldiers loaded in wagons. They moved up the pass at Scotch Plains now New Providence Road and moved down Valley Road through Watchung and Warren to rejoin the main army at Middlebrook. The pass was called "bloody gulch" for many years after the war by local people who remembered the wagons loaded with hemorrhaging soldiers.

General Howe made no attempt to cut off Stirling's retreating men or pursue the Americans into their positions in the Watchung Hills. This lack of aggression was a pattern that the general repeated after other battles. It may well have been that he was haunted by the astonishing losses his forces took on Bunker Hill earlier in the war. He later explained his lack of action to the House of Commons,[13] *"To have attacked General Washington in that strong post, I must necessarily made a considerable circuit of the country and having no prospect of forcing him, I did not think it advisable to lose so much time as must have been employed on that march during the intense heat of the season."*

This time he was correct. An American newspaper summed up the conditions at that time, "Our army is encamped in the old spot, [Middlebook] only large bodies are posted at all the passes, and in some advantageous places below the mountains. It is suspected that the enemy would force our camp if possible, but to attack us in the mountains is a thing devoutly to be wished by everyone that desires to see the destruction of the British Army."[14]

The Westfield Meeting House, a Presbyterian Church at Broad and Mountain Avenues frantically tolled its bell to warn of the approach of thousands of Redcoats and Hessians. Outraged and frustrated by not being able to draw the weak American Army into a battle the British behavior abruptly changed. These previously well disciplined soldiers, restrained by their officers, degenerated into shameful looters and wanton destroyers of property. Claims recorded by many residents detail the extensive damage done to civilian homes and property.

The enemy forces viewed the Presbyterian Church at Westfield as a symbol of radical patriotism. They threw down the bell from the steeple and slaughtered sheep and cattle in the building. The jubilant troops camped overnight in Westfield on the church grounds and along Willow Grove Road to Rahway Road and Grove to Central Avenue. Many of the unwelcomed guests spent the night in homes and shops of the Patriot neighborhood.[15]

The British and Hessian forces marched out of Westfield at 9:00 AM the next morning with their prisoners and wagon loads of plunder and headed to Rahway by way of Rahway and Central Avenues. Brigadier General Charles Scott with Morgan's Riflemen harassed the rear flank of the British columns and attempted to free the prisoners being taken to the infamous Sugar House Prison in New York. The Americans broke off the strike after losing two officers and a sergeant. That evening, June 27, the enemy camped on the south side of the Rahway River.

Washington took full advantage of the time that Stirling's forces had allowed him to withdraw the Continental Army and get back to the security of Middlebrook. Fearing a possible counterattack he dispersed regiments to defend the vital passes through the Blue Hills at Westfield, Scotch Plains, (New Providence Road), Watchung, (Somerset Street), Bound Brook, (Chimney Rock Road) and Bridgewater (Routes 202/206).

After assessing American strength and defenses, Howe decided to abandon the campaign across New Jersey. The British Army evacuated New Jersey on June 30, 1777 and crossed over to Staten Island and New York. The invasion and attack on the Rebel capital at Philadelphia would have to be via a sea route around the Delmarva Peninsula and up Chesapeake Bay. That did not occur until September 1777, three months later.

The stand taken by Stirling's forces at The Short Hills and Ash Swamp had saved Washington's Army. The British had failed to gain entry into the interior of New Jersey. This evacuation was a welcomed relief to civilians throughout the state and they rejoiced the following week by celebrating the new nation's first birthday.

The reports of losses at the Short Hills vary widely, with each side exaggerating the losses of the other. The British and Hessians admitted to 70 men killed, wounded or suffocated by the heat and 13 taken prisoner by the Americans. The only officer they lost was Captain John Finch who brashly attempted to capture the American cannon. An intelligence report received by Washington, an entire afternoon of June 22 was needed to remove an estimated 500 wounded soldiers to hospitals from the dock in the city and officers were heard to admit that they had not suffered so severely since Princeton. The Patriots considered the loss of three of their four French cannon was a serious blow. These weapons provided the first evidence to the British side that the American rebellion was receiving direct military aid from France.

Perhaps the most reliable number of American losses was published later in the *Continental Journal* a record of the daily proceedings of the Continental Congress. It reported losses of three field pieces, 20 killed and 40 wounded.

British reports claim far greater American losses with upwards of 200 men, including three officers, were either wounded or taken prisoner. Ottendorfs Corps who had formed Stirling's advanced guard appeared to suffered the most. Out of 80 men, 32 had been killed or taken Howe's aide Maunchhausen reported that he counted 37 rebel wagons carrying wounded into the Blue Mountains via the pass at New Providence Road in Scotch Plains. The road was known as Bloody Gap for many years as a direct result of this incident. Maunchhausen estimated that the Americans lost 400 killed and wounded.[16]

The Scene Today

Heavily wooded locales have replaced the plowed fields of 1777 but the Short Hills viewed from Oak Tree Road look much the same as they did to Cornwallis and his Redcoat columns. At the Plainfield Country Club Golf Course the high ground which was the location of the American cannon emplacements stretches from the 4th to the 13th Greens. From here the defenders could fire down on the enemy advancing along Tingley Lane. The grounds of the club occupy much of the crest of the Short Hills. Looking west from this promontory the first ridge of the Watchung mountains appears exactly as it did during the war. Trees obscure the heavily populated towns of Plainfield and Scotch Plains which lie below.

The roads followed by both sides during the battle are intact but heavily built over in places. The route from Strawberry Hill along Green Street, crosses over both the Garden State Parkway and U. S. Routes 1 and 9. Oak Tree Road and

Inman Avenue are busy thoroughfares but New Dover Road, Woodland Avenue, Rahway Ave and Raritan Road with scattered upscale houses and much open land, retain much of their original appearance.

The area around the Short Hills abounds with historic sites and restored colonial houses. On the corner of Oak Tree and New Dover Roads near where the Ottendorf Corps made its stand is a five acre site with unusually well detailed markers that describes the battle. A photo mural of New Jersey Brigade soldiers adorns the wall of a bank adjoining the park.

Not far from the Frazee House on Old Raritan Road an eight foot antique sandstone monument topped by a replica Revolutionary War cannon stands at the entrance to Ashbrook Golf Course. Each side of the memorial features a panel telling the story of the battle. Also depicted is a map of the battle and pictures of General Stirling on horseback and wounded soldiers being evacuated in wagons after the battle.

Washington Rock the General's observation place set in a 52 acre State Park on top of the first Watchung Mountain is in nearby Greenbrook Township. There a dramatic scenic overlook provides a thirty mile panoramic view of the eastern plains of New Jersey as far as Staten Island. George Washington directed the Battle of the Short Hills from here. Curiously the renowned artist Charles Wilson Peale made a sketch in his diary. It shows the General on the rock during the battle. Peale included himself in the picture.

Below Washington Rock is the site of the Vermuele Plantation. It was the campsite for the New Jersey Militia for most of the war. Camps were strategically placed here to guard both the route between Quibbletown and Scotch Plains and the stony brook pass leading through the first Watchung ridge to the present day Borough of Watchung. The Vermuele Mansion built in 1803 still stands here on an eight acre Green Acres Park located on Greenbrook Road in North Plainfield.

While the battle of The Short Hills was a tactical defeat for the Americans, it was really a significant strategic victory of the Revolutionary War. Stirling's valiant stand against a vastly superior force provided the time for Washington to move the Continental Army back to the safety of the hills at Middlebrook and avoided the British victory that would have doomed the struggle for independence. Washington's tactics and strategy at the Battle of The Short Hills earned him the respect of Lord Cornwallis who, four years later after his surrender at the final decisive American victory of the war at Yorktown said, "But after all, your Excellency's achievements in New Jersey were such that nothing could surpass them."[17]

Chapter Five

The Twin Forts, Montgomery and Clinton Tragedy to Triumph, 1777.

Defense of the Water Highway from New York to Canada

High on a cliff fifty miles upriver from New York City the ruins of two forts overlook the Hudson River at a narrow point. This is the Hudson Highlands where the hills reach a height of over 1,000 feet. Forts Montgomery and Clinton, known as the Twin Forts were built on this strategic site early in the Revolutionary War to prevent an invasion up the river by warships. On October 6, 1777 a small American force was left alone here to defend the critical waterway which ran north 300 miles to Canada. If the British controlled it New England could be separated from the other states and the war would be lost.

This vastly outnumbered Patriot corps confronted Sir Henry Clinton with his overwhelming force of British, Hessian and Royalist regiments and a fleet of warships. This fierce engagement and tragic American loss has come down in history as a strategic victory. Historians credit this battle for creating a bump in the road that delayed Clinton from reaching Saratoga and joining Burgoyne's large Army invading south from Canada. Burgoyne was defeated at Saratoga. This enormous victory is generally regarded as the turning point of the Revolutionary War.

Over half of the small American force of 600 soldiers at the Twin Forts were killed or captured on that fateful day. The percent of American losses, in what history calls The Battle of Fort Montgomery, surpasses Gettysburg, Normandy and other bloody and decisive battles in our nation's history. [1]

After the battle the British invaders destroyed the forts so they could not be used again. History glorifies victories and this battle was long regarded only as a bitter memory by the inhabitants of southern New York State who lost family and friends in the struggle. Nothing was ever built on the site and it was forgotten for the next 150 years. The remote place became overgrown with trees and dense foliage. Piles of stones and building foundations the remnants of the forts soon became completely hidden under dense underbrush. The ruins were invisible even from Highway 9W. Built in the 1920s the highway passes directly through the grounds of Fort Montgomery only a few yards from the redoubt where the Patriot survivors made their last stand.[2]

In May of 1775, only a month after the first shots of the war at Lexington and Concord the Continental Congress in Philadelphia began taking active measures to guard the Hudson River. Barnard Romans, an engineer, was sent out by Congress to find the best location for building fortifications. He recommended that a single strong fortification be build on what appeared to be an impregnable site. It was on a rugged cliff a hundred feet above the river and surrounded by mountains that were considered to be impassable.[3]

The new bastion was named Fort Montgomery after the General Richard Montgomery who was killed at the Battle of Quebec the previous year. Construction began in March, 1776, but soon met with problems and delays. General Washington directed material and manpower to projects that he considered more critical. Defensive works in and around New York City were urgently needed to keep the British Army from breaking out of the City. The loosely disciplined Militia regiments assigned to the construction work at the fort were constantly on the verge of mutiny because of the lack of supplies and accommodations. They often went home to tend their farms and returned when they were able.

Lord William Alexander Stirling of New Jersey was sent to report on construction progress and detected a serious problem. Enemy cannon could fire down from an adjacent higher hill and easily destroy the fort. Construction began on the second fort on higher ground. It was named Fort Clinton after New York General and Governor George Clinton. Thereafter, the two forts became known as the "Twin Forts" and their history merged.[4]

The position of the two fortresses made a frontal attack on the forts from the river virtually impossible. The battery of heavy cannon could blast any ship attempting to pass below. Popolopen Creek, which flowed into the river through a deep gorge between the forts, offered Fort Montgomery natural protection on the south side.

Beneath the twin forts, the river is only a few hundred yards wide. The Bear Mountain Bridge today spans this narrow place on the river. Ingenious army engineers stretched a huge chain across. It was cast in the forges of western Orange County and made of 850 huge iron links, each weighing 35 tons. The chain, supported by pine logs, would stop any ship that could not be demolished by the batteries firing down from the forts above. Fort Montgomery's chain preceded another which was later stretched across the Hudson at West Point later in 1778. Several links of the West Point chain are exhibited on the parade ground of the Academy.[5]

To complete the defenses a small flotilla of American warships, which included the frigates *Montgomery* and *Congress*, tacked from bank to bank behind the chain. With gun ports open, they were ready to deliver broadsides into intruders. All of these formidable defenses focused on an attack by ships and not a land assault. It was believed that an attack through the impassable mountains on the rear of the forts was unachievable.

During the fall of 1776 and the spring and summer of 1777, construction progress was slow, although the chain was completed. In May, Washington wrote to Brigadier General Alexander McDougall, the senior American commander in the Hudson Highlands.

> *"The imperfect state of the fortifications of Fort Montgomery gives me great uneasyness, because I think that from a concurrence of circumstances, that it begins to look as if the enemy intended to turn their view toward the North river (Hudson River), instead of the Delaware. I therefore desire that General George Clinton and yourself will fall upon every measure to put the fortifications a state that they may at least resist a sudden attack and keep the enemy employed until reinforcements may arrive."* [6]

In early 1777 Colonel Dubois, commanding the 5th New York Regiment was assigned to Forts Montgomery and Clinton.[7] His under manned regiment of about 300 men and a few militia units were at the forts. Construction had not been completed at either fortification This split force of about 600 men, some without muskets, was all that stood between Manhattan and Fort Ticonderoga 120 miles north.

Despite their precarious position during the spring of 1777, the troops at the twin forts enjoyed a warm spirit of camaraderie and a high quality of life. Archeology at Fort Montgomery has uncovered the remains of well constructed barracks, complete with fire places and glass windows. Pension applications filed in later years by veterans' widows show that families often visited and clothing and supplies were frequently issued. During the summer, soldiers were offered cash advances against their bounties to purchase personal items from settlers (civilian peddlars who followed the army).[8]

The troops followed the same schedule each day. The exhausting work included cutting wood, building the entrenchments and erecting barracks. It was the same hard labor that most were accustomed to do as farmhands. A workday of twelve hours was common for those who were not sick. Work began at six in the morning and except for breakfast and lunch breaks continued until sunset. Patrols along the river often broke the monotony of this routine.

Disease spread rapidly among the soldiers at the Twin Forts. Having spent their lives in the sparsely settled countryside, soldiers lacked the immunity needed to stay well in the densely settled confines of the forts. Dysentery and smallpox proved to be even greater dangers than the enemy. During the Revolutionary War, about nine soldiers with smallpox died from the disease for every one killed in battle. Muster rolls for the 5th Regiment while at the forts in May and June of 1777, list about twenty percent of the men as sick. Washington began the inoculation program for smallpox in 1777 long after the disease became an epidemic in the Continental Army.

While the camp buzzed with concern about being unprepared activities were not being focused on preparation for an enemy flotilla to attack up the river. The 5th Regiment occupied itself with capturing and punishing Tories and apprehending deserters. Many Orange County Loyalists, emboldened by the resurgence of the British Army strength, were supplying and even attempting to join the Redcoat regiments. Officers spent their days trying them in court martial hearings. During these months, farmers from the militia deserted to go home to take care of their crops and families. They usually returned and were accepted back without question or with a token punishment.

By July 1777, Washington was certain that there would soon be an invasion up the river. He urged George Clinton to call in the local militia to Peekskill on the east side of the river and on the west side to the Twin Forts and Suffern, the entrance to Smith's Clove, the corridor through the Ramapo Mountains. The next day Clinton reported that if a sudden assault were to occur, there would not be time enough for regular army or militia reinforcements to reach them. With most of the Continental Army preparing to defend the nation's capital at Philadelphia or massing at Saratoga to meet Burgoyne's assault from Canada. The remnant army in the Hudson Highlands would be on their own.

The 5th New York Regiment was still at half strength despite vigorous recruiting efforts. This portended disastrous consequences. In July, Colonel Dubois reported that his entire 5th Regiment consisted of only 218 privates available for duty out of 358 soldiers. Men were sick, "on command" (assigned elsewhere) or on recruiting duty. An astounding 56 men were listed as sick. Dubois realistically predicted that the forts were defenseless if they were incomplete and not manned by a force of at least two thousand. [9]

All of the diversions left few men to complete building the defenses of the forts during the summer. In the limited time that was available, the soldiers of the 5th Regiment struggled alongside the patriotic but independent militia men. Tory prisoners were forced to work. The men dug trenches, moved cannon, built firing platforms and cleared fields of fire. Despite these exuberant efforts, the lack of manpower left the redoubts and other defensive fortifications far from complete as autumn approached.

Bad news continued to reach the forts. Fort Ticonderoga was recaptured and the Redcoats continued to roll south. Their advanced units were soon within 35 miles of Albany, the seat of the New York Colonial government. In desperation, more of the troops along the Hudson were sent north to defend this city and to counter the threat of a final defeat.

The 5th New York Regiment of 300 soldiers stood alone at the forts. Militia came in large numbers from sparsely settled nearby Orange County towns to reinforce them. The Patriot forces at the Twin Forts were divided equally, 300 to each fort. This number was even too few to man the guard posts along the perimeter of the defenses. Fort Montgomery which was much larger than Fort Clinton was especially vulnerable.

During the first three weeks of September, events in New York City gave the beleaguered troops at the forts a brief, but false, sense of security. Instead of moving up the Hudson as expected, most of the British fleet sailed south and up the Chesapeake to attack Philadelphia. Fortunately, their departure left Sir Henry Clinton in New York City without the strength to defend the city, and attack up the river at the same time.

However, a sudden turn of events reversed this good fortune and struck terror in the hearts of the Patriot defenders in the Hudson Valley. On September 25, 1777 a task force of 60 ships with 3,000 Redcoats appeared in New York Harbor. These reinforcements had arrived from England. Now, with this massive buildup of strength, Sir Henry was fully prepared to launch an invasion up the river to link up with Burgoyne's large force coming down from Canada and win the war.

On October 3, terrifying news reached the Twin Forts. Sir Henry Clinton was on the way. Enemy regiments on board transport ships were sailing up the river to attack. They had already reached Tarrytown, ten miles below Forts Clinton and Montgomery. The defenders at the twin forts honed bayonets and cleaned musket barrels to prepare themselves for what might be their last days.

A Heroic Defense by the Outnumbered Patriots

Why was such a strategically vital position as the Twin Forts so lightly defended and neglected by American commanders at this critical time. Other calamitous events in the war were occurring at the same time and considered to be of greater urgency than the defense of the Hudson Highlands.

Most of the strength of the American Army had been drained out of the lower Hudson Valley to counter what seemed to be an even greater emergency. General John Burgoyne, with 13,000 fresh British regulars and Hessian (Brunswicker) troops, newly arrived from England was moving down Lakes Champlain and George and threatening Saratoga. On August 21, 1777 General Putnam pulled out the entire 2nd and 4th New York Regiments which were posted along the river and sent them north to join General Horatio Gates to defend Albany. This would be the next British objective if Saratoga fell.

American defenses along the river were weakened further when Putnam sent an additional 2,500 troops south at the request of General Washington to join the main army defending Philadelphia. This sapped most of the Continental Army's strength from the Hudson River defenses. The under strength 5th New York Regiment together with a few local militia units was so short of men that guard posts along the perimeter of the forts could not be fully manned. The New Yorkers were decimated by transfers and were virtually abandoned to fend for themselves at the Twin Forts.

There were other reasons why the forts were so lightly defended. With General Gates attempting to stop Burgoyne at Saratoga 110 miles to the north, it was unlikely that there would be a sudden attack on the forts from that direction. It was believed that Sir Henry Clinton sailing up the river from the south would first attack the main body of 1,200 American troops under General Israel Putnam five miles south in Peekskill on the opposite bank of the river.

The American generals believed that the forts even in an uncompleted state were impregnable. Ships attempting a bombardment from below would be stopped by the huge chain and boom stretched across the river and repelled by the battery of heavy American cannon on the cliffs above. An amphibious landing would require the enemy to scale the 100 foot high cliffs to reach the forts. A thrust by land through the rugged mountains at the rear of the forts was not even considered a possibility. Most of these assumptions were tragically wrong.

The Twin Forts Montgomery and Clinton -A Deadly Surprise

While American military leaders were certain that the Twin Forts would not be surprised by a sudden attack it was likely that there could be some action there if the fighting spread north. Massed troops were on the heights in preparation and all cannons were trained over the river. From this position the British ships might bombard and then launch an amphibious invasion and try to scale the heights.

The Patriot defenders on both sides of the river anticipated an invasion up the Hudson. Everyone, even the lowest private understood the master plan of the British invaders and their objective to move north up the river and through the Hudson Highlands to link up with another large force invading south down the chain of lakes from Canada.

Brigadier General James Clinton was the senior commander at the new forts. Colonel Lewis Dubois led the 371 men of the 5th Regiment. One hundred artillery men from Colonel John Lamb's Regiment supported Dubois. Two hundred militia troops could hastily be called in from nearby Orange County towns.

This action is often referred to as the "battle of the Clintons," since all three senior commanders had the same name. General Sir Henry Clinton led the British forces, James Clinton led the New York Regiments and his brother, Governor George Clinton, was in command of all New York forces. Some believe that James and George were distant cousins of Sir Henry.

On the morning of October 4, 1777, the apprehensive defenders at the undermanned Twin Forts felt a sense of relief. As expected the enemy struck the

Patriots on the opposite side of the river near Peekskill where the main body of American troops under General Putnam stood ready for a major confrontation. However, this was a false, diversionary maneuver designed to divert the attention of the Americans away from the real objective- the Twin Forts. This feint completely deceived General Putnam who further weakened the forts by ordering additional men across the river to protect Peekskill.[10]

The Americans at Fort Montgomery were now certain that the battle would be on the other side of the river. The next evening, October 5, Major Samuel Logan was sent out with about one hundred men to try to locate the enemy and to see if any had crossed the river from Peekskill. Early on the morning of October 6, Logan's patrol was astonished to witness Sir Henry Clinton's main army of 2,100 British assault troops, shrouded by dense fog, landing at Stony Point, six miles below the forts. Informed of the weakness of the forts by local Tories, the Redcoat forces had moved to the west side of the river. Attacking here would give them the advantage of surprise since the attack was unexpected by land. If they could get through the mountains they could strike the lightly protected rear of the Twin Forts.

Major Logan, whose mission was only to scout and report, fell back to the fort with the dreadful news. Historians lament that his patrol could have made a standalone and stopped the invaders at a narrow, rocky ravine called "The Torn" at Dunderberg Mountain, through which the main body of attackers had to pass. With fog obscuring the landing place, Logan was unable to estimate accurately the size of the invading force and returned to the forts by nine o'clock in the morning. While he told the Clintons that they were being threatened by a major land assault, his report was incomplete and provided no hard intelligence of the number of enemy troops or when or where they might strike.

That morning, after the landing had taken place, General Putnam sent a belated warning message to George Clinton at the twin forts. It arrived too late to help him:

> *"I am this moment returned from Fort Independence (Peekskill) and find that the party of the enemy that was said to have landed last night is without foundation. I am informed that the enemy have landed betwixt Kings Ferry and Dunderbarrack, if that the case they mean to attack Fort Montgomery by land (which I am sure of) shall immediately reinforce you."*

First Clash At Doodletown

At this point the thirty men of the 2nd Company of the 5th New York played a pivotal role in the action. This unit, led by Patton Jackson, a 34 year old Lieutenant and Corporal John Allison was sent on a reconnaissance patrol at 10:00 AM. They were ordered to move along the main route leading south along, the Haverstraw Road, to try to learn more about enemy strength and movements.

This company was selected for this perilous mission because of its high number of seasoned combat veterans with knowledge of the terrain. Most of them lived in this part of Orange County. They knew the narrow mountain passes through the rugged wilderness and had passed through here many times on previous patrols and on visits home.

This small detachment moved cautiously south about two miles down the road to a stream at the crossroads hamlet of Doodletown. Here, they came upon advanced elements of the entire British Army hidden in the bushes. Facing overwhelming numbers, in an amazing display of courage, the brave little band stood fast and from only twenty-five yards away, attacked with a withering barrage of musket fire. When the enemy saw that there were only a few men, they returned the gunfire from their concealed positions. Three of the patriots fell in the sharp exchange of musket fire. It was at this moment that the surviving 27 Patriots realized that they faced the entire Redcoat Army.

These were the first shots fired in the battle of Fort Montgomery. When the sounds of this gunfire were heard back at the forts, it immediately alerted the defenders that the assault had begun. Drums beat to arms and defensive measures shifted men and artillery to the unfinished rear of the forts. Patton Jackson and his men also observed that the British Army at the crossroads in Doodletown was following the advice of the local Tories and dividing its force to strike the forts on two fronts. This critical intelligence was quickly relayed back to the defenders.

As the 2nd Company fell back, they again made another stand from behind a stone wall less than a mile away from the rear of the forts. For as much as a full hour, they stood alone holding off the 1,200 Redcoats who had split off at Doodletown to attack Fort Clinton. All evidence of the stone wall that had marked the boundary of a farmer's field has disappeared over the years, but a monument has been erected to mark its location. Surrounded by picnic tables on the north side of the Bear Mountain Inn, a bronze plaque mounted on a large boulder reads:

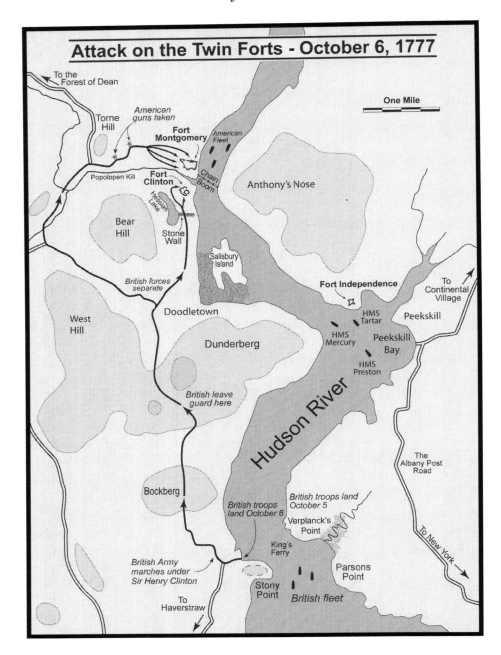

Attack on the Twin Forts - October 6, 1777

One Mile

To the Forest of Dean

Torne Hill

American guns taken

Fort Montgomery

American Fleet

Anthony's Nose

Popolopen Kill

Fort Clinton

Chain Boom

Hessian Lake

Bear Hill

Stone Wall

Salisbury Island

Fort Independence

To Continental Village

British forces separate

Doodletown

HMS Tartar

Peekskill

West Hill

Dunderberg

HMS Mercury

Peekskill Bay

HMS Preston

British leave guard here

Hudson River

The Albany Post Road

Bockberg

British troops land October 6

British troops land October 5

Verplanck's Point

To New York

King's Ferry

British Army marches under Sir Henry Clinton

Parsons Point

Stony Point

British fleet

To Haverstraw

When the British attacked forts Clinton and Montgomery Oct. 6, 1777
the first fighting occurred over the outworks located at this point.

To gain time, in the hope that reinforcements might arrive from Putnam's regiments to relieve the forts, Governor Clinton sent a hundred Continental and militia troops to reinforce Jackson's beleaguered patrol at the stone wall. With this support, the 2nd Company continued to halt the British advance with galling barrages of musket fire. Outnumbered ten to one, they were outflanked and forced to fall back, sniping from behind trees and rocks. A canon in the west redoubt of Fort Clinton covered their retreat.

The British lost the advantage of surprise as soon as the 2nd Company had alerted the forts that they were dividing their forces at Doodletown to make a two-pronged assault. Sending back this critical information gave the Americans a short time to prepare for a separate attack on each fort. There would be a direct frontal assault on Fort Clinton while another large unit would swing left around Bear Mountain to strike Fort Montgomery from the west. Troops were redeployed to the outer redoubts, (star-shaped defenses along the ramparts), and artillery was rushed out to the rear approaches of the forts where the assault had not been expected.

Back at the forts, the defenders were stretched out in a thin line and clustered in the redoubts. By three o'clock in the afternoon, they looked out on a terrifying sight. The entire Army of over 2,000 British regular, Hessian and Tory regiments stood massed before the forts with bayonets fixed.

The intrepid 2nd Company, 5th New York Regiment of the Continental Line served with valor on the morning of October 6, 1777. They located the main body of the British Army and stood fast against overwhelming numbers in the courageous engagement at Doodletown. The sound of this gunfire alerted the Twin Forts of the impending attack. In falling back, they delayed the enemy advance by taking a second stand at the stone fence. The intelligence they sent back, that an army of over two thousand British, Hessian and Loyalist assault troops were making a two-pronged assault on the rear of the forts, foiled the enemy's surprise and allowed the defenders to deploy their firepower immediately to the best advantage. This long day was far from over after they reached the other Patriot defenders in the outer redoubt of Fort Clinton.

5th New York Regiment Reenactors on the site of the stone wall, now on the grounds of the Bear Mountain Inn, where the 2nd Company made its stand after the s kirmish at Doodletown.

It takes about an hour to reach the rushing, but fordable, Doodletown Brook from the forts. The town lies along the unpaved Doodletown Road on the opposite bank. Only the remnants of stone foundations remain. Today it is a popular destination for hikers, birdwatchers, local historians and botanists. The site is accessible from many surrounding trails. Plaques identifying the structures and orientation signs are located on the site. Park Commission signage includes a map of the area.[11]

Pleasant Valley Road, which is a stretch of the old Haverstraw Road, intersects Doodletown Road at the stream. This is where the British Army, after marching over Dunderberg Mountain, divided its forces to launch the dual attack on the forts. Across from this site, on the north side of the stream, is where the valiant 2nd Company skirmished with the British invasion force. The dense foliage here would have provided cover for both sides.

The enemy started to swarm around their flanks of the reinforced 2nd Company at the stone wall and the outnumbered Americans were finally overrun. They began to run out of ammunition but were able to maintain a steady barrage of musket fire as they were slowly forced back to the outer defenses of Fort Clinton. Their incessant gunfire and the roughness of the terrain again served to slow the British approach. Colonel William Allison sent out another 100 men, but ordered them to return when they were driven back to within "a few yards" from the outer defenses of the fort.

Today, the half- mile between the stone wall and the west redoubt of Fort Clinton extends from the picnic grounds at the Bear Mountain Inn and crosses over Route 9W. There it becomes part of the Appalachian Trail and passes through the Bear Mountain Trailside and Wildlife center on the site of Fort Clinton. Foundation stones still outline the site of the redoubt

To reach Fort Montgomery from Fort Clinton it is necessary to descend down a steep ravine to the gorge of the broad, swift Popolopen Creek that separates the Twin Forts. At that time, a wooden pontoon footbridge crossed the creek at bottom of the path. The steep, narrow path down into the ravine still exists under the shadow of the Bear Mountain Bridge, the majestic modern bridge which crosses this narrow point of the Hudson at the Twin Forts. [12]

Climbing up the opposite bank, you emerge into the main area of the fort, amid barracks, the powder magazine and the main battery of 32 pounders. These cannons were too heavy to reposition and remained trained out over the river to repel the warships and the amphibious landing, which never came.

Men were thinly stretched along the uncompleted walls and others clustered in three redoubts, (enclosed defensive works) along the ramparts. Many of the militia had rushed to the fort from their farms only a few hours before. Many were still arriving. These ragtag farmers were poorly equipped with old homemade firearms and no bayonets. Many had no weapons at all.

A Long Afternoon at the Twin Forts

As the action raged at the stone wall, half of the enemy force approached the rear of Fort Clinton, the other half which had split off at Doodletown passed around the rear of Bear Mountain. They still hoped to surprise the defenders of Fort Montgomery. British Lieutenant Colonel Mungo Campbell led his force of 900 soldiers through the ravines and the gorge of Popolopen Creek to the rear of Fort Montgomery.[13] To slow this wave of attackers, George Clinton sent out 120 men with a brass cannon, under the command of Captain Ephraim Fenno.[14]

Fenno's artillerymen rained down a devastating barrage of grapeshot and managed to repel the invaders several times. However, vastly outnumbered, they were finally enveloped as repeated bayonet charges hit them from both sides. Many American artillery men fell and Captain Fenno was taken prisoner. Their retreat was covered by a second cannon. Both guns were spiked but captured as the troops fell back. The site of this heroic stand at the gorge became known in history as the "Hell Hole." By three o'clock in the afternoon, the enemy force of 2,100 British Grenadiers, Regiments of Foot, Highlanders, Dragoons, Hessian Chasseurs and loyalist brigades massed in the rear of the Twin Forts before the Patriot defenders. Their number was now reduced by their losses at the stone wall and the "Hell Hole."

The survivors of the 5th New York Regiment took positions along the incomplete and poorly situated wall and in the west redoubt at the rear of Fort Montgomery. They planned to fall back to the north redoubt if overrun. This reinforced position on the ramparts commanded the fort and would bear the brunt of the attack.

The defenses had been strengthened by moving twenty smaller cannon to the rear of the fort. The immobile main battery of 32 pounders remained trained out over the river. An abbatis (a defensive obstacle made of felled trees with sharpened branches pointed outward) had been formed in front of the walls to slow the attackers. Out in the river British warships prepared to bombard the forts.

Both wings of the British Army were now in position to attack each fort separately. General John Vaughan would lead the assault on Fort Clinton.[15] After overrunning the valiant troops at the stone wall, his men stumbled over the rocks and hacked their way through the abbatis in front of the fort. These 1,200 men the Grenadiers, Light Infantry and Scottish Highlanders were the equivalent of today's elite special forces.

Mungo Campbell's force attacking Fort Montgomery included many Americans Loyalists. This unit, the "Loyal American Regiment" had 400 men and was under the command of Colonel Beverley Robinson.[16] The Tory Robinson was an affluent landowner from the nearby town of Garrison, New York. He knew the terrain and his advice in planning the attack was invaluable. Looking out from the north redoubt, the Patriot defenders could see hundreds of sinister figures with bayonets emerging from the dense foliage. After beating their way through the "hellhole" against Fenno's cannons, the attackers now stood 40 yards from the defenses of Fort Montgomery.

Few Americans had bayonets. With no time to load a musket, the bayonet was essential in repelling aggressive frontal assaults. Many of the militia who rushed to the forts from their farms did not have weapons of any kind. The three redoubts of Fort Montgomery were spaced 125 yards apart; and with so few troops, the Americans were unable to man the walls between these ramparts.

By three o'clock in the afternoon, Vaughan and Campbell had completely surrounded both forts. Still, there was a possibility reinforcements would arrive from General Putnam across the river with the main American force. Governor Clinton sent a third and last frantic appeal for reinforcements. The main attack then began.

For the next three hours, the enemy rushed up to the walls repeatedly, taking heavy casualties and being continually beaten back by sprays of grapeshot from the patriot cannons. The long afternoon stretched into evening and still the thin line of defenders resisted with incessant musket and cannon fire from behind the broken rampart walls and redoubts.

Unable to dislodge the American defenders, Mungo Campbell himself approached the fort at 5:00 pm with a white flag of truce. He offered the struggling defenders a chance to surrender. George Clinton sent out Colonel William Livingston to meet him. The arrogant Campbell demanded that the forts "Surrender in five minutes or die by the bayonet." Governor Clinton, not to be intimidated, instructed Livingston to make a similar counter offer.

Eight hundred British soldiers with fixed bayonets then prepared for a final frontal assault. As Campbell gave the command to charge, an American sniper who had kept him in his sights after the parley killed him instantly. Tory Colonel Beverley Robinson was the next in command and rapidly reorganized the charge. This final massed assault by the combined force of British Regulars and Loyalist troops succeeded in overwhelming the weary Patriots who could not defend the entire length of the walls. The first ones over the wall were the green coated American Tories from the Loyalist Regiment. The beleaguered defenders may have recognized their neighbors among them.

As afternoon turned into evening more waves of attackers smashed through the walls and engaged the outnumbered Americans in savage hand-to-hand fighting. Many of the defenders were now locked in close combat against some of the Tory soldiers they knew by name. The Twin Forts were under attack from all sides as the British warships rained heavy cannon fire from the river.[17]

General Vaughan, having taken heavy losses, mounted a final frenzied bayonet attack on Fort Clinton. This fort, while smaller than Fort Montgomery, was more strongly built and surrounded by rougher terrain. Many British officers singled out by marksmen began falling. The American defenders continued to fight stubbornly as they fell back over the parade ground. They rallied one final time to discharge a murderous volley from their muskets but then the Redcoats swarmed through Fort Clinton. No order was ever given to withdraw.

At the west redoubt of Fort Montgomery the exhausted American defenders continued to resist but were finally overpowered by sheer numbers and fell back to the north redoubt to make a final desperate stand. Major Abraham Leggett was in the north redoubt and recalled years later, "They came on very furiously and were beat back the second and third time."[18]

Finally, the Americans began to crumble; and the action turned into a struggle to escape. A relief force of 500 men sent by Putnam finally reached the forts but found them to be completely over-run and beyond any help that could be given. By six o'clock, the fighting was over. Still there was never an order to withdraw or surrender.

Fortunately, dusk was turning to darkness and those not wounded and fleet-of- foot, were able to escape the slaughter. To get away, they had to pass through the British lines and mix in with their foes. Some knew the way through the ravines and woods and they joined others in hacking their way northward in the fading light to lose their pursuers. Others desperately slid down the sides of the steep hill to the river where they were picked up by friendly boats. The long afternoon finally ended with most of the American force killed, wounded or captured.

American losses at the Twin Forts were appalling. A muster roll taken after the battle shows that in many companies half of the privates were killed or captured. In the 5th Regiment, 14 officers, 10 sergeants, 9 corporals and 122 privates were missing. A total of 263 Americans were taken prisoner.[19]

Colonel Lewis Dubois the commander of the 5th Regiment, was bayoneted in the neck but managed to escape. Among the senior officers, Governor Clinton stood fast in the midst of the fighting and finally was persuaded to leave when the north redoubt was over run. He managed to slide down the cliff to the river where he was rescued by boat. His brother Brigadier General James Clinton was wounded by a bayonet in the thigh. He escaped by climbing on the barges that supported the great chain where it crossed the river. The small patriot flotilla of two sloops was torched to prevent them from falling to the enemy. The destination of the survivors was New Windsor, six miles up river, where they would attempt to regroup.

The triumphant enemy forces paid dearly for their victory. Governor Clinton wrote to George Washington three days later *"I have good authority to assure your excellency the enemy suffered great loss at Fort Montgomery; they had 7 field officers and a young noble man volunteer mortally wounded and by the accounts upward of 300 rank and file killed."* The British listed their toll as 42 killed and 142 wounded. Though the British forces had great superiority in number, credit should go to their clever strategy and full use of their advantages. They exploited the knowledge of the local area and effectively used the added troop strength provided by their Tory allies. They used the element of surprise with a feint attack on the opposite side of the river and an assault by land on the rear of the forts. Having no cannons, they brought down the forts using massed bayonet attacks against opponents who were only armed with slow loading muskets.

Many of the patriots lived nearby and sought refuge on their farms. David Rose of the militia lived less than a mile from the battleground and reached his home with two other soldiers. His wife Hannah hid them in a barn. When an enemy patrol arrived, she refused to disclose their hiding place. Torn away from her hysterical children, she was seated on a horse with a noose around her neck. The officer leading the enemy patrol mercifully freed her, saying that there had been enough bloodshed that day.[20]

Lieutenant Henry Pawling, encircled by bayonets was captured with Patton Jackson in the north redoubt. He wrote an account of events after he became a prisoner. Angry Tory officers threatened and beat the captive officers who they personally knew and stripped them of their coats, hats, shoes, watches and anything else of value. Pawling describes the view from his cell window at Fort Montgomery on the morning after the battle. *"We saw the enemy carrying our dead on poles, naked with their heads and heels hanging down and we saw the enemy walking about the fort with our clothes selling them to each other."* The bodies of the fallen patriots were dumped in a lake outside the walls of the Fort.[21]

The next day, captives Pawling, Jackson and the other officers and men who had been captured were herded onto boats to be transported down the river to New York City. Driven at bayonet point to the dock, they were forced to pass two thousand hostile loyalist civilians who shouted insults and threatened to hang them. Imprisoned in the notorious Sugar House Prison and held captive on prison ships on the East River many died from starvation and sickness.

The day after the battle British sappers (engineers) severed the great chain. This allowed the British fleet to begin a sweep up the Hudson to link up with Burgoyne's northern army now approaching Albany only 40 miles north. The next week the victorious Redcoats renamed Fort Clinton, Fort Vaughan after their commander and used it as their headquarters in the Hudson Highlands for the next three weeks. All the buildings of Fort Montgomery were burned and destroyed.

Visitors and Archeology

Dr. Timothy Dwight, an army doctor, made the first recorded visit to the abandoned site in May of 1778 only seven months after the battle. He reported that the forts were completely destroyed and people living nearby collected heaps of bones and built fires to reduce them to ashes. He was appalled by the many bodies of the fallen Patriots that had been dumped in a pond outside the fort. The water had receded leaving their bodies exposed. He reported, *"The clothes they wore when they were killed were still on them and proved that they were militia; being the dress of ordinary farmers."* Archeologists place the location of "Bloody Pond" in a swampy spot just outside the north wall of Fort Montgomery. This tragic place is now covered by Highway 9W.[22]

Benson Lossing, the intrepid traveling historian and artist was the next notable visitor in 1848 70 years later. He found the grounds covered by grass and cedar trees and inaccessible without a hatchet. He found the remains of the grand battery where the heavy artillery was pointed down the river at the time of the action.[23]

Reginald Bolton and Edward Hagerman did the first archeological survey at the forts beginning in 1916. They reported finding "a wild thicket with pine, hemlock, cherry and other species of trees, with many growing out of old building foundations." They uncovered the remains of ramparts and buildings and uncovered a rich treasure trove of artifacts. From 1967 to 1971 Ed Lenik and Jack Mead, Director of the Trailside Museum, located on the grounds of Fort Clinton, directed an ambitious archeological dig. He drew maps, diagrams and uncovered thousands of artifacts.[24]

1916 excaation at Fort Montgomery

In 1997, local citizens formed the Fort Montgomery Battle Site Association and arranged for the Palisades Interstate Park Commission to clear the site. In 2004 a large scale archeological study was conducted by the State of New York to stabilize the ruins and to provide descriptions of the fort's buildings and the daily lives of the soldiers who occupied it during the Revolutionary War. Details of the structures built by the American Army were recovered during the excavations and a large collection of artifacts was recorded and described. The forts were not rebuilt but preserved as ruins.[25]

A visitors center and museum was opened in 2007. After 225 years the area was transformed into a fascinating place for visitors. The original foundations and earthworks are all identified with pathways and interpretive signage. A tunnel under Route 9W provides access to two western redoubts. The center houses a museum of artifacts found on the site and a three dimensional map model. An excellent orientation film on the fort can be viewed.

The anniversary of the battle is commemorated each year and is attended by hundreds of people. The battle is reenacted and activities in the life of soldiers at the time are portrayed by the 5th New York Regiment whose forbears so valiantly defended the fort in 1777.[26]

Chapter Six

An Unknown Dark side of a Cruel Winter, Jockey Hollow, Morrristown, New Jersey, 1779-1780.

In the Shadow of Valley Forge

Jockey Hollow in Morristown, New Jersey was the location of an event of the war that truly tested the heart of the new nation. The tragic place was a remote woodland in the hands of private owners for about 150 years after the last soldier departed. Conditions were far more severe here than at the encampment the previous year at Valley Forge, Pennsylvania in the winter of 1777-1778. But Jockey Hollow has never rivaled the fame of Valley Forge. New Jersey historians have always lamented its neglect. Researching original source documents and viewing both places in light of events after the war provide some explanation as to why for many years the camp at Morristown was overlooked.[1] While the winter at Valley Forge was not especially severe, the inability to feed and clothe the 14,000 men led to an appalling toll of 1,895 deaths due mostly to "putrid fever" (typhus), smallpox and dysentery.[2] The camp was in an isolated place in a district of iron mines and forges, not an agricultural area and far from supply depots.

There were 86 recorded deaths at Jockey Hollow. This lower fatality rate can be attributed to the lessons learned at Valley Forge two years earlier. Despite the harsh conditions, Jockey Hollow had a better water and wood supply which made it possible to accommodate as many as 12,000 soldiers in an area half the size of Valley Forge. Hut building and administration were greatly improved along with the professionalism of the officer corps. Many of the senior officers, however were absent during the hard winter. Curiously corporal punishment Jockey Hollow was excessive when compared to other times during the war. The camp was near a substantial community in the center of a bountiful agricultural area that despite the apparent advantages of its location completely failed to sustain the army.

After the war the saga of Valley Forge simply made a better story for the American public due to a success soon after. The winter there, viewed by many as the low point of the war, was followed a few months later by the Battle of Monmouth. There for the first time the fledgling American Army stood up to seasoned British regulars, the best trained and equipped army in the world.

This turning point in the war and the birth of the Continental Army is popularly believed to have been achieved largely by the training of raw soldiers by Baron von Steuben at Valley Forge. This legend had great public relations value especially since the site was only 18 miles from Philadelphia the nation's capitol for several years after the war. Valley Forge became a major tourist attraction and in 1911 a railway station was opened to accommodate the flood of visitors. Today four million people travel to this site each year. Tucked away in the back hills of New Jersey, Jockey Hollow now attracts 262,000 visitors after languishing for years without acclaim and finally becoming a National Park in 1933. [3]

The camp near Morristown had bad memories for both the public and the army in the years that followed the war. Two major mutinies by entire state brigades occurred here and another mutiny in nearby Pompton. These uprisings sullied the image of quietly suffering soldiers. The place reminded people that the beleaguered troops at Jockey Hollow received meager support from civilians who often chose to sell food and supplies to the enemy rather than accept devalued Continental dollars. This avoidable breakdown of the supply chain in a bountiful country was shameful.

The local population smarted for years over the memories of the encampments. The Army brought smallpox which killed a quarter of the civilian population. The starving soldiers stole livestock and tore down fences and outbuildings searching for firewood

There were two major encampments at Morristown during the Revolutionary War, The winters of 1776-1777 and 1779-1780. This caused confusion and actions that occurred during the two winters became comingled. Valley Forge fitted neatly into a single winter. One could easily relate to this single period other military and political events. [4]

Morristown is the location of two significant historical sites, the camp at Jockey Hollow and the Ford Mansion that served as Washington's Headquarters during the encampment. By 1873 the once elegant home was in disrepair and in danger of being dismantled or used for a boarding house. In that year a group of New Jersey citizens bid $25,000 at auction and saved this significant landmark.

Joined by others they formed the Washington Association. The Association became the caretaker of the home. They restored it with little public funding and began collecting artifacts, books and manuscripts. Over the next half century the mansion grew to a substantial library and a museum that contains weapons, maps, furniture and other objects of cultural interest. By 1890 the house was attracting many visitors and has continued to be a popular destination. [5]

The farmland at Jockey Hollow three miles south of the mansion continued to languish in obscurity in the hands of private owners for about a century and a half. In 1921 the Wick house was offered as a gift to the Association but in those hard days of the Great Depression it was refused by the Association for the lack of funds to maintain it.

By the 1930s it was evident that it would soon be built over. Mayor Clyde Potts of Morristown joined forces with Lloyd W. Smith a wealthy local investment banker with a strong interest in the history of the area to try to save the hallowed site. Smith ended up buying most of the tract and together with other owners, the town and the Washington Association, the place was offered to the U.S. Department of the Interior. Herbert Hoover signed a law in 1933 that established Jockey Hollow, Fort Nonsense and the Ford Mansion at the country's first national historic park

Destination Morristown

During early December 1779, the officers and men of the Continental Army streamed into the camp. Most of these men were seasoned veterans. They had fought in the invasion of Canada in 1775 and at the battles of Long Island, White Plains, Trenton, Princeton, Saratoga and Monmouth. Two years earlier many had wintered at Valley Forge, Pennsylvania. Some of the men had spent the winter of 1776-1777 in Morristown and were now returning. At that time, the Army was smaller, the weather was less harsh and a few had been quartered in the homes of the town. These veterans wrongly predicted a benign winter.

Most of the Continental Army marched into Jockey Hollow from the north. The main body of troops came from West Point or other places in the Hudson Highlands. Stark's Brigade came from Rhode Island. They moved down Smith's Clove, now Route I 87, through Suffern, New York and Pompton, New Jersey on the way to Morristown. The long columns of soldiers passed through this village with a few houses formed around a town green where cattle grazed in the warmer seasons. Mount Kimble Road led out of the town. It was a narrow back road, slick from rain and ice storms that had left two feet of hard crusted snow on the ground. They then trudged three miles south and came into a bleak, windswept 2,000-acre forest in a mountainous valley, known locally as Jockey Hollow. Other brigades from the middle and southern colonies had already gathered there.[6]

The New York Brigade also approached from the north. On returning from the campaign against the Indian Nations they had made a 100 mile detour to their home state. Only six months before Iroquois Indians and Loyalists under War Chief Joseph Brant has massacred forty eight men of the Goshen Militia at Minnisink, New York. The New Jersey Brigade had the shortest trip from Union County, about 15 miles from the winter camp.

Other brigades marched in from the Princeton area from the south. They passed through Pluckemin, Bernardsville and Basking Ridge and then plodded along the western edge of the Great Swamp down Lees Hill Road the main street of Harding Township As they neared the center of the town the long lines of weary men walked past houses that still exist and bear markers with 18th century dates. The columns turned left at the town's center onto Glen Alpin Road. This road runs two miles west before turning into Tempe Wick Road which leads into the entrance of the Jockey Hollow campground. Two original roads, in use since 1776, still lead into the campsite Jockey Hollow Road from Morristown and Sugar Loaf Road from Mendham in the west.

Eight infantry brigades arrived at the camp. They came from Pennsylvania, Maryland, Delaware, Connecticut, Rhode Island, Massachusetts, New Jersey and Virginia. All had reached their final destination for the year. It was known locally as Jockey Hollow. For the next seven months they would suffer through more than 28 snowstorms during the longest and most severe winter of the revolution and the entire eighteenth century. Quartermaster General Nathaniel Green assigned an area to each brigade.

George Washington selected this desolate Morris County location. Protected on the east by three ridges of the Watchung Mountains and the impassible Great Swamp the site had obvious logistical, topographical and geographic military advantages. It was. Its elevation hundreds of feet above the plains that stretched to British lines in Staten Island made it impregnable in the days when men and horses moved all supplies and cannons.

From the first ridge of the Watchung Mountains advancing troops of the main British Army, headquartered, 30 miles away in New York City could be detected. This served as an early warning to prepare to defend the passes through the Watchungs at Westfield, Scotch Plains, Watchung and Bound Brook, New Jersey.

A marker on Jockey Hollow Road reads, *Between here and the British Army in New York City lay a land of divided loyalty. Washington kept several brigades out there patrolling "on the line." The soldiers never knew who was patriot or Tory. And mistakes could be fatal. The Watchung Mountains took no sides but divided the armies from one another.*

Most of this heavily wooded tract covered the 800 acre farm of Henry Wick a prosperous farmer who was away serving in the militia with the Morris County Cavalry. The lands of Wick and his neighboring farmers could also provide most of the timber that was needed to construct cabins to house the army through the winter. If more troop support was needed, the New Jersey Militia could be called upon. They had the reputation of being more dependable than most citizen soldiers. Despite these benefits the severity of the winter and the ability to sustain the Army with clothing, supplies and food was tragically underestimated. Every day the troops needed 10,000 pounds of bread and beef to survive.

Until log huts could be built, there was no shelter for the men in the wilderness. Tents pitched after scraping through the snow that soon became knee deep provided the only protection. Both tents and blankets were in short supply. Many of the cold, hungry and barefoot men had little choice but to lie down on an armful of straw and huddle together for warmth. Most were clad only in threadbare remnants of uniforms.

Quartermaster Green assigned campsites 100 yards long and 300 yards deep to each brigade. The huts stood on a sloping well-drained hillsides intersected by footpaths and camp streets that varied in width. The paths were used hundreds of times to carry water and firewood and to walk to the parade ground and stand sentry duty. Except for trees, this place today looks exactly as it did during that winter.

Reconstructed huts at Jockey Hollow

Brigadier General John Starks mixed brigade of Connecticut and Maryland troops occupied the southeast on the slope of a hill called Mount Kimble. Brig General William Maxwell's New Jersey Brigade was positioned near the upper Passaic River about a mile southwest of the center of the camp. The New York

Brigade was assigned to the northern end of the camp along the main road which led north to Morristown. General Henry Knox along with the Artillery Brigade encamped a mile west of Morristown on the Morristown-Mendham Road. Officers' huts were placed on higher ground near their unit's campsites.

A descriptive sign marks each encampment. One example is one at the New York site which reads: *Brig. Gen. James Clinton with the New York brigade of the 2nd, 3rd, 4th and 5th Regiments, a total of 1,267 men, spent the winter of 1779-1780 in huts here on this hillside. They were encamped here from December 12, 1779 to May 12, 1780. The official uniform of these troops was blue, faced with buff with white buttons and linings.*

Within two weeks of their arrival soldiers began cutting down oak, walnut and chestnut trees to finish and move into huts. When this supply of timber ran out, they began pulling down farmers' fences and outbuildings for boards. This caused a furor among the local population. The huts were completed by the end of the month. These crude dwellings could be seen stretching south for a mile from the north end of the camp toward the town of Basking Ridge.

George Washington Arrives

General Washington arrived in Morristown on December 1, 1779 and moved his staff into the Ford Mansion in Morristown. Washington faced many challenges at this time. The Continental Army was beginning to disintegrate. Enlistments were expiring, men were beginning to desert, food supplies were not reaching camp through the impassible roads and discipline was breaking down. After returning from long furloughs officers were resigning at an alarming rate.

Many senior officers left camp before the holidays to go home for several weeks. Some did not return until spring. The reason offered for their absence was that they were returning to their home states to recruit replacements for their decimated units. With so few officers remaining at the camp during the winter, brigades shared their leadership. James Clinton's New York Brigade exchanged duty officers with the force commanded by General John Stark. Sergeants and low- level officers were responsible for the army during most of the hard winter.

Brigade Orders, January 30, 1780, *His Excellency is displeased that there are so many officers on Furlough on so much as there is not a sufficient number to preserve order and perform the common Rottation of Duty So Several companies are left without a commissioned officer. He directs that a distribution of the remaining officers be made that no company be without a commissioned officer.*

Orderly books, the daily record of orders and details of camp life show that strict discipline was observed at Jockey Hollow despite harsh conditions. Guard duties were assigned each day. Parades, musters, inspections, drills and punishments were regularly held on the Grand Parade ground. General Washington and members of the Continental Congress visited the camp parades, where inspections were held. This involved the entire army.

Brigade Orders December 17, 1779, *An inspection of the Brigade will commence in the 2nd Regt on Tuesday the 21st instant for which purpose the Regt. will be under arms at 10 OClock. Each officer commanding a company will have two rolls prepared, one of which will be delivered to the Inspector….the whole of the troops are to attend and appear clean with their arms and accoutrements in good order and have their knapsacks on their backs containing every article of cloathing in their possession.*

As the soldiers stood at attention shivering on the parade ground, General Baron Von Steuben personally inspected each of the eight state brigades wintering at the camp. After reviewing the New York Regiments, the Baron reported, "*The most shocking picture of misery I have ever seen, scarce a man having wherewithal to cover his nakedness in this severe season and a great number very bad with the itch.*" Quartermaster General Nathaniel Green wrote, "*Poor fellows, they exhibit a picture truly distressing-more than half naked and two thirds starved.*" Washington himself criticized General James Clinton by saying that his New York troops were "*in bad an order as possible.*" While he excused their tattered clothing, he deplored their rusty and broken muskets.

A severe snowstorm hit the camp on December 28, 1779, and the weather continued to worsen in the new year. Howling winds tore apart many of the tents. Five more snows fell in January. Drifts reached over twelve feet high and caused the roads to disappear in many places. In December, most of the American forces were now together for the first time in six months but there were smaller armies in New England, New York, Pittsburgh, Connecticut and Charlestown, South Carolina. With this deployment, Washington ordered an immediate assessment of the state of readiness of the army. A complete muster would sort out those who officially, on record, had signed up for the three year period or for the duration of the war.[7]

By January 1780, a month after arriving at Morristown, many men were on duty on patrols to the front lines and guarding the passes to the east of Morristown through the Watchung Mountains. Others worked building a fortification overlooking Morristown. This earthwork, started by the previous encampment in the spring of 1777, took on the name of Fort Nonsense since it was believed that the project was maintained for the sole purpose of keeping the soldiers busy.

General Orders, 28th Dec 1779, *A sergeant, corporal and 12 men from the Connecticut line with their arms, packs, blankets and three days provisions to be sent to Pluckimin (Pluckemin, Bedminster Township, N.J.) tomorrow to cut wood for the Hospital for two weeks. A corporal and six men from the same line to be sent as a guard to the forage Yard at Vealtown. (Bernardsville, N.J.)*

That month Joseph Martin a sergeant in the Connecticut Brigade wrote that, "*We got settled in our winter quarters at the commencement of the new year and went in on our old Continental line of starving and freezing. We now and then got a a little bad bread and salt beef (I believe chiefly horse beef for it was generally thought to be such at the time). The month of January was very stormy and a great deal of snow fell, and in such weather it was a mere chance if we got anything at all to eat. Our condition at length became insupportable.*" His Brigade, the Connecticut Line, mutinied in May.[8]

One way to lessen the number of mouths to feed and reduce the number of desertions was to grant furloughs to the soldiers. Officers were given short leaves of absence provided they promised to stay on another year Three-month furloughs were offered to all men whose enlistments were expiring after three years, provided they reenlist for the duration of the war. Others were given leaves of absence of shorter duration. Sergeant Martin went home to New Haven and had to beg for food and shelter along the way. Corporal John Allison of the New York Brigade was granted leave from February 15 to March 15. He beat his way home 40 miles over New Jersey snow blocked roads to Haverstraw, New York, to visit his pregnant wife and infant daughter.

Thousands of soldiers at Jockey Hollow had now been in service for three years. Many enlisted in early 1777. When they signed up, the term of enlistment was "for three years or the duration of the war." Since three years had passed, they assumed their obligation was over and expected to leave this frozen misery. However, the Continental Congress interpreted the terms as requiring the men to remain for the "duration of the war." Men who had only signed up for only three years were honorably discharged in December. This added to the anguish of those who were forced to remain. This issue was never clarified during the excitement and patriotic fervor three years before. Now, the only way to go home was to desert and risk a death penalty. Troops continued to desert from Jockey Hollow at an alarming rate, and mutinies of entire state brigades were festering.[9]

The lines of huts offered little protection as the cruel winter went on. Bitter winds pierced the wooden walls and froze hands and feet. During those weeks, many regiments were reporting that only fifty men were ready for duty out of a total of four hundred men. Many men were too cold to desert. Without warm clothing and far from home, they could never survive the trip home. Soldiers were starving and freezing to death at the same time.

Maintaining Discipline

While the diaries of many officers expressed sincere sympathy for the plight of their wretched soldiers struggling to survive, punishment at Jockey Hollow was frequent and severe. Even the compassionate General Washington became inflexible when it came to maintaining discipline. Most offenses involved either desertion or the pilfering and plundering of livestock and other possessions from civilians. Offenders and deserters, when apprehended, were given trials by court-martial and were routinely punished by flogging. The death sentence was given to long term deserters, those defecting to the enemy with their weapons or leading a mutiny.

Despite severe punishment, typically a hundred lashes, the suffering troops began to raid homes and steal livestock from neighboring farmers in order to stay alive. Joshua Guerin, a farmer whose home was only a half mile away from the cabins at the northern end of the camp was compensated by the army in devalued Continental dollars for the theft of sheep by soldiers.

Many men risked the death penalty by returning home to care for their starving families and neglected farms. In most of America, at that time, the absence of men for the entire year and especially at harvest time could mean starvation for their wives and children. Without food, clothing or pay, the situation became so desperate that the high desertion rate threatened the future of the beleaguered Continental Army. Punishments became more frequent and severe. Six privates from the New York Brigade were tried for desertion only two weeks after arrival. All were convicted and each received 100 lashes. This was the first of many harsh sentences that followed at Jockey Hollow, during that winter. Flogging was the usual punishment. It was brutal but effective since it kept men alive to fight again.

In the first six months at Morristown, the orderly books for the New York regiments show twenty-one floggings. Most of the court martial proceedings were held for offences such as desertion, theft, drunkenness, card playing or in the case of officers, ungentlemanly behavior.

Executions demanded a larger audience. The entire population of the camp reported to the parade ground to witness these tragic spectacles. The punishment of death in the Continental army was carried out either by hanging or firing squad. Those sentences that were soldiers preferred a soldier's death-the firing squad.

Beginning in1777 and lasting for the duration of the war, desertion was a vexing problem for the commanders of the Continental Army. About one of every three private soldiers deserted at some time during the war. However, most men continued to believe that desertion was a disgrace. They served despite despair, disillusionment, monotony and longing for home. These haunting thoughts, aggravated by a constant struggle for food, clothing, medicine, pay, caused many to go home.

The whipping was always done in front of the entire brigade to the sound of repeated drum rolls. The whip was formed of small knotted cords that cut through the skin with each stroke. Whippings encompassed intervals of two or three days, so that the wounds would became inflamed and more painful with each application.[10]

Officers did not escape punishment. The orderly book for the New Jersey First Artillery Regiment for March 26, 1780 reports that, *The Court Unanimously found Capt. Leut. (Theopheliss) Park Guilty not only of fraud but of repeated forgerness and Sentence him to be Casheared with Infamy, by having his Sword brock over his head on the Publick parade in front of the Regt. To which he belongs by the Adjt. Of said Regt.*

The War Men

After five years of combat, the men who had unintentionally enlisted for the duration of the war had at first been disappointed by their vague enlistment terms but camaraderie and intense patriotism had developed in the ranks and this was the last time most of these veteran soldiers attempted to leave the army. Too proud to desert, these resilient men stayed on. They became known as "War Men" the label given to those who were bound to serve until the war ended. The "War Men" bravely accepted their fate and willingly and loyally continued soldiering until the war ended four years later. During those years these men became the backbone of the Continental Army. They were the corporals, sergeants and combat-hardened veterans who bonded together to form the professional army that led to the final victory at Yorktown.

At the end of the war, Washington acknowledged the thousands of "War Men" who stayed on for the duration of the war. *"Those gallant and persevering men who resolved to defend the right of their invaded country so long as the war should continue. For these are the men who ought to be considered as the pride and boast of the American Army."*[11]

Supply roads were snowbound until mid-March, and farmers refused to sell the little food available. Most would not accept depreciated Continental currency which had become almost worthless. Sixty dollars in Continental script was only worth one dollar in hard money. An ordinary horse cost $20,000 in Continental currency.

The problem was simply that the Continental Congress, without the power to tax, could not obtain credit to provide enough food and clothing to support an army. By the spring of 1780 the war had been dragging on for five years. For merchants, the hope of redeeming any credit seemed unlikely. Washington grudgingly considered imposing martial law. This drastic step would have allowed the army to simply seize cattle and grain from civilians.

While the bitter cold had caused much suffering, the worst problem was that the depleted Continental Army was starving to death. The entire camp was going without food for four or five days at a time. Corn used to feed horses was eagerly consumed. Pet dogs disappeared from the camp. Some men began eating bark and boiling shoe leather. Conditions were appalling by mid-March. Beginning early in the year weapons and tattered clothing were being stripped from the sick and given to men on duty.

Fortunately, patriotic New Jersey officials cooperated by providing a large quantity of food for the camp in January. This rare and benevolent act provided a temporary respite and served to cut down on the rampant plundering by soldiers that was destroying the morale of the civilians. This gracious move by New Jersey officials helped for a brief period and may have saved the entire army from disbanding at that time.

In less than a month, the famished army had eaten its way through these supplies and now began going without food for four or five days at a time. Starvation lasted until the camp was disbanded in May.

Mutiny of the Connecticut Brigade

The abnormally cold winter had frozen fields and destroyed fruit trees. Cattle had perished for lack of food. In May, anger over enlistment terms and no pay for five months boiled over into a mutiny by the Connecticut Regiment. On the night of May 25, a hungry soldier argued with a sergeant and his entire regiment joined him in defiance. In the scuffle that followed an officer was accidentally wounded by a bayonet. The men then aimed their weapons at other officers rushing to his assistance. An officer from the adjoining Pennsylvania Regiment rushed in with his men to keep order. The Connecticut mutineers reluctantly returned to their huts after one of their officer recorded their complaints and offered to take them to General Washington.

Washington was angry and deeply disturbed, but understood the reasons for the uprising. In order to avoid large scale punishments but still set an example he ordered the execution of only one of the ringleaders. Of all the offenses committed by officers and men during the dreadful winter encampment, mutiny was feared the most. It had the potential to quickly destroy the Continental Army and with it the dream of independence.

General Orders, May 25, 1780, *The criminals now under sentence of death are to be executed tomorrow morning at Eleven OClock near the Grand parade. Fifty men properly officered from each brigade to attend. The camp collourmen from the Pennsylvania, Connecticut and New York Line under the direction of a sergeant will dig the graves this afternoon.*

Stiff Resistance Halts the British Invasion of New Jersey

The rebellion of the Connecticut troops and intelligence reports from Tories led the enemy to believe that the Americans were too weak to continue fighting and the British began to plan for an invasion of New Jersey. In the spring the Hessian General Wilhelm Knyphausen and Sir Henry Clinton in New York City and Staten island believed the Continental Army had been so weakened by the severe winter that they could easily invade New Jersey.

On June 7, 1780 the German general landed at Elizabeth with 5000 men and another 3000 in reserve. Alerted by a lookout on the Watchung ridges beacon fires were lit, alarm cannons fired and mounted couriers summoned the New Jersey Militia. The British forces were surprised by stiff resistance when they reached Connecticut Farms which today is Union, New Jersey. The invaders were repelled by The New Jersey Brigade under General William Maxwell which was heavily supported by the militia of that state. Two weeks later Knyphausen's force returned to Springfield and again met stiff resistance from the New Jersey Militia and the Rhode Island regulars under General Nathaniel Greene. After burning the town the enemy forces again withdrew to New York. They had expected to find the Americans more vulnerable.

Washington was confused at this time. Would the British strike again through New Jersey or try to move up the Hudson to divide the new nation. He covered both of these possibilities. On June 25th and 26th 1780 after six months at Jockey Hollow he moved most of the army 15 miles north of Morristown to Pompton, New Jersey. This location was nearer the Hudson River and from there he could move in either direction if attacked. The New York Brigade marched north on another perilous mission to the Mohawk River Valley, where Indians and loyalist raiders were again devastating the settlers on the New York frontier. Generals Greene, Maxwell and Stark were left at Springfield. By spring, the entire Continental Army was reduced to fewer than 4,000 men. Except for a few detachments, the Continental Army never returned to Jockey Hollow.

While the Patriots had survived the winter they were still no match for the well organized British regulars and still unprepared to meet them on the battle field on equal terms. After Jockey Hollow the American cause wavered, not for lack of patriotic spirit but because of the loss of confidence in the army due to its decline. Without any inspiring victories Washington and his army left Morristown depressed. However, if the army had not survived the winter of 1779-1780, France may not have entered the war and the joint forces would not have won the final decisive battle of the war at Yorktown in 1781.

Mutiny of the Pennsylvania Line

The camp south of Morristown was destined to play a final role in one of the war's saddest events. The next winter, 1780-1781 the Pennsylvania Brigade under Brig. General Anthony Wayne returned to Jockey Hollow to occupy the empty huts. Their morale was abysmal. They were trapped in service by the vague enlistment terms and were without adequate food, shelter and clothing and pay. They erupted into the war's first full blown mutiny on New Years Day, 1781.[12]

On the evening of New Year's Day 1781, the Pennsylvania Line seized the artillery and ammunition, and prepared to leave the camp. Attempting to restore order Capt. Adam Bettin was killed and two other officers were wounded. Wayne himself, popular though he was with both rank and file, could not persuade the mutineers to lay down their arms. The rebellious troops then marched toward Philadelphia carrying their grievances directly to the Continental Congress.

A stone monument on the site of the uprising reads, *In memory of Captain Adam Bettin shot in the mutiny Jan.1 1781. Erected by the Morristown Chapter D.A.R.*

General Wayne caught up with the mutineers and accompanied them to Princeton. The men still declared they were loyal and would oppose the British if they attacked New Jersey. They turned over to the American side two emissaries dispatched by Sir Henry Clinton to lure them to join the British forces. This display of loyalty, the firm stand taken by the mutineers, and at the same time the justness of their complaints all had effect on representatives of Congress and the Pennsylvania State authorities who came to Princeton to negotiate the whole question.

An agreement, concluded on January 7, 1781, provided that enlistments for three years or the duration of the war would be considered as expiring at the end of the third year and that clothing would be issued to the men discharged and that prompt action would be taken to reimburse the soldiers for back pay. More than half the mutineers were released from the army, and the rest furloughed for several months as a result of the final settlement. Their main grievances removed, many of the men later reenlisted for new bounties.

These terms achieved the objective of the uprising, but mutiny could not be tolerated nor could the favorable terms of the settlement be allowed to set an example for others. Washington took harsh measures. A ringleader from each regiment was tried for mutiny. Two of them were executed by a firing squad made up of their fellow mutineers.

What is remarkable about the Revolutionary War is that mutiny was rare and never escalated into a rebellion involving more than one military unit. Despite the atrocious conditions under which they served few abandoned their loyalty to the struggle for liberty.

Jockey Hollow Revisited

The Camp at Morristown can be approached from all directions and most of the troops arriving there in 1779 traveled south from the Hudson River Valley in New York. The best way for a visitor to appreciate the strategic advantages of the location is to approach it from the east. From that direction you will travel through the natural barriers that shielded the camp from an enemy advance from New York City. The three Watchung Ridges of the Appalacian Mountains and the Great Swamp made the camp virtually impregnable.

The crossroads hamlet of Meyersville is on the eastern edge of the Great Swamp. Traversing the swamp, one can begin to appreciate how daunting this quagmire appeared to troops attempting to cross it over 200 years ago. This impassible four mile wide, 6800 acre morass which served as the final protection for the feeble Continental Army has remained unchanged over the ages. The impenetrable cattail marshes could not be traversed until the early twentieth century, when a road was built across the swamp. One finds it difficult to realize that you are less than 25 miles from the teeming canyons of New York City.

Today it is a lush wildlife refuge and the home of 26 endangered bird and animal species. Sheep graze in the meadows, bog turtles swim in the ponds and ubiquitous white tailed deer cross its many paths. The road becomes submerged in heavy rains. This environmental gem has wooden boardwalks and blinds for bird watching wild ducks, great blue herons and red tailed hawks. Wildlife is even more abundant at dusk, and also when the seasons change. In the 1950s, the Great Swamp narrowly escaped becoming a jetport for the New York metropolitan area.

The Visitors Center at the park's entrance houses a life size interior of a soldier's cabin and period artifacts. A short film that vividly reenacts camp life and the suffering during the encampment can be viewed in a small theater.

The original house of the Wick family stands a few yards away from the Visitor's Center. The atmosphere of authenticity created by the working farm kitchen, hand -crafted artifacts and furniture is remarkable. The exterior of weathered hand split shingles and the vegetable garden takes you back to 1779. Standing in Tempe Wick's bedroom, one can feel the presence of the young girl. Historians at the site do not believe the story of her hiding her beloved riding horse in the house. Jude Pfister, Chief of Cultural Resources at Morristown commented "I think it is insupportable to claim that Tempe Wick hid her horse in her house. It makes for a great story, but that is all. There is no support for any such act and when you are in the house the plausibility of such an episode evaporates. She did something in reference to the mutiny, but exactly what is lost to history and myth."

Tempe must have drawn a lot of attention from the thousands of homesick men living on the family's lands. General Arthur St. Clair used the house as his headquarters, sharing it during the winter with the 20 year old Tempe and her mother and father. It was occupied as a private residence until 1935 when the National Park Service acquired it.

Wick House c. 1747-Jockey Hollow, Morristown N.J. National Historic Park

A sign directs you onto Cemetery Road which joins Jockey Hollow Road and makes a three mile loop through the camp. Most of the soldiers' huts occupied the hillsides to the north of the Wick house. At the time of the encampment this area was completely stripped of trees which were used to build huts. Today the location is enchanting. Open fields and split rail fences stretch to the wooded hills beyond.

Along the Jockey Hollow Road loop is an open field. A reconstructed log army field hospital once stood here but was torn down in 1979. Behind the hospital site is the civilian cemetery. This is not where the 100 men who did not survive the winter at the camp are interred. More likely they lie randomly around the encampment or on nearby church grounds. Behind the first Presbyterian Church in Mendham, a town adjacent to Morristown, are 27 Revolutionary War soldiers who died from smallpox epidemic during the earlier winter of 1777. Burials were purposely obscured so the enemy could not detect the losses.

On Sugarloaf Hill, overlooking the former site of the hospital, is a row of enlisted men's log huts. It was the campsite of the Pennsylvania Brigade. The huts, while austere, were built to uniform specifications. A marker at the site reads, *Soldiers of the Pennsylvania Line built these hearths in the winter of 1779-1780. The rest of the encampment vanished decades ago, victims of disuse and decay. These huts are copies, based on the ghosts of the post holes and foundation log sstill found in the ground. But only the hearths survived just as they were then. The little momentos-buttons, knives, pipe stems-have all been sifted out of the ground and studied to recapture the life of Washington's soldiers.*

On the other side of Sugarloaf is the large open field of the Grand Parade Ground. Here, the army paraded for inspection, was assigned patrols and guard duty and witnessed punishments and executions.

The forest has returned to Jockey Hollow. While there is little evidence left in areas overgrown with trees and dense foliage, many markers noting brigade campsites are found along the route. Footpaths used by the soldiers hundreds of times to carry water and firewood, or to walk to the parade ground and stand sentry still traverse the campground.

On the west side of Jockey Hollow Road, where it intersects with Grand Parade Road is the campsite of the New York Brigade. A descriptive sign there reads:

> *Brig. Gen. James Clinton with the New York brigade of the 2nd 3rd, 4th and 5th Regiments, a total of 1,267 men spent the winter of 1779-1780 in huts here on this hillside. They were encamped here from December 12, 1779 to May 12, 1780. The official uniform of these troops was blue, faced with buff with white buttons and linings.*

Jockey Hollow, to preserve its original appearance is purposely devoid of any heroic monuments. It is best visited in the winter. On a cold snowbound day the site appears much as it did to ragged and hungry soldiers as they stood on guard in the icy wind.

Chapter Seven

Lost Opportunities on a Highway to Hell
Battle of Monmouth, New Jersey- 1778

A Commemorated Event, but Mysteries Remain

It cannot be said that the battle of Monmouth Court House has been forgotten or neglected in American history. The engagement at Freehold, New Jersey, 50 miles south of New York City, in June of 1778, was the longest and hardest fought engagement of the Revolutionary War and the last major encounter in the north. It was the only battle of the Revolutionary War in open field where the main forces of both armies and the greater part of the highest and most renowned officers participated. While it is one of the most commemorated battles in American history, curiously, it is best remembered only for specific dramatic and heroic episodes. These occurrences have shrouded this battle in the golden haze of the mythology and patriotic rhetoric that covers many of America's most cherished legends of the War for Independence. Patriotism and valor triumph over weakness and treason and the courage of the American woman is exemplified.

Historians over the past 200 years have focused on reducing the battle to these intriguing incidents while some chapters of the conflict remain obscure or enmeshed in controversy. A fresh look at this New Jersey campaign in its entirety reveals a number of events that could have led to a final decisive victory for either side.[1]

This confrontation between the top commanders of each side, General George Washington and Sir Henry Clinton is replete with legends. The battle at Monmouth Courthouse is the point in the war when the world image of the American army was transformed from that of a tattered band of ill-trained farmers to that of a disciplined, well led, professional military force. Molly Pitcher personified the bravery of the American woman when she took the place of her fallen husband. Washington confronted and turned around the retreating patriots lead by the treacherous General Lee. The training by Baron Von Steuben during the dark days at Valley Forge paid off. Washington's Continentals stood toe-to-toe with the best army in the world and bloodily repulsed a series of powerful attacks to fight the British to a standstill, thereby passing their first major test.

Versions of these events have been portrayed repeatedly but the details and consequences of the movement of the clashing armies before and after the battle belong in this anthology of lost history. A full understanding of this critical battle is still needed to move beyond the legends and myths that obscure it. The question about which side was victorious is still being debated.

Many questions remain. Why did King George's mighty army in America which could have mustered 18,000 men in the spring of 1777, not attack an emaciated Continental Army less than half its size at Valley Forge? Why were the British forces in their massive evacuation allowed to spend a week crossing the Delaware River in flatboats when they could have caught by the Americans who were only a day's march away? A strung out British Army, interspersed with supply trains and civilians in columns miles long, slowly passed through New Jersey for nine days and marched over 50 miles and were largely unopposed by Washington's rejuvenated Continental army.

What caused British forces, still intact after a day of intense fighting, to sneak off under the cover of darkness? Why didn't Howe confront the Americans from the height at Middletown? Why were the Redcoats, exposed on a barren strip of sand on the Sandy Hook peninsula, awaiting transport, not attacked or bombarded from the Highland of the Navesink? A close examination of the more obscure phases of the conflict in original military documents, diaries and public records on both sides can serve to dispel these mysteries. Why didn't the invaders make their stand on the high ground of Middletown and Navesink, only 20 miles from Monmouth Courthouse, where they would have had a tactical advantage?

The Redcoats Enjoy Philadelphia during a Merry Winter

Following the dreadful defeat of the Continental Army at Brandywine in the fall of 1777, the British army moved a few miles north to capture the Patriot capitol of Philadelphia. Here they found snug winter quarters. The large, affluent loyalist population welcomed the Redcoats and their Hessian allies were to the city. The army enjoyed a delightful winter with bountiful food and drink, festive celebrations in their honor and the companionship of charming Tory ladies.

Only 20 miles north of the city on a bleak hillside near the Schuylkill River called Valley Forge, the vanquished Americans were leaving bloody foot prints in the snow and eating bark. Nearly naked Continental soldiers, who were wrapped in thin blankets and huddled around smoky fires of green twigs chanted "We want meat! These are the unforgettable images of the suffering and endurance at that camp during the winter of 1777-78 when 2500 patriots died from exposure and disease. This army of skeletons received few provisions from a bountiful countryside with abundant resources. Their countrymen, who demanded their protection, preferred to sell provisions to the enemy rather than accept Continental paper money. The Patriot Army received even less assistance from an insolvent Congress in exile in nearby York, Pennsylvania.

British leaders in Philadelphia became apprehensive as the spring of 1778 approached. France had entered the war six months before and it would be possible for the French Fleet to blockade the mouth of Delaware Bay. The British forces in Philadelphia, supplied from the sea, would then be trapped in the city. The remainder of the army, about 18,000 troops was in New York City. The French Navy could also intercept any supply ships that sustained these forces. British strategists in London and America believed it would be more prudent to maximize his strength by massing all of His Majesty's occupation forces in one place- New York.

It seems incredible that General Howe, the Commander -In -Chief of the British Army in America, with a large fleet to cover the city with cannons and a superb army did not make the least attempt to attack the American campground at Valley Forge during the winter. This was an easy opportunity to end the war. The desolate base, with its starving and freezing army, depleted by desertions and expired enlistments, was only a day's march away. Starving the Americans into surrendering in only a few days was possible by surrounding Valley Forge.

There was no escape route for Washington's men. Many would be lost from exposure if they tried to break out and there was no topographically advantageous place anywhere near that would offer a strong defensive position. American Generals Lafayette, Von Steuben and De Kalb were astonished that the most feared army in the world, which outgunned and outnumbered them, did not take advantage of their frailty. This puzzled even the Tories in Philadelphia who questioned the behavior of their saviors. Surely, Howe was acquainted with the debilitated state of the American Army at the time. The many Tory merchants and spies who had access to the camp constantly updated him on the deplorable conditions at Valley Forge.

What were General Howe's excuses for missing this obvious opportunity to end the American rebellion? He blamed his immobility on the lack of reinforcements from England and what he professed as an even greater problem, horse fodder.[2] Howe's justification is found in his journals. In April 1778 he wrote to Parliament, *"The enemy's position continues to be at Valley Forge and Wilmington. Their force has been diminished over the course of the winter by desertion and by detachments to the back settlements where the Indians make constant inroads.: but the want of green forage does not yet permit me to take the field, and their situation is too strong to hazard an attack with a prospect of success."*[3]

Howe was obviously procrastinating. His record as a military leader was mixed. He drove the American forces out of New York in 1776 and soundly thrashed the Continental Army at Brandywine on the Philadelphia Campaign, but still he had a reputation for lacking aggressiveness. He failed to pursue Washington's army after defeating it at White Plains in 1776 and instead returned to New York City to enjoy the winter. The Battle of Bunker Hill may explain his temerity. His army of seasoned professionals, outnumbered a raw American force by two to one. The British were victorious but took enormous losses. Howe had underestimated the ability of the Patriots to withstand repeated frontal assaults and to retreat only when their ammunition was exhausted. Worst of all, he had overrated the ability of his own Redcoat troops.

One may gain better insight by considering Howe's personal circumstances. The General was a "short timer." In military jargon, this is a person who is nearing the end of his service. "Short timers" through the ages had the reputation of being so focused on getting out of the military intact that they were reluctant to take risks or even to enthusiastically perform routine duties.

The staggering defeat of a large part of the British Army at Saratoga, New York in October 1777 was a shock to Great Britain. Howe's decision to capture Philadelphia rather than join up with General Burgoyne at Saratoga was regarded by many as the reason for the defeat. This loss was the beginning of the end for British rule in America. While Burgoyne was in command at Saratoga, Howe was the senior officer in America and this appalling failure happened on his watch. Howe took tough criticism from a disappointed Parliament and believed that he had lost the confidence of King George. He submitted his request to be relieved of his command when the Army reached Philadelphia the same month. Knowing that he would sail back to England in the spring, the short timer bided his time during the winter enjoying the festivities in Philadelphia instead of attacking the beleaguered Americans before that gained strength in the spring. Constant reports of the daunting conditions in the Valley Forge area must have further convinced him not to take his troops into harm's way.

It was the custom in that era for European armies to go into winter quarters each year for a time of inactivity. Howe was not an incompetent military commander but preferred the outmoded European approach to warfare. In his view, combat was an enterprise that should not be conducted during inclement weather. He unabashedly delighted in this practice and thoroughly relished his winters in New York and later in Philadelphia.

Another likely explanation for the British commander's curious behavior was that the beautiful Mrs. Loring distracted Howe. Elizabeth Loring became Howe's mistress while the army wintered in Boston. She followed him to New York and later to Philadelphia. This attractive, fair- haired, 25 year old lady was known as 'The Sultana." She was overly fond of drinking, gambling and other indoor sports. Elizabeth was the wife of Loyalist Joshua Loring Jr., a commissary of prisoners. Mr. Loring seemed comfortable with the arrangement as long as he kept his lucrative appointment. She is credited with distracting Howe many times, to the advantage of the Patriots.

Was the general enthralled by his young mistress or was he simply acting in accordance with the rules of European warfare? Rather than pressing on with the hostilities by pursuing and crushing Washington's disheartened army, he decided that dancing and gambling in the salons of the colony's largest city was more pleasurable than trying to survive on a cold battlefield. A decisive British victory over the rebels could have ended the war here. But despite this opportunity to deal a lethal blow to the Continental Army, Howe did not strike. In May, Sir Henry Clinton replaced Howe and assumed command of His Majesty's forces in America.

A Joyful Departure from the Vale of Misery

The warm days of May revived the spirits of the weary soldiers at Valley Forge. Morale soared as supplies of food and clothing began to arrive at the camp, thanks to the efforts of Quartermaster General Nathaniel Greene. This exuberance was fueled by a new *espirit de corps* inspired by the discipline and pride instilled by Baron Von Steuben. The appearance of 600 fresh troops from New England added to the exuberance. A feeling of euphoria swept through the ranks of the Continental Army and they were spoiling for a fight. On June 10, 1778 the Patriots were delighted to receive marching orders and eagerly prepared to leave the squalid huts and haunting memories of the dismal winter. They left behind 3000 sick and disabled men at this grim place.

During the winter General Friedrich Wilhelm Von Steuben, a Prussian officer, with dubious credentials, trained the American regiments in a form of European battle drill he adapted for American troops. Von Steuben's training technique was to create a "model company." This group of 120 chosen men successively trained other companies of similar size. Steuben's eccentric personality greatly enhanced his mystique. He trained the soldiers in his full military dress uniform, swearing and shouting at them in German and French.

Von Steuben also established standards of sanitation and camp layouts that would be standard for other large encampments later in the war. Previously there was no set arrangement of tents and huts. Men relieved themselves where they wished. When an animal died, it was stripped of its meat and the rest was left to rot where it lay.

Perhaps Von Steuben's biggest contribution to the American Revolution was providing training in the use of the bayonet. Americans used the bayonet mostly as a cooking skewer or tool rather than as a lethal weapon. They depended on muskets, only 20% accurate, to win battles. The fearful bayonet charge was the most effective offensive tactic in the war for both sides. Von Steuben's introduction of it was crucial to American victories. In the Battle of Stony Point, in 1778, American soldiers attacked with unloaded muskets and won the day solely by a massed bayonet charge.

Because of its triangular shape the bayonet inflicted wounds that were impossible to suture. Injuries usually resulted in death by bleeding or infection. These weapons were not sharp which made them even deadlier. When thrust into an opponent they tore, not cut, through the opponent's body. Triangular bayonets were outlawed by the "Geneva Accords on Humane Warfare" in 1864.

Washington was confronted by still another unexpected threat. After surviving the crushing defeat at Brandywine followed by the devastating winter at Valley Forge, a political issue erupted that had an even greater potential to end the struggle for independence. In London, Parliament was alarmed by the defeat of a large part of the British Army at Saratoga and the entry into the war by the French. At the urging of Prime Minister Lord Frederick North, the House of Commons and the King agreed to significant concessions which they were certain would appease the American people and end the war.

Parliament proposed that the rebellious colonies be granted the freedom of self government and have representation in Parliament. They would agree to withdraw all military forces and pardon all American military and political leaders. All acts of Parliament affecting America, dating back to 1763, would be repealed. Duties on tea and other products would be removed as well as other forms of taxes. In other words, by this remarkable display of conciliation, Great Britain was willing to agree to all the conditions that America demanded when it went to war-except one. The proposal did not include independence. The proposition was sent to General Washington and a group of commissioners sailed to America to meet with the Continental Congress.[4]

Washington was at Valley Forge when he received the proposals. The incredulous general at first regarded the documents as forgeries but then apprehensively forwarded them to the Continental Congress. Would the war weary American people be tempted into acceptance? Any support at all could create unrest and a lack of enthusiasm to continue hostilities. Without the patriotic fervor of the people the Continental Army would crumble.[5]

The Commander-in Chief wrote to Congress in April of 1778, *"The enemy are beginning to play a game more dangerous than their efforts by armies which threaten a fatal blow to the independence of America and of course to her liberties...They are endeavoring to ensnare the people by specious allurements of peace...Nothing short of Independence could possible do."*

In Philadelphia at this time, a colossal commemorative extravaganza was being celebrated to bid farewell to the esteemed General Howe. During the festivities Washington sent Lafayette out with 2,500 men and eight cannon, on the first independent command of his career. The young general's mission was to reconnoiter the area around the city to learn of any enemy preparations to attack Valley Forge. Howe responded by dispatching 7,000 of his elite special forces of grenadiers and dragoons to surround the patriots. This force was led by the three top commanders, newly arrived Sir Henry Clinton, Hessian commander Knyphausen and Howe himself.

The Americans were camped on Barren Hill, a place 10 miles from the city, at present day Conshohocken, Pennsylvania. As the arrogant generals left the festivities, they promised the ladies to return to the city for dinner with the young general a prisoner. Lafayette wisely managed to escape the trap after finding no evidence of preparations to attack Valley Forge.

The commissioners sent by Parliament presented the conciliatory proposals to Congress in June 1778. Congress rejected the offer and would not settle for anything less than full independence. The failure of the peacemaking effort had an immediate and grave effect on Britain's military and the Loyalist population in Philadelphia. General Sir Henry Clinton, during his first week in command at Philadelphia was disappointed that his government was willing to capitulate and had delayed evacuating the city pending the outcome of the negotiations. With the failure to agree on the terms, he was then forced to depart from the city without delay.[6]

The Loyalists were devastated by the failed negotiations. Without any possibility of returning to normalcy they had to abandon their property and possessions and flee with the army into exile. Those who remained were faced with imprisonment or even death at the hands of infuriated Patriots who they had persecuted during the occupation of the city.

Directly across the river from Philadelphia in New Jersey were signs of activity that caused Washington to alert four New Jersey Militia battalions in Burlington County and issue orders for them to "annoy" any British forces that were encountered. These 800 men were commanded by Major General Philemon Dickenson. These local troops were soon joined by General "Scotch Willie" Maxwell's brigade of 1,000 Continental Line soldiers. Maxwell was also ordered to harass the enemy if they made any attempt to move overland through New Jersey.

In May, 600 British light infantry men had crossed over the Delaware River from Philadelphia to Bordentown, New Jersey. They burned down a store house filled with army supplies and the houses of Patriot leader Francis Hopkinson, a signer of the Declaration of Independence. The homes of New Jersey militia leaders Colonel Joseph Borden and Colonel Joseph Kirkbride also went up in smoke. After plundering other houses they threatened Trenton, four miles north. The marauders suspected that they might encounter strong opposition by the New Jersey Militia and turned back. This raid, into the threshold of the Garden State, could be the harbinger of a plan by Sir Henry Clinton's to cross over to New Jersey with the Redcoat army.

General Washington now led a rejuvenated army that had actually increased in number to more than 13,000 men. He was faced with a critical strategic decision at this time and considered a number of options. He could simply reoccupy Philadelphia and allow Clinton's force to evacuate unopposed through New Jersey to New York City. Or he could move the army 100 miles, to the north of New

York City, to protect the vital water highway up the Hudson River to Canada. This water way, if captured would split New England from the other states and soon lead to an American defeat. Other alternatives would be to harass the enemy troops if they attempted to pass through New Jersey or engage them in a full scale battle.

Washington called his generals together for a council of war on June 17, 1778, after he became convinced that Clinton would evacuate Philadelphia. He asked for their suggestions about proceeding with the campaign. His policy in the early years of the war had been to avoid a total showdown with a stronger army that outmanned and outgunned his forces. A decisive defeat would effectively end the war. Now the odds were better. The exuberant Americans were not greatly outnumbered and the foe was fleeing from an occupied city. The enemy was withdrawing, without a battle, to open country where they would be on the defensive. Washington decided to abandon the practice of strategic withdrawal to preserve his army and to pursue the British forces.

His plan was to send out a large advanced force of 3,000 men to attack and harass the enemy columns but not engage the British Army in a general action. He would keep the main army back until he could better assess the situation. The decision to risk a major battle would be deferred for another eight days after the American Army had advanced deep into New Jersey.

Major General Charles Lee, second in Command to General Washington, was opposed to any course of action that involved fighting. He vehemently insisted that taking any offensive action was risky. He advocated letting the British escape to New York and maintained that hazarding an engagement with the most fearful army of the day was irrational.

Lee was an experienced professional military officer whose opinion was highly respected. He had served with the British Army in the French and Indian war and afterward saw action in the Portuguese and Polish Armies. He was credited with repulsing the British attempt to capture Charlestown, South Carolina in 1776. When Lee volunteered to join the Continental Army early in the war, Congress was delighted to have this seasoned senior officer on the Patriot side.

At that time he had aspirations of becoming Commander- in - Chief. Congress chose Washington to lead the army. He was from a southern state, which would be politically advantageous, and he was willing to serve without pay. Lee again appealed to Congress for Washington's position after the military setbacks of 1776. He chided other officers for not remembering the tragic defeat of America's raw army at

Brandywine the previous year and ominously warned that the new nation could not afford to lose another major engagement. He favored deferring any combat until the French entered the war. At first, Baron Von Steuben and most of the other generals agreed with him but they later changed their opinions. [7]

A Reluctant Exodus from the Rebel Capitol

Sir William Howe, senior commander of His Majesty's forces in America came to recognize that his strategy of breaking the back of the rebellion by capturing the capitol of the new nation had failed. After resigning, he sailed back to England and left all the tribulation behind. He was replaced on May 23, 1778, by Sir Henry Clinton. Clinton, age 40, was a cautious yet courageous officer who often placed himself in danger during combat.

Clinton faced the first major challenge of his command as soon as he learned of the failure of the peace proposals that were being presented by the parliamentary commissioners to the Continental Congress. He had to move the army out of

Clinton's Army begins it's march across New Jersey

Philadelphia and join the rest of the British forces in New York City. A divided army in two locations was at a strategic disadvantage with France entering the war. The move became urgent when a French Fleet headed for the mouth of Delaware Bay where it could blockade the city. Without supplies from the sea the American Army could come down from Valley Forge and besiege the city. Clinton would have preferred transporting the entire force by ship but found there were too few available. He loaded 3,000 Loyalist refugees and all other men, women and children unfit to march, on the vessels that were on hand. Two Hessian regiments with a mutinous reputation also sailed with them. They would be less of a risk if confined on board ships. [8] Everyone else would take a land route.

A staging area was prepared in New Jersey directly across the river from Philadelphia. It was on Coopers Creek at Gloucester Point four miles below Camden. The British began their evacuation of the city by crossing the Delaware

River on June 9, 1778. The passage to Gloucester Point was made in open flatboats and took over a week. Clinton, in command for less than a month, was compelled to lead what amounted to the most a massive retreat in the Revolutionary War.[9]

Reports of the departure from the city began arriving at Valley Forge but no action was taken to prevent the British forces from gaining a beachhead in New Jersey. Maxwell and Dickenson were in the immediate area with a force of 1,800 troops. Washington with the entire Continental Army was only 20 miles away, less than a two day march. They left Valley Forge only a day after the last British troops departed. The Americans could have easily headed for the crossing a few days earlier and pounced on the enemy at the crossing when it was helpless. This was a missed opportunity of great significance.

On the morning of June 18, the last of the British were observed leaving Philadelphia. Little time was wasted in entering the city that had been occupied for eight months. American scouting parties arrived the same day. Captain Allen Mc Lane of the Delaware Militia did not meet any opposition when he led a mounted patrol through the streets and rounded up 40 stragglers from the British Army.

The most influential city in the new nation was in appalling condition. Shops were closed, homes abandoned and the streets were choked with filth. Twenty five Loyalists were also captured and convicted for aiding the enemy. Two were hung. On the first day of occupation Washington appointed General Benedict Arnold to govern the city. At that time Arnold was regarded as an outstanding military leader for his role in the Canadian Campaign of 1775 and at the great victory at Saratoga. He was severely wounded at Saratoga while leading a frontal charge during the battle.

Washington left Valley Forge with the main body of the American Army the day after the last Redcoat troops had departed from Philadelphia. During the next two days they marched 40 miles up York Road to Doylestown, Pennsylvania and then headed east to Coryell's Landing, now New Hope, Pennsylvania. They crossed the Delaware River to Lambertville, New Jersey over the next four days then moved inland five miles to the hamlet of Amwell. That night, despite heavy spring rain, spirits were high in the Patriot ranks. The Commander -In- Chief ordered that a gill (one quarter pint) of spirits be given to each man. This was enough to induce a bit of euphoria but not drunkenness. The officers were issued greater quantities.

Washington was still uncertain as to which route the enemy would take. They could cross New Jersey to New York City through the Brunswicks, Perth Amboy and Staten Island. Their other option was to take a shorter southern route through Monmouth County to Sandy Hook. There, they could be transported 10 miles across New York Bay by ship.

The 12 mile long British procession crossed the Delaware River from Philadelphia to Gloucester Point, New Jersey, and headed northeast toward New York. Eleven thousand Redcoats and Hessian troops with more than 1000 loyalist civilians and hundreds of camp followers trudged along the sandy roads of southern New Jersey The baggage train had 1,500 wagons overloaded with weapons, equipment, supplies, personal baggage and booty stolen from Patriot homes and businesses. New Jersey commanders Maxwell and Dickenson had labored hard to sabotage their routes. Bridges were destroyed and trees felled across roads. The exposed formation plodded along at an average of only four miles each day and followed paths to avoid the many swamps along the way.

Howe anticipated that his columns would be constantly harassed by local militia and light infantry units of the Continental Army. As a security precaution he divided the armed units of the army into two parts led by his top generals, Knyphausen and Cornwallis. Half the soldiers marched in front of the wagons and the other half followed. The vast parade headed toward the Burlington County towns of Mount Holly, Columbus, and Bordentown. Hessian Jaegers were sent ahead six miles inland to seize the town of Haddonfield.

The Armies Move Out on Converging Paths

The main army reached Haddonfield the first night and the next morning marched another six miles to Evesham Township. There they met with the first resistance when a small party of New Jersey Militia ambushed part of the column. The event was so inconsequential that no mention of it appears in British journals.[10]

Another detachment moved up King's Highway, now the path of the New Jersey Turnpike, and camped at the Friends Meeting House at Moorestown. Along the way the invaders plundered everything they could find including household goods, grain, horses and cattle. Many of the villagers had the foresight to hide their property in the swamps. When the raiders reached Mount Holly they destroyed the iron works and burned the home of Colonel Israel Shreve, commanding officer of the 2nd New Jersey Regiment. General Clinton did not wish to alienate the civilians along the way and reprimanded his troops, but the devastation and looting continued unabated.

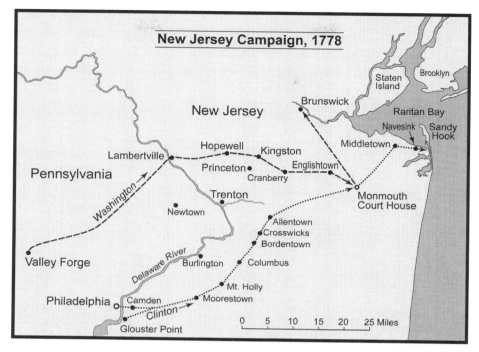

The main army then passed through Evesham and Moorestown. The British columns merged on June 22, at Mount Holly. The invaders found the town deserted. Residents there had fled with their possessions. The people had been raided before when the British passed through in the opposite direction in 1776 pursuing the vanquished Continental Army after the fall of New York and they knew what to do.[11]

The terrain north of Mount Holly was a patchwork of streams and swamps. New bridges had to be built and causeways constructed. Men in the stalled ranks began to suffer from the oppressive heat. After a march of seven miles the columns reached Slabtown, now Columbus and Mansfield, New Jersey. There they learned the ominous news that Washington's army had left Valley Forge and was heading east on a path that could converge with theirs.

Clinton conferred with Cornwallis as they rode together in the main column. They agreed that their army was at a disadvantage. It was encumbered by the vast entourage and needed greater mobility to be an effective fighting force that could turn on the agile Americans nipping at their heels. Divesting the train of everything that was not essential to combat might be necessary. About 1500 wagons train were loaded with plunder along with baggage, portable bakeries, laundries and blacksmith shops, large quantities of hospital supplies, boats hoisted onto wagons and collapsible bridges. All of this was followed by a vast mob of Tory refugees and camp followers. The women in the group were especially troublesome. They frequently strayed away from the columns to collect loot from the homes along the way. Clinton concluded that turning away the civilians and jettisoning equipment would show a strong signal of weakness to his soldiers and completely demoralize them.[12]

Captain Johann Ewald led a regiment of Hessian Jaegers 15 miles to Bordentown and Crosswicks. Along the way his men were picked off by the steady musket fire of scattered Americans concealed in the spring foliage on both sides of the road. The Germans were plagued by mosquitoes, bridges without planking, filled in or polluted wells, intense heat and humidity. Ewald wrote in his diary, *"the skirmishing continued without letup. Many men fell and lost their lives miserably because of the intense heat And due to the sandy ground thru which we passed, a pathless brushwood where no water was to be found on the entire march."*[13]

At Crosswicks an advanced unit of dragoons reached a torn up drawbridge with the draw raised at Watson's Ford. Today this place is where Route 206 goes over Crosswicks Creek. Thisdrawbridge dates back to 1714. Here the invaders finally met with stiff resistance The New Jersey Militia was prepared to defend the crossing from redoubts with a six pounder cannon. British sappers (engineers) tried to repair the bridge with planks torn from a nearby barn but the militia regiments of Colonels Frelinghuysen, Van Dyke, and Webster poured volleys of musket and cannon fire on them. Four Redcoats fell and several were wounded. The main force of the army, that was following, began coming up to the bridge and succeeded in taking it. The sappers were able to make repairs and over the next day elements of the main army streamed over the patched up bridge. Remains of the American redoubts were still visible in 1899 and portions of the bridge still exist today.[14]

This comprehensive account that appeared in the Mt. Holly Herald on July 19, 1924, is a description of the action at this point. Before daylight on the morning of June 23, 1778, a large party of [British] foot troops moved through Bordentown and outt he White Horse or Trenton Road to the drawbridge. General Dickinson had some redoubt thrown up noth of the bridge, and the flooring had been removed and the draw raised. Under cover of darkness the foot trops approachedandhaving ripped the planks and weather boards from a neighborhood barn, proceeded with zeal to repair the bridge. The militia got under arms and double quick to the bridge. But the picket who were already there opened fire on the enemy and drove them back with the loss of four killed and several wounded. The militia remained there under armsfor the rest of the night and the next day. If General Washington then moving to interceptthe movement of the British to New York, could have taken position on the north bank of the creek, he would have had a much more advantageous position than at Monmouth.

A second attempt was made by Hessian troops to cross the creek at Watson's Ford where the remains of earth works still exist. Finally a column of dragoons passed through Bordentown at dawn the next day and arrived at another bridge over Crosswicks Creek. It was located where today Route 130 in Yardville crosses over the creek. Lieutenant Colonel John Graves Simcoe's Queens Rangers engaged the 2nd New Jersey Regiment and the 12th Pennsylvania Regiment there. The Rangers captured the bridge with the loss of four or five men. The clashes at Crosswicks were also considered so trivial to the British Army that no mention of the events appears in any formal military document. The action, however, is described in the diary of John Peebles, an officer in the grenadier company of the Royal Highlanders known as the "Black Watch."

> *"Tuesday 23d. The army marched at 4 o'clock in three divisions.... We, the middle division came by the Sign of the Rising Sun to Crosswicks about 6 miles. The advanced corps had a little skirmish at the creek where a party of Rebels had partly broke up the bridge and made a little stand with some cannon, but were soon drove off and pursued with little loss-The Queens rangers had a Captn. wounded.*

During these skirmishes, three cannon-balls fired by the Americans struck the north wall of the Chesterfield Friends Meeting House at Bordentown. One still remains embedded in the wall to this day. The Rising Sun Tavern was opened in 1761 and was used as a Hessian outpost in1776.

Very early in the morning of June 23, 1778, General Leslie entered Bordentown with the advanced corps of the Fifth British Brigade and Hessian Jaegers and marched toward Crosswicks. To clear his way the supply train with its many wagons and refugees was sent ahead of the fighting men. The army continued on to Imslayville where Clinton spent the night at the house of a Mrs. Bunting. Apparently, he had begun to succumb to the intense pressure of the forced march and went to bed drunk. During the night he had a nightmare and ran from the house. He was caught and forcibly returned to bed by his aides.

The next morning, the British forces continued north about 10 miles to Allentown, New Jersey, where the road forked. The northern route led to New Brunswick and Staten Island and a single southern path to Sandy Hook. By heading north they would risk being attacked as the long entourage crossed the Raritan River. Washington was nearer to the river and could reach it first. They also found the problem of swampy land, on the way to New Brunswick that would be difficult to pass through. Curiously, they could not find any local Monmouth County guides who knew the way. This stretch follows the path of the present day New Jersey Turnpike.

Since Clinton's primary objective was to get his army safely to New York, he might avoid converging with the advancing American Army on the shorter road to Sandy Hook. This route ran east through a small village with less that 100 inhabitants called Monmouth Courthouse. It was later named Freehold, New Jersey. Clinton decided that the better option was to head for Sandy Hook and cross a few miles over Lower New York Bay, by ship, to Manhattan,

On June 25, the procession began the 18 mile march from Allentown to Monmouth Courthouse. The British columns stumbled over sandy roads in the intense heat that reached 100 degrees. Almost a third of the Hessian's were overcome by heat and collapsed along the roadside. Some died of sunstroke. Raids by detachments of the American advanced force intensified. A force under Major Joseph Bloomfield of the New Jersey line made repeated strikes on the British rear and took 15 Hessian prisoners. The exhausted British army lumbered into Monmouth Court House on June 26. [15]

At this point they had they had taken eight days to move 55 miles from Philadelphia. They had trudged through ankle deep sand or marshes under burning sun or driving rain. Their heavy woolen clothes were drenched with sweat from carrying packs that weighted 60 to 100 pounds. They constantly had to build new bridges to replace the ones destroyed and clear trees felled across roads to block their way. Clinton's army lost around 550 deserters on the way from Philadelphia, the equivalent of an entire battalion. Four hundred and fifty of the deserters were Hessians soldiers who decided to make America their home and joined American regiments.

It is surprising that Washington's forces missed the chance to wreak more havoc and destruction on the long vulnerable British procession as it moved through New Jersey. Other than the minor stand at Crosswicks and Bloomfield's attack beyond Allentown, most of the action by the Patriots had been limited to sporadic raids by small detachments and the obstruction of bridges and roads. The combined brigades of Dickenson and Maxwell, with the strength of 1,800 men, were roaming close to the slow moving columns. Once the enemy reached Bordentown, the main body of the American Army was never more than 25 miles away.

At the same time the British Army arrived at Monmouth Courthouse, the entire American Army massed at Hopewell about eight miles from Princeton. Washington stayed in the house of Joseph Stout. At Hopewell the Patriots prepared for action. Muskets were cleaned and two days of extra rations were cooked. At the Stout house Washington called his generals together again for a council-of-war., Generals Green, Wayne and Lafayette supported a more aggressive approach despite Lee's objections. The strategy decided upon was a compromise. A large advanced force would attack the British rear. The main army would follow closely to support it. An advanced force of some 4,000 troops was allocated to harass and delay the British Army before they reached the safety of New York. Washington guessed right. Clinton would take the southerly route to the city.

Regardless of the diverse opinions of his generals Washington's hidden agenda at this time was to maneuver his army into a full scale battle at Monmouth Courthouse within a few days. Five months had passed since France had joined the American cause. For most of that time all these new allies had seen was a shrinking Continental Army, barely surviving a harsh winter at Valley Forge. Washington desperately needed a victory or even a show of strength to renew their confidence and encourage additional support. The open country here also ensured that a major engagement would be fought on terrain that was not advantageous to the enemy. If allowed to continue, in only a day the British could reach the high ground at Middletown and Navesink where they would have a tactical advantage.

On June 25 the main body of the American Army moved out of Hopewell and marched seven miles to Rocky Hill and Kingston, New Jersey. The regiment of Anthony Wayne and Enoch Poor were added to Lee's advanced guard. The main army left Kingston for Cranbury after sunset on June 25.

Washington offered the command of the detachment to Major General Charles Lee as he was senior in rank to his other generals. Lee lacked confidence in the success of the plan and refused the appointment. He continued to advise waiting until the arrival of the French army to take any offensive action. Again, Lee warned the other officers that after the calamity at Brandywine the American Army could not afford to lose another major engagement. After a council-of-war with his generals, the Commander- in- Chief decided that the best strategy was to strengthen the advanced force to 5000 troops.

Their mission to destroy bridges, block roads and harass and delay the long procession of British troops and civilians fleeing to New York was broadened to draw the enemy into battle. The command of the advanced force was given to the eager, 21 year old, Marquis de Lafayette. When Lee learned that the advanced force was to include nearly half of the army he reversed himself and asked for the command. Washington complied with his request and Lee relieved Lafayette of the critical position. It would be Lee's task to first attack the rear of the British column so that the main American army could come up and engage in a full battle.

Why was Lee chosen for this critical task when he did not support the plan and in effect was a political rival? Washington with his martial background honored the military tradition that throughout history has steadfastly honored the custom of seniority and did not question the appointment. To this day, date of rank determines assignments, often regardless of qualifications.

The main army caught up with the advance guard at Englishtown on June 27, Washington informed Lee of his intention to attack. The weather was unsettled and the high day-time temperatures gave way to heavy rainstorms.

On the morning of Sunday, June 28, the British were camped along Dutch Lane and the Freehold-Mount Holly Road while the main American Army was camped at Manalapan Bridge, four miles west of Englishtown. At dawn Dickinson warned Washington that the British army was on the move. Lee's force was already approaching the British rear guard a few miles north of Monmouth Courthouse. Washington sent orders for him to immediately begin the assault and bring the British withdrawal to a halt. He would then bring up the main strength of the American army along the Monmouth Road to support him. Clinton then suspected that Washington would attack him in strength and ordered Knyphausen to move north up the Middletown road. The Battle of Monmouth Courthouse had begun.

Sweltering Armies Clash at Monmouth Courthouse

At 8:A.M. on June 28, 1778, General Charles Lee's advanced brigade of 5,000 men with 12 cannons struck the British rear guard a few miles north of Monmouth Courthouse. Lee's forces, west of the Middletown road, could have made an effective attack on the slowly moving column. A coordinated plan could have halted the British withdrawal to the north east and allowed the main American army under Washington to move up to join the attack. Apparently Lee gave no specific orders to his commanders and they used their own discretion as they moved toward the road that led to Middletown and missed another opportunity to strike the redcoats at a vulnerable time.

Lee rapidly lost control and his officers became confused. He did not notify the other officers of his plans to attempt to encircle and capture the 1,500 man British rear guard. The fighting became disorganized and after the British began bombarding Lee's disorganized troops they began to run away back toward the main army. The British exploited this drawback and pursued them. Cornwallis's wing of 14 battalions and a regiment of Light Dragoons were sent out to annihilate Lee's men before Washington could move up to the battlefield.

General Washington advancing up Monmouth Road with the main American

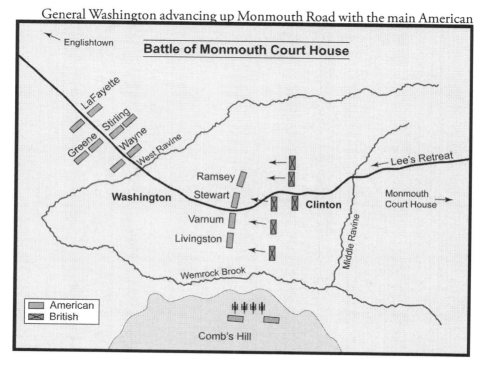

army expected to encounter the rear of the British force. Instead, to everyone's surprise, he met Lee in a full retreat with a disoriented mob and with the British in hot pursuit. The temperature was 96 degrees in the shade as the 5,000 weary and thirsty men tramped back along the road back to Englishtown. The American troops swarmed along the roads. They were puzzled and disappointed by the order to fall back.

Washington soon met Lee leading the flight of a large group of escaping soldiers. Memorably, this is the only occasion in the war in which Washington is said to have sworn. In a heated argument Lee insisted that the American forces were at risk and actually believed that he was saving the army by pulling back. There are several versions of the exhange between the two generals. Washington's language was reported as "strongly expletive" and "a terrific eloquence of unprintabe scorn."

Virginia General Charles Scott when asked if he had ever heard Washington swear replied, *"Yes, sir, he did once, it was at Monmouth and on a day that would have made any man swear. Yes. sir, he swore that day until the leaves shook on the tree.... Sir, on that memorable day he swore like an angel from heaven"*

Washington then galloped forward and began rallying Lee's disordered troops. He succeeded in forming a defensive line that delayed the pursuers so that he could bring up the rest of the army. General Charles Lee was later convicted by a court-martial of disobeying orders and neglect of duty during the battle. The hearing was held six days after the battle in New Brunswick. He was sentenced to one year's suspension from duty. After he refused to accept the suspension he was expelled from the army. Many months later, Lee wrote a strongly worded letter to Congress in protest but the lawmakers closed the affair by informing him that it had no more need of his services. Lee never held another military command and died in 1782. Was his conduct at Monmouth Courthouse motivated by his disagreement with Washington's offensive strategy or his flawed leadership in combat or was treachery his motive?[17]

A Hot Battle Rages on a Scorching Day

After Washington formed the troops into a defensive line, General Nathaniel Greene rushed up with four cannons that were placed on high ground known as Combs Hill. The Visitor's Center at the battlefield now stands on the site. The enemy also brought up artillery. The exchange resulted in one of the largest and most intense artillery duels of the Revolutionary War. Mounted infantry and grenadiers, the special forces of the day, finally broke the American lines.

As the British charged over a bridge at Spotswood Middle Brook they were opposed by Americans occupying the Perrine Farm Ridge with ten cannons. The British also brought up ten cannons and howitzers and positioned them in front of a hedgerow to try to silence the American cannons at the bridge. The exhausted Redcoats first charged into volleys of American grapeshot, then faltered and their attack subsequently collapsed.

Cornwallis mounted an attack on Comb's Hill less than a mile to the south. Well trained ranks of disciplined Redcoats advanced menacingly toward Greene's position. The force included the enemy's best units, British and Hessian grenadiers, light infantry and Cold Stream Guards. The attack was met by fire from the American artillery on Combs Hill, as well as accurate volleys from the muskets of Greene's troops. The guns raked the hedgerow as the British attempted to advance up a ravine slope. Within minutes five high-ranking officers fell and Cornwallis's men began suffering heavy losses from the intense fire. The attackers stumbled back down the slope. The artillery battle continued to rage on for hours, but the intrepid patriots had stood toe to toe and had beaten back the best soldiers of the world's mightiest army.

During this failed attack, Anthony Wayne's Pennsylvanians, protected behind a long hedgerow, drove the British back three times with grapeshot and musket fire. An overwhelming fourth attack overran Wayne's position and forced his units to fall back to the main American line.

When the British artillery began to fall silent, Washington counter attacked with two New England Battalions and engaged retreating Royal Highlanders. Wayne led three Pennsylvania regiments back across the bridge but was again driven back after heavy hand- to- hand fighting with the British Grenadiers. The bitter standup fight went on in the sweltering heat until the late afternoon when Clinton ordered his troops to withdraw.

The British made no further attempts on the main American lines, although continued to bombard them until 6 P.M. At this point, the British fell back to a stronger defensive position east of a ravine. When Washington saw that Clinton was retreating, he ordered an advance of his entire army toward Monmouth Court house and instructed the Virginia regiment to attack their right flank from Combs Hill. The oppressive heat, and hilly terrain brought the exhausted American columns to a standstill and darkness brought an end to the battle. At 6:00.P.M Washington ordered the advance halted. Men were allowed to rest on their arms on the battlefield but were warned to be prepared to resume fighting in the morning. Washington slept on the field that night with Lafayette at his side.

During the battle a camp follower, Mary Ludwig Hayes, (who was later known as "Molly Pitcher,") brought water to the fighting men from a nearby spring. According to one story, she was the wife of an American who came to battle with her husband, bringing water for swabbing the cannons and for the thirsty crews, took a soldier's place after he fell, and fought beside her husband. Under heavy fire with men falling about her. The artillery unit was about to fall back when she courageously saved the gun position. There is a common misconception that her husband was the soldier that fell, but research has proven this to be incorrect. The

story is based on a true incident but has become embellished over the years. Two places on the battlefield are marked as sites of the "Molly Pitcher Spring."

According to most accounts the British suffered some 300 casualties and the Americans lost 350 men. Close to 100 men on both sides are thought to have died of heatstroke during the battle.

Molly Pitcher at the Battle of Monmouth

However, recent conclusions have shown that both sides probably lost many more soldiers. The Americans likely lost close to 700 soldiers, and the British perhaps a thousand soldiers. Monmouth was the largest field battle of the war. The contest went on for many hours.

Captain John Peebles a Scottish Grenadier, who fought in the battle, noted in his diary, *"In this action the Grenrs. suffer'd considerably having 13 officers killed & wounded and about 150 men killed wounded & missing. The Guards likewise lost above 40 - and the several other Corps that came up lost some men either by the Enemy or the heat & fatigue of the day, which was very distressing - The total of killed wounded & missing [was] near 400.*

The Battle of Monmouth Courthouse was technically a draw. Essentially, both sides had accomplished their objectives. The Patriots had held the field and could claim a strategic victory and a political triumph. Their army had applied its Valley Forge training and stood as an equal to the British in a major European style battle. Although failing to win a decisive victory in New Jersey they had inflicted severe casualties on the finest British regiments. Monmouth proved that Patriot troops if properly led could stand against the best army in the world. The battle marked the first time in the war that the Continental Army was able to hold a battlefield and fight the full force of the British army to a standstill without the advantage of surprise.

The British were unable to defeat the Americans in open battle but were successful in withdrawing to New York with their army and baggage train intact.

There, they could join the rest of the British Army and under the protection of the fleet, await the outcome of the French entry into the war. While both sides missed opportunities to win the war on this campaign the British were awakened to the maturing capacity of the American Army.

The Redcoats Vanish

The exhausted British soldiers were allowed to rest for a few hours after the fighting broke off in the evening. They were aroused at 10: P.M. and ordered to start marching northeast on the dusty lane that led toward Sandy Hook. General Knyphausen's Hessians protected the wagon train and were the first to leave the battlefield. By 9 PM they had advanced three miles to a place beyond Lincroft called Nut Swap. They set up camp here, three miles from Middletown. By midnight the last of the Redcoats had departed from Monmouth Courthouse. General Clinton followed with the main body of the army and reached Nut Swamp at sunrise.

The British left their dead and wounded behind. Four officers and forty men remained in town with surgeon to tend them. Others were taken to Tennant Church that was being used as a makeshift hospital for the wounded of both sides. Soldiers killed on the battlefield were collected by the Americans and buried in the Tennant Churchyard. Those who died from wounds in the town were interred in a pit near the village center. Clinton withdrew his army so silently that he was already well on his way when the American sentinels discovered his flight. By the morning he left a gap of six hours between the two armies. During the afternoon he sent Washington a message, under a flag of truce, thanking him for caring for his wounded men.

Scottish Grenadier Captain John Peebles who wrote an unusually well detailed and lucid daily account of the battle and entire campaign best described the hasty and quiet departure of the British during the night.

"Sunday 28th June ... it was thought improper to advance any farther upon the Enemy who were strongly posted, & the Troops were accordingly order'd to retire to cover the Village of Monmouth where the Wounded & Sick were brought to in the Evening - where we remained till near 12 oclock at night, & leaving those of the wounded that were too ill to remove, with a Surgeon & flag we march'd forwards to join the other divisions of the Army whom we overtook near to Middletown about 9 o'clock of the morning of the 29th."

Washington did not attempt to pursue the retreating enemy. They would soon reach a strong defensive position on the high ground at Middletown that stretches into the highlands of the Navesink. As they neared the shoreline they would come under the protection of the guns of the fleet. The area was infested with sympathetic Tories who would provide other assistance. Rather than tarry in Monmouth County, Washington wanted to move his army north of New York City to defend the Hudson Highlands. The general wrote to Congress to justify his position.[18]

> *"Being fully convinced by the gentlemen of the county that the enemy cannot be hurt or injured in their embarkation at Sandy Hook, the place to whence they are going, and unwilling to get too far removed from the North (Hudson) River, I put the troops in motion early this morning."*

Colonel Henry Lee agreed with his commander's strategy: *"the enemy having united his columns on the heights of Middletown, an attempt to dislodge him would have been blind temerity."* Lee goes on to say, however, that if the hilly terrain had not favored the British with such a vast advantage, this would have been the most advantageous place to attack on the entire retreat across New Jersey.

Ironically, D'Estaing's arrived with the French fleet five days too late and narrowly missed a chance to disrupt the amphibious evacuation. Without the transport ships to ferry them across to Manhattan, the British forces could have been trapped on the narrow, seven-mile long, barren Sandy Hook peninsula with no supply lines or water. The Patriots were in position to rain cannon fire on them from the hills on the mainland.

The British also may have missed the chance to face off and continue to fight from the high ground. The army remained intact, and provisions from the ponderous wagon train could sustain them in a major engagement. This was the opportunity to lure the entire Continental Army into a decisive battle, which was the strategy of the invaders since early 1776. Clinton must have had some remorse about fleeing from Monmouth and may have feared criticism. In his report of the battle to Lord George Germaine, Britain's Secretary of State claims to have waited at Navesink two days in the hope that the Americans would pursue him.[19] This is simply not the case. His only agenda was to reach New York as quickly and safely as possible.

British Forces Head for Sandy Hook

The morning after the battle the enemy procession moved through the area that today lies in the town of Colts Neck. Washington sent Generals Morgan and Maxwell with the New Jersey Militia units to attack the rear of the retreating enemy, preventing further devastation of property and to encourage deserters. On the road to Middletown Captain Ewald and his Jaegers reported being cut off on all sides as they moved toward Middletown and the high ground to the east.

> *"The line of Baggage was likewise attack'd by a small party about 10 or 12 miles from Monmouth, & had a few men kill'd & wounded. The last night's march about 14 miles NE thro' a thick wood & a sandy road almost the whole way, cross'd a creek about 5 miles from Middleton, march'd two miles further & halted till next morng. The face of the Country now changed from level to hilly"*

To follow the route of the British retreat from Monmouth Courthouse to Sandy Hook today, start at Freehold on West Main Street and head out of the center of town to Dutch Lane. The flat sandy road east was ideal for rapid evacuation of the British wagon train. Dutch lane continues for about six miles through was once called Montrose and connects with Revolutionary Road just below Vandenburg where it falls off a few degrees to the south. Turn east onto Conover/ Liard Rd to the grave of Private Michael Field in a small roadside memorial park. Field, was in the 1st Regiment, New Jersey Militia. He was wounded and captured in the battle and left here when the British Army moved on. Whether he perished from his wounds or was slain by his captors is not known. He died on June 29, 1778.

This is the present day town of Colt's Neck. The area is renowned for its beauty the fertile farmland originally a farming community is now covered with equestrian farms, fruit orchards and palatial homes. The British route continues over Laird Road to Phalanx, where the troops crossed a ford at Swimming River. Swimming River Road is wider today after being dammed to form the Swimming River Reservoir. No sign of habitation is visible on the river on this pristine lake. The river is an estuary of the Navesink River, upstream from Red Bank in Colts Neck Township.

The route continues northeast along the Lincroft –Middletown Road. The location of the British Camp here at Nut Swamp was discovered in 1992 when a deep search metal detecting team collected a number of musket balls in the Sunnyside Recreation Area. The ordinance appeared to be military and possibly British. The pattern and number of artifacts collected indicated that the place was only a resting place and used only for a very short period, possibly overnight. There is no evidence of a swamp in this residential area.

Captain Peebles describes the second day of the march, *The 1st. Division march'd at day light thro' a hilly strong Country & came to Middleton about 3 miles, in the Environs of which the army Encamp'd - This little Village surrounded with hills is about two or 3 miles from Rariton Bay, and about 12 miles to the light house [at Sandy Hook] - from the Hills you have a fine view of the Bay the Hook, the Fleet, Long Island, Staten Island & Amboy - In the afternoon the heavy division moved a few miles towards Neversink and about 10 o'clock at night the first Division followed, creeping & halting on a crooked road till 2 oclock of the morning. when we stop'd & took a nap whh. was much wanted"* –

The British army marched on the evening of June 30, their second day out from Middletown, toward today's Borough of Highlands. This path can be followed today by taking King's Highway east to the village of Navesink. The terrain rises here and along the roadside are a number of historic markers that all say that the British Army camped on both sides of the road on their way to Sandy Hook after the Battle of Monmouth. This is the "Heights of Middletown." The high ground here would have provided the Redcoat Army with a tactical advantage that could have defeated a pursing Patriot forces.

Peebles describes the last camp of the army before it began crossing over to Sandy Hook on Wednesday July 1. *'The army Encamp'd in a strong position, occupying the Hills from 2 to 4 miles eastward of Middleton & making a communication with the Bay in which the Fleet are lying within the Hook ... the Enemy may be expected, who are still hovering about us, showing themselves in different places in our front & right, some popping shots, now & then ..."*

King's Highway becomes Monmouth Avenue and intersects with Navesink Avenue (Route 36). The British continued a few hundred yards then turned toward the Shrewsbury River down Linden Avenue to Water Witch Avenue. These short streets descend a steep hill down into Huddy Park in the Borough of Highlands. By crossing over the park to Gravelly Point Road the weary troops reached the river beach.

Advanced parties had sent word back that Sandy Hook was separated from the mainland by the narrow inlet. Captain John Montresor, Chief Engineer of the

British forces began building a pontoon bridge across the narrow channel. The pontoon bridge was built along the riverbank in this area across the narrow 60 yard channel to Sandy Hook. The river here is much wider now. A 1781 survey of Monmouth County, drawn by I. Hill, shows the channel the channel running through a swamp. The place was dredged to create the wide main channel that serves as the outlet to Sandy Hook Bay from the Shrewsbury River. Gravelly Point is a mile north of the Rt. 36, Sandy Hook- Highlands Bridge. Somewhere along this stretch was the site of the pontoon bridge. The bridge crossed over to Plum Island on Sandy Hook near the toll gate to the present day beaches that swarm with thousands of people during the summer months.

The British fleet arrived in the waters outside of Sandy Hook on the morning of the same day and then sailed inside the bay to anchor and embark the army. Captain Peebles reported that the ships could be viewed by the British soldiers as they moved down the hill to the present Borough of Highlands. For the next five days, the army crossed over the pontoon bridge or was ferried over the narrow channel on flatboats, to Sandy Hook where they would embark on the ships.

Sir Richard Howe commanded the fleet that greeted Clinton's expedition from Philadelphia. The ships arrived at Highlands during the morning of June 29 to ferry the British forces to New York. The armada consisted of six men- of -war and frigates and sloops The ships anchored outside of the Hook and then sailed inside the Bay. The men- of war offered a reassuring sight to the troops that evening as they descended down to the beach at Gravelly Point. The exact site of the anchorage is unknown but local historians agree that it was either Horseshoe Cove or nearby Spermacetti Cove on the inside of Sandy Hook.

A marker on Sandy Hook near these anchorages reads, "British Embarkation –On July 5th, 1778, armies under General Sir Henry Clinton passed this point to reach British ships, at anchor off Horseshoe Cove, which evacuated them to New York. This completed their withdrawal through Middletown from Freehold after the Battle of Monmouth seven days earlier."

Captain Peebles describes the last leg of the march, *"The army march'd between 5 & 6 from yr. respective ground by different roads to the point of the Highland that joins the Hook, & there is a Gut of water across the low Sandy part next the main, a Bridge of flat boats was made for the Troops to pass some embark'd on board of flat boats & rode off to their ships but the greatest part of the army crossed at the Bridge & march'd along the Hook towards the Light House & went off in flat boats to their ships in the afternoon; it was night before the whole got on board. - a great number of horses on Sandy Hook yet not embark'd into the Vessels that are to carry ym. up - the day cool, march about 6 miles in the woods before we came to the point & about 3 or 4 miles on Sandy Hook, deep sand - provision drawn on board a very irregular & ill managed Embarkation".*

It took three days to embark the sick and wounded, civilians, supplies, weapons, horses and wagons. The troops were the last to embark. Peebles remarked that the process was somewhat chaotic. The fleet sailed over lower New York Bay and through the Narrows to the safety of Manhattan.

While waiting their turns to board the ships the ominous sound of gunfire was heard in the distance. Peebles reported, *"Saturday 4th. the weather clear'd up towards noon - all the officers horses sent off ... great expedition this in Embarking our things so fast, -- hear'd a great deal of firing in the Eveng. Of Cannon & Small arms at a distance which we suppose is the Americans rejoicing on the anniversary of ye. Independence. The firing seems to be somewhere about Brunswick ... orders to be ready to move at break of day."*

What the Redcoats heard was the thunderous sound of guns of the Continental Army carried eastward by the wind from New Brunswick. The Patriots were celebrating the second anniversary of the Declaration of Independence. After a generous distribution of rum the soldiers paraded for review in front of their Commander -in-Chief. They wore a sprig of mint in their tricorn hats as a symbol of hope. Then regiments lined up and each fired their muskets in turn, down through the ranks and back.

The last of the British departed from Sandy Hook Bay by ship for New York on July 5. When they arrived in the city they began preparing the defenses in expectation of an attack by the French Fleet. This naval assault was cancelled in favor of a joint assault on Newport Rhode Island. New York City remained the principal base for British forces until the end of the war in 1783. The Continental Army was positioned in New Jersey and New York on both sides of the Hudson River for the rest of the year. In December the Army moved to Middlebrook, New Jersey for the winter of 1778-1779.

The Scene Today in the Monmouth Courthouse Area

Monmouth Battlefield the site of the largest one-day battle of the war when measured in terms of participants is one of the best preserved Revolutionary War sites in the nation. The fields and forests that now make up the park cover a scenic rural, 18th-century landscape of hilly farmland and hedgerows that encompasses miles of hiking and horseback riding trails, picnic areas, a restored Revolutionary War farmhouse and a Visitors Center. This 2,928-acre New Jersey state park is located today on the border of Manalapan and Freehold Township. It lies approximately 12 miles east of Exit 8 of the New Jersey Turnpike on Business Route 33.

The park offers an ongoing variety of interpretive and educational programs including nature and history hikes, birding and lectures on the details of the battle. During the 1990s, public and private sources funded extensive battlefield restoration. During the battle, the Craig farmhouse was the home of John and Ann Craig and their three children. Its 1746 kitchen is Dutch-framed, while the two-story addition is English-framed. The Craig farmhouse and the exterior of the 1745 Rhea-Applegate dwelling have been restored. At the same time the central part of the battlefield was rehabilitated with the reconstruction of period fences, lanes and a woodlot.

In June of each year there is a reenactment of the battle. In 2003 Monmouth Battlefield celebrated the 225th anniversary of this historic event. Thousands of spectators gathered to witness the full- scale recreation of the occasion that was punctuated by cannon barrages and cavalry charges. The park's Visitor Center is located on Combs Hill, the site of a Continental artillery battery during the battle. On exhibit at the center are there are artifacts that were recovered by archeologists from the battlefield and interpretive displays.

The battlefield can be explored from parking areas at the Visitor Center and along Monmouth County Route. 522. It remains a working landscape with farms that grow corn and soybeans and cultivate extensive fruit orchards. While strolling on the grounds, visitors can learn more about the battle through wayside informative signage on Perrine Hill, Combs Hill, and the Hedgerow.

The Battle of Monmouth involved 35,000 soldiers and traversed an area of nearly 20 miles so archeologists were perplexed as to where to search for evidence that would substantiate the many accounts of the fighting and troop positions.

The area that encompasses the heart of the action alone covers three square miles. The first known map of the action was drawn by a British officer, Lt. Col. John Simcoe. It was likely done from memory shortly after the battle since the Americans held the ground. The land features and topography were determined to be inaccurate. A more accurate version, dated the day of the battle was done by Michel Capitaine du Chesnoy, cartographer for Layfayette. I was likely done by eye and shows a correct depiction of the terrain. The troop positions and movements are shown but cannot be completely verified.

Artifact locations were identified using a metal detection technique in 1992. This site is the first Revolutionary War battlefield to ever to be fully excavated.[20] The work enabled the location of specific events during the fighting along with eye witness accounts and the position of specific British and American army units. The exact place where Proctor's Artillery Company fought and where Mary Hays (Molly Pitcher) serviced a cannon alongside her husband were   identified.

The nearby area abounds with structures that stood at the time of the battle. In nearby Englishtown the restored Village Inn was General Lee's quarters. The Old Tennent Church was used as a field hospital by the Continental Army. Many of the men, from both sides, who fell in the battle rest in its graveyard. In Freehold, the British wounded were cared for in the still active St. Peter's Church. The Covenhoven house which served as the headquarters of British commander Sir Henry Clinton stands on Main Street.

The State Park opened in 1978. People concerned with the deteriorating conditions formed the Friends of Monmouth Battlefield in 1990. Landscapes were being overwhelmed by foliage that obscured historic views and buildings were on the verge of collapse. The Friends initiated the annual Battle of Monmouth reenactment as a way of bringing attention to the threatened national historic landmark. The historic event is observed on the third or fourth weekend of June each year. It has become the largest annual living history event in New Jersey.

The Monmouth County Historical Association at 70 Court Street in Freehold Borough, houses a collection of documents that includes personal accounts, journals, pension applications and original letters.

Reflecting on the New Jersey Campaign of 1778, it is curiously replete with occasions where both sides missed tantalizing windows of opportunity that could have inflicted heavy losses and been decisive in bringing the war to an earlier end. This lack of a decisive confrontation created a stalemate that lasted for the next five years.

If the Americans had been more aggressive they could have pounced on Clinton's vulnerable procession as the troops and civilians crossed the Delaware River. A vigorous assault there would have disrupted or entirely stopped the British campaign across New Jersey. Bolder strikes on the plodding miles long wagon train strung out during the eight days that it took the British to reach Monmouth Courthouse from the Delaware River did not occur although Washington's army was only about 20 miles away during that entire time.

During the final evacuation at Sandy Hook British forces could have been annihilated by a bombardment from the high ground of the Highlands of the Navesink. Continental gunfire raining down on the defenseless Redcoats trapped on the barren and exposed strip of sand would have been a disaster for the troops waiting to be evacuated. The arrival of the French Fleet there only a few days later could have finished off the smaller English Navy that was helplessly anchored while arduously loading troops and supplies.

The litany of lost opportunities continues for the British side. General Howe with its formidable task force in Philadelphia could have easily beaten the depleted, starving and freezing Continental Army during the hard winter at Valley Forge. Instead, Howe's Army and its German mercenaries chose to enjoy a benign winter in the captured Patriot capitol. Sir Henry Clinton also missed a chance that his side had sought for the previous three years, an all out, face to face, engagement with the Americans.

The British Army that crossed New Jersey in 1778 was completely self-contained with superior troop strength, weapons and supplies. It had the infrastructure to engage in the all out battle that the evasive, Fabian Washington had avoided for the previous eight months. Then he was available and could have been drawn into battle at Middletown Heights on the way to Sandy Hook where British forces could be well entrenched amid favorable high terrain.

The Battle of Monmouth was the longest sustained battle of the Revolutionary War and probably the best fought by the entire Continental Army. Standing alone, and personally led by Washington, the Americans strategically and tactically displayed unusual competence and by holding the field could claim victory.

Reexamining the battle and the events that preceded and followed it leads to the conclusion that in fact both sides performed quite well. They had both successfully emerged from great hardships before the engagement to fight a battle on one of the hottest days ever recorded in America. Clinton survived the exhausting march across New Jersey and Washington's men stayed alive after a debilitating winter at Valley Forge.

Chapter Eight

The Last Stand of the Iroquois Nations
Newtown, New York-1779

Native Americans Join the War

In the summer of 1779, the American Revolution divided into two wars with much of the military action shifting to the southern states. In the north, George Washington, with the main body of the Continental Army camped at Bound Brook, New Jersey was in a stalemate with a well entrenched British Army in New York City. The Sullivan- Clinton campaign against the Six Iroquois Nations and their Loyalist allies that year was one of the largest offensives of the Revolutionary War but it remains unfamiliar to most people today. A significant battle occurred during the campaign at Newtown, New York, near present day Elmira. It was the last time a large and unified Native American force opposed the Patriots. A commemorative monument stands two miles away from the site of this engagement. The steep hill where the battle raged is unmarked. Today it stands on private property.[1]

From the start of the war the Indians joined forces with the Tories, Americans loyal to England. Together they began to devastate the frontier settlements of the new nation. By 1779, this issue was regarded as a greater threat than the regular British Army campaigning in other parts of the country. Public outcry over atrocities by the Indians caused Congress to direct a reluctant General Washington to take offensive action. By August of that year more than 6,200 soldiers, about a quarter of the entire Continental Army, was committed to subduing the Indian tribes and their Tory allies.

This expedition against the native people captured the imagination of the entire nation. It generated tremendous interest and was openly discussed and followed in the newspapers of the day. The strangeness and distinctiveness of this campaign against the red men in the frontier wilderness, with the curious sights, bizarre experiences and shocking barbarity, produced more curiosity than any other event in the Revolution. It defeated the Loyalists and destroyed Iroquois villages, crops and orchards. The Indians would never fully recover. Many of these significant events stand in the shadow of American history.

It was a crusade of vengeance. Retaliation for the carnage on America's frontier that in those days was as close as eastern New York State, Pennsylvania and Virginia which at that time included West Virginia, Ohio and Kentucky. Several established towns were near this troubled region. American settlers were flocking in increasing numbers to these regions that the indigenous people had traditionally occupied. The colonizers built cabins and stockades and ploughed fields. They regarded the lands of the native people as unoccupied wilderness. These acts confirmed the suspicions of the Indians that whites not only intended to remain but also would continue to aggressively encroach upon their ancestral tribal land that extended through western New York State and lower Canada. In this territory were hundreds of villages and hunting grounds.

The Iroquois Nations was a confederation of the Seneca, Cayuga, Mohawk, Onandaga, Oneida and Tuscarora tribes. Unlike the nomadic plains Indians, theirs was an agricultural society with an organized central government. They lived in cabins in permanent settlements, raised crops and kept livestock. The Indian way of life was very much the same as the white settlers. Indian culture, highly developed in many ways, did not follow the conventional methods and rules of European warfare generally observed by both the British and Americans who were appalled by their shocking brutality. Warriors never attacked without having a great advantage or where victory was certain. They rapidly fled if they were losing. Their preferred tactic was the surprise raid by a small party that would massacre, plunder then disappear into the woods. They usually attacked isolated villages or ambushed an enemy who was outside of a protected place.

Mohawk Village in central New York-1780

Iroquois braves routinely scalped and mutilated bodies of the fallen enemy. After being tortured, prisoners were brutally killed. Women and children were kidnapped and some were adopted by Indian families to replace their losses. In return for fighting they expected to be rewarded with prisoners and plunder. Victory for the Indians meant the right to regard all property of the vanquished as booty. They gave no quarter and did not expect to receive any.

Early in the war, both sides had tried to gain the support of the Native Americans by giving them generous gifts of weapons, clothing and manufactured implements. After 200 years of contact with the white man, they had grown to depend on these items. British efforts in wooing the native people were much more ambitious than American attempts. The Crown through their Department of Indian Affairs, a large and well organized agency, often provided food and shelter during difficult times. The Indians revered Sir William Johnson, Superintendant of this agency. He spoke their languages, understood their culture and was adopted as a member of the Mohawk tribe.[2]

The indigenous people accepted gifts from both sides and professed that they would remain neutral and vowed they would take no part in the war. They claimed to view the conflict as problem among white men. The Six Iroquois Confederation, however, soon perceived that the best way to protect their homeland would be to join the British side.

The Indian tribes united under Joseph Brant a charismatic Mohawk Chief known as Thayendanegea to the Indians. The son of a German settler and a Mohawk mother he attended a charity school for Indians, which later became Dartmouth College. He was an Anglican and a Freemason and assisted in translating part of the Bible into Mohawk. His political connections with the British, his oratory skills and his bravery and skill in combat during the French and Indian War led to his becoming the strongest military leader among his people. Brant led many of the raids on American settlements.[3]

Joseph Brant's sister Mary also known as "Molly" was the common law wife of the British Superintendent of Indian Affairs Sir William Johnson, the top official in the region, and mother of their eight children. She was the leader of the Society of Six Nations Matrons. These politically powerful matriarchs actually appointed sachems could veto the decisions of chiefs. Molly Brant was strongly pro- British and had a son in the loyalist militia. The union of Molly and Sir William cemented the Anglo Indian alliance.[4]

The Seneca tribe was the most belligerent of the nations. Skilled in wilderness warfare they were led by Sachems Cornplanter and Old Smoke. These powerful warrior chiefs joined forces with Joseph Brant to form the General Council of the Six Nations, a group of 50 Sachems chosen by the matrons of each clan.

The Indians were supported by Loyalists of the British militia commanded by Lieutenant Colonel John Butler a British Army Officer. He had spent his life on the frontier had commanded Indian warriors and knew the languages. When the Revolution started, Butler along with many other Loyalists fled to Canada. He left his wife and two children behind at their homestead in what is today Fonda, New York. The Rebels who confiscated his estate seized them and confined his eldest son in irons in an Albany jail. This provided the ardent Tory with a strong motive for retaliation. Butler accepted the brutal Indian methods of warfare. He described the slaughter and torture of prisoners and civilians along with kidnapping and routine pillaging as being "comfortable to Indian tradition."[5]

In September 1776, the alliance between the British and the Indian Nations was formalized. John Butler met with the Indian Grand Council at Fort Niagara The fort was a stronghold on Lake Ontario not far from Niagara Falls and controlled the entrance to the Great Lakes. Except for the Oneidas and Tuscaroras all chiefs of the Iroquios Nation agreed to enter the war on the side of Great Britain.

It was a very advantageous time for the Indians to make this commitment. The American forces after the devastating defeat at Quebec at the end of 1775 had retreated all the way south from Canada down the lakes. Fort Ticonderoga was recaptured and General John Burgoyne's army of 15,000 British regulars and Hessians were advancing to within 30 miles of Albany. At this time the British Fleet was massed in New York harbor. Supply ships disembarked a huge army of 32,000 British and Hessian Troops on Staten Island and soon after, captured New York City. Washington's untrained and poorly equipped army, weakened by losses, fled across New Jersey. These events convinced Brant and Johnson that the American rebellion would soon be smashed.

During 1776 Guy Johnson, who had succeeded his father-in law Sir William as Superintendant of Indian Affairs, took Joseph Brant to England to enhance the alliance with the Indian Nations. In England, Brant was presented to King George III. The King presented him with a silver gorget (an ornament worn on an officer's uniforms that evolved from armor that protected the throat.) He was further honored by receiving a captain's commission in the Canadian Loyalist Corps. During his visit the charismatic Brant became the toast of London society. His portrait was painted wearing a plumed headdress and carrying a tomahawk. He returned with the English fleet and provided the Indian Confederation with an eye witness account of the overwhelming strength of crown forces in America. [6]

British commanders began using the Indians as spies and scouts but were reluctant to use them in larger scale offensive operations. Warriors were undisciplined and difficult to control in combat. After plundering and taking scalps most braves simply became bored and headed home. They were of greater value for their relentless harassment of American frontier settlements. The British believed these raids would eventually weaken the Continental army by causing it to divert its forces. However, the attacks did not dissuade settlers from becoming Patriots since war parties did not distinguish Loyalists from Patriots and molested all white men. This alienated many who were sympathetic to the crown.

The beginning of the total commitment of the Iroquois to pro- British forces in the Revolutionary War began with participation in Burgoyne's invasion. His army was threatening Albany. If successful, this drive could divide New England from the other colonies and effectively end the American Rebellion in the fall of 1777.

A British force under Brigadier General Barry St. Ledger approached from the west along the Mohawk River to link up with Burgoyne. They were stopped at Oriskany, New York on August 6, 1777, in one of the bloodiest battles of the Revolutionary War in the North America. Fort Stanwix on the Mohawk River blocked a major invasion route from Canada. St. Ledger forces besieged it. An American relief force under General Nicholas Herkimer, numbering around 800 men of the Tyron County Militia and a party of Oneida Indians, attempted to raise the siege. St. Ledger sent a force consisting of a New York Loyalist regiment and Indian allies to intercept them. Led by Brant and Butler this force ambushed Herkimer's force in a small valley about six miles east of the fort near the present-day village of Oriskany.[7]

During the battle, Herkimer was mortally wounded. The Patriots suffered 450 casualties but held the fort. The Loyalists and Indians lost approximately 200 dead and wounded fighters. An apparent Loyalist victory was spoiled when their camp was sacked and supplies and possessions taken by the Patriots. While the Americans suffered horrible losses, most military historians regarded Oriskany as a Patriot victory. St Ledger witnessed the determination of the Americans and failed to capture the fort. He headed back to Canada and never joined up with Burgoyne.

Oriskany was one the few battles in the war where almost all of the participants were North American. Loyalists and Indians fought against Patriots in the absence of British soldiers. For the Indians the battle marked the beginning of a civil war. The Oneidas were allied with the American cause and fought against tribes of other Iroquois nations. While other sites claim the honor, the first display if the stars and stripes may have been at Fort Stanwix on August 3, 1777. The garrison had no flag, so they made one according to the prescription of Congress by cutting up sheets to form the white stripes, bits of scarlet cloth for the red stripes, and the blue ground for the stars was composed of portions of a cloth cloak belonging to Captain Abraham Swartwout, of Dutchess county, New York.

After the battle, Butler was authorized to raise a full battalion of Loyalist rangers and Indian warriors to support Burgoyne whose invasion of New York was faltering. Before Butler could reach Burgoyne the British were defeated at Bennington, Vermont, then completely collapsed and surrendered at Saratoga. The defeat of the huge British force is regarded as the turning point of the Revolutionary War.

During this campaign, British officers, schooled in European style warfare, were appalled at the barbarity of the Indian allies and attempted to instruct the chiefs in the rules of battle protocol. The terror continued. Along the Mohawk three girls were picking raspberries in a meadow. Four warriors hiding in the woods appeared and shot at them. Two of the girls were found scalped and tomahawked. The third, shot in the shoulder, escaped to report what happened.

The same day that the girls were murdered a slaying occurred at Fort Henry, on Lake George, a hundred miles east. Jane McCrea was the 20 year old daughter of a Presbyterian minister. A loyalist and the fiancé of a lieutenant in the Queen's Loyal Rangers, Jane was staying at the home of Mrs. McNeal waiting for the lieutenant to arrive with Burgoyne's army. Indians stormed into the house and carried off the women. When Mrs. McNeal was brought into the British camp she saw a warrior holding a bloody scalp. She recognized it as belonging to Jane McCrea's whose mutilated body was found a short distance away.

This murder by one of Burgoyne's Indians was one of the most notorious atrocities of the war. The American public was enraged by the story of the beautiful young girl attacked by Indians serving with the British forces and the news swept through the states. The murder had such great propaganda value that enlistment rates dramatically improved. American Major General Horatio Gates, who would soon be defeating Burgoyne at Saratoga, condemned him for the horrible fate of Jane McCrea and hundreds of other men, women, and children who were murdered by his Indian troops. For fear of upsetting the British Army's tenuous relations with the tribes, Burgoyne did nothing to punish the killers and the Indians viewed the act as normal part of warfare. James Fenimore Cooper used the story of Jane McCrea as the theme for his novel *The Last of the Mohicans*.

After the defeat of Burgoyne's Army at Saratoga the Indian tribes moved west to gather at Fort Niagara for the winter of 1777-78. Here John Butler and Joseph Brant began to plan a campaign of large- scale organized raids on the American frontier settlements in New York and Pennsylvania.

Blood and Barbarity on the Frontier

Butler's Tory Rangers and Brant's warriors hoped to achieve several objectives by harassing the American frontier. Terrorizing patriot settlers might convince them to change sides and become loyalists for protection. Raids would also hamper the rich harvests that supplied the American Army with most of its grain. Creating chaos on the frontier would force the Continental Army to send troops west. This would substantially weaken the rebels who needed all their strength to repel the main British Army occupying their capitol city, Philadelphia. British leaders were well aware that even a threat of an Indian raid had an immense psychological effect on civilians. Constant pressure on the frontier could eventually erode all support for the cause of independence.

Raids on American settlements began in early 1778. Butler equipped war parties at Fort Niagara and rewarded them when they returned from raids. In the first three months of 1778, 70 warriors returned with scalps and a few prisoners. Two thousand gallons of rum were bestowed on the victorious braves in April, and another 5,300 gallons were provided in the months that followed.

Indians usually surprised farmers working in their fields and hunters or travelers alone in the wilderness. Anyone working outside the walls of stockades was targeted. Warriors rarely attempted to attack a fortification unless they had an overwhelming advantage. They typically remained in an area for a brief time. After slaughtering or kidnapping the inhabitants, burning crops and killing or driving off livestock they moved to another location after a few days.

The bloodiest attacks of the Indian Nations occurred during 1778, in Orange County, New York, in northeastern Pennsylvania's Wyoming Valley near Wilkes-Barre and in the Cherry Valley, south of Canajoharie, New York.

In April 1778, friendly Indians warned settlers in the Cherry Valley that Joseph Brant had gathered 1,500 warriors and Loyalists along the Susquehanna River, 40 miles south. This force had already begun destroying isolated farms, killing and scalping men and taking women and children captive. In May, Chief Brant attacked Cobleskill at Cherry Valley with a force of 350 warriors and loyalists.[8] The town was defended by 100 militiamen. The Patriots attempted to turn the enemy away with a bayonet charge but gave way to the onslaught of frenzied warriors wielding tomahawks and war clubs. The town was burned and all food supplies were captured. Americans suffered 25 killed and wounded.

The Wyoming Valley, lying between Scranton and Wilkes-Barre, Pennsylvania was attacked in July. The lush valley had settlements that stretched along the northern branch of the Susquehanna River for 25 miles. The rich farmland was a major source of food and supplies for the American Army. It was an isolated area away from any populated centers and far from the protection of the Continental Army. The people of the Wyoming Valley were ardent patriots who maintained a strong militia even though many of the male inhabitants had left to join the Continental Army

Colonel Butler and Chief Brant arrived in the Wyoming Valley in June with 464 Indians and 110 rangers reinforced by 50 cannons that were floated down the river on rafts. The settlers were alerted to their approach by an attack on 12 unsuspecting field workers. Four workers were killed and another four taken prisoner. Two of the prisoners were tortured until they died.

The next day Colonel Butler set up an ambush and directed that a small American fort be set on fire. The Americans believed that this was a retreat and charged ahead. Butler instructed the fierce Seneca braves to lie flat on the ground to avoid observation. The Americans advanced to within one hundred yards of them firing as they ran. The Seneca suddenly sprang to their feet and fired a volley. They then changed the battle by engaging the Americans in the type of fighting at which they excelled- Indian style hand- to- hand fighting.

The fanatical fight lasted about forty-five minutes then turned into a frantic Patriot rout when the inexperienced citizen soldiers of the militia panicked and ran. After that the warriors began to look for survivors. The victorious Loyalist Rangers and Iroquois braves killed and tortured an unknown number of prisoners and fleeing soldiers. Butler reported that 227 American scalps were taken. More than 300 Americans were killed. The Iroquois raiders hunted and killed fleeing Patriots before torturing to death the thirty to forty who had surrendered.

News of the battle caused a panic on the entire frontier. Settlers in the surrounding counties evacuated. About 1,000 homes and all of the American forts in the Wyoming valley were burned in the days following the battle.[9]

Later that year, on a cold, snowy day in 1778, 200 of Butler's Rangers and about 400 Seneca warriors led by Joseph Brant and Cornplanter approached the town of Cherry Valley about 10 miles from Cooperstown, New York. A timber palisade built around the village meeting house protected a temporary garrison of 300 Continental Army soldiers commanded by Colonel Ichabod Alden.

Most of the officers of the regiment were quartered nearby in private homes and attempted to return to the safety of the stockade. Colonel Alden was chased by Joseph Brant. Alden stopped and tried to shoot his pursuer when he was within reach of the gates. His damp pistol repeatedly misfired and he was killed when a thrown tomahawk hit him in the forehead. The attackers cut down another sixteen officers trying to reach the stockade. The people of the town fled and left behind their homes, possessions and food supply. The Indians hunted for those who had escaped. All the houses of the town were burned and plundered. The Continentals still held the fort and the invaders retreated after three hours. In addition to the loss of Colonel Alden and his men 30 civilians, mostly women and children, were scalped and killed.

The *New Jersey Gazette* reported on November 25, 1778, "*The enemy killed, scalped, and most barbarously murdered, thirty-two inhabitants, chiefly women and children. They committed the most inhuman barbarities on most of the dead and all the officers and continental soldiers, were stripped and drove naked before them. Several accounts indicate that during the fighting, or shortly thereafter, Lieutenant Colonel Stacy who was second in command of the fort was stripped of his clothing, as if about to be murdered, but his life was spared after he appealed to Brant a brother Freemason. After the mayhem the raiders disappeared into the forest.*"

In the spring of 1779 the leaders of the Indian Nations began to hear reports of troops massing for an invasion deep into their homeland. These were the American forces of Sullivan and Clinton gathering at Wyoming and Otsego near Cooperstown, New York. When Brant heard these warnings from reliable sources he sent expeditions to these places to attempt distract the buildup and to steal cattle.

Brant himself led a band of 260 Indians and 27 white men to Minisink, New York, ten miles west of Goshen, on the upper Delaware River, The settlement was undefended and the settlers had hidden their cattle in the woods. Guided to the town by a local Loyalist, Brant spent the day burning the town's houses, barns and its church. The raiders took four scalps including that of the schoolmaster who attempted to shield his students. The chief mercifully tried to restrain his warriors from killing women and children.

Colonel John Hathorn's 2nd Orange County militia regiment was alerted and its 120 men rushed from nearby Goshen and Warwick to rescue the town. They caught up with the Indians as they were leaving. Brant managed to circle around the minutemen and ambushed them from the rear. After intense hand- to-hand fighting the citizen-soldiers were overrun. The warriors took 40 scalps and only 30 Americans survived. Chief Brant and his forest fighters lost seven men. The Presbyterian Church in Goshen had 30 widowed members as a result of this action and the battle of Fort Montgomery two years earlier.[10]

These disastrous raids on Wyoming, the Cherry Valley, Minisink and other vulnerable frontier places forced thousands of American pioneers to abandon their homes and head back east. Constant reports of the massacres of prisoners and other atrocities began to enrage the American public and the issue became a political problem. Congress dreaded a defensive war on the frontier that extended hundreds of miles from Virginia to Canada. With the British army poised to invade again from New York and rampaging through the southern states, there were not enough Continental Troops to do the job.

The Slaughter Must Be Stopped

After the attack on the Cherry Valley, Congress and Washington reluctantly began to accept the fact that a western campaign was essential. He started planning a major offensive against the Iroquois nations in 1778. In early 1779, Washington at his Middlebrook, New Jersey headquarters developed a detailed strategic plan for a quick strike during the coming campaign season.

This frontier war was directed at the Indians and not the British Army. The plan was to destroy Indian villages and burn their harvests late in the season when there was not enough time to raise another crop before winter. Then there would be no food supply to sustain their raids and the Indian Nations would be forced to retreat west and beg provisions from the British. The Commander- in- Chief called for *"total destruction of their settlements and the capture of as many prisoners of every age and sex as possible"* Indian lands, he stated, *"were not to be merely overrun but destroyed."*[11]

Washington sought an experienced officer to lead the venture. After several officers declined, the command fell to New Hampshire's General John Sullivan. Sullivan was a seasoned general who was on the invasion of Canada and in the battles at Long Island, Trenton and Princeton in New Jersey. General Sullivan agreed with his commander's goals and saw his mission as convincing the Iroquois "that we have it in our power to carry war into their country."

The slaughter at the Minisink in July 1779 was the final act of aggression that would be tolerated by the new nation. Three weeks after the raid the Continental Army marched into upstate New York to destroy every Iroquois village in their path. Washington instructed Sullivan to march from Easton, Pennsylvania with three brigades. When they reached the Susquehanna River in central Pennsylvania they would follow the river upstream to Tioga. This village is now Athens, Pennsylvania, on the New York border. Sullivan's army totaled 4,000 men. He faced a major logistical challenge. His forces would operate for many weeks beyond the supply lines and would have to live off the land. Washington promised complete support. He allowed Sullivan to hand pick his troops and draw exorbitant quantities of supplies from the depleted resources of the main army.

Brigadier General John Sullivan
(1740-1795)

Washington ordered New York General James Clinton to assemble another brigade of 1,500 men at Schenectady, New York. They would move west along the Mohawk Valley and pass down to Otsego Lake to a staging point at Cooperstown. The plan was for Clinton's New York Brigade to meet Sullivan at Tioga and together destroy all Indian villages his route.

Sullivan's column left Easton on June 18 and marched 58 miles to an encampment in the Wyoming Valley. The progress of the invaders was slowed by both the mountainous terrain and the heavily laden flatboats carrying supplies for the expedition down the Susquehanna. They arrived at Tioga on August 11 and began construction of a temporary fort at the confluence of the Chemung and Susquehanna Rivers. The Fort was named Fort Sullivan in honor of their senior commander.

An astonishing engineering achievement took place along the route of Clinton's Brigade. His force arrived at Cooperstown, at the source of the Susquehanna River, with 250 bateaux carrying three months supplies. These flat bottomed boats were built for use in shallow water, but loaded down with provisions could not be floated on the river during the dry season. General Clinton ingeniously ordered a dam to be built across the mouth of the lake to build up a head of water. After five weeks the dam was broken and the bateaux were launched in the flood. The supplies could then be floated without difficulty forty miles down the river to their destination at Tioga.

After leaving behind a 200- mile swath of destroyed Indian settlements and crops, Sullivan and Clinton joined up at Tioga on August 22, 1779. The worst fears of the Indian Chiefs were realized when they learned that they would be confronted by seasoned regiments of the Continental Army under veteran officers, not untested militia. Sullivan's and Clinton's 4,500 soldiers were now poised to march toward the villages in the heart of the Indian lands in New York State. At a Fourth of July party, before the invasion began, the confident officers toasted, "*Civilization or death to all American savages.*"

The Battle of Newtown and the Invasion of the Iroquois Heartland

In early 1779 the British Army was completely focused on subduing the American rebellion along the east coast. The British Army offered little assistance as the Americans mounted a major campaign against the Native Americans. Except for support from Butler's Rangers, the tribes were on their own to defend their villages. The American invaders were then poised to head northwest from Tioga toward the capitol of the Iroquois at Genesee, New York. At this time Indian leaders prepared to make a desperate last stand to prevent the complete destruction of their homelands.

On August 20, 1779 they gathered a force of 1,200 men. The defenders included mostly warriors. These fighters were supported by a regiment of Loyalist militia and a few British Army Rangers under Captain Walter Butler which was a disappointing show of force for the Indians considering that all of the homelands of the Six Nations were in jeopardy. Many braves had stayed behind to protect their own villages. Butler was dismayed at the poor turnout and tried to dissuade the Chiefs from confronting an obviously stronger force. He tried to convince them that their present strategy of strike and run harassment was very effective and should be continued. The Sachems refused to follow his guidance.

They built a defense line along the base of a half-mile long ridge along the Chemung River where they hoped to surprise the American Army and block their path. The site was 14 miles from the Patriot departure point at Tioga- the site of the village of Newtown, six miles east of present day Elmira, New York.

The Indians were commanded by some of their top leaders: Joseph Brant, Cornplanter and Old Smoke. The Loyalist contingent was led again by the intrepid John Butler. With inferior numbers, an ambush would be the only way to stop the American assault. This narrow pass between a steep ridge and the river was well suited for the trap.. The unsuspecting Continental soldiers would be forced into this chokepoint. The braves built a three foot high stockade made from the logs of torn down houses and concealed it with foliage. The barricade stretched for a half mile across the pass.

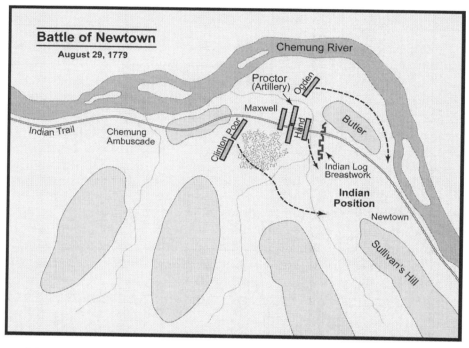

The unsuspecting American task force plodded west over rough pathways and the slippery river bank along present Route 17. The Americans were encumbered by supply wagons, pack horses and eight pieces of artillery. Sullivan had demanded exorbitant amounts of supplies for the campaign. Most military leaders considered that the provisions were far more than were needed, which would slow down the encumbered invading columns and cause the loss of opportunities for surprise strikes.

Five thousand men, in columns that stretched for miles, marched toward the trap. Major James Parr's Rifle Corps led the entourage with orders to "reconnoiter mountains, defiles and other suspicious places ahead to prevent the enemy from launching a surprise attack or ambush." They were followed by two musket battalions led by Brigadier General Edward Hand. Next came the artillery with four light 3 pounder bronze guns, two 3 pounder iron guns, two 5 ½ inch howitzers, and a coehorn mortar. This portable mortar was designed to be movable by as few as four men. A traveling forge and three ammunition wagons followed the guns.[12]

Brigadier General Enoch Poor's New Hampshire brigade marched to the right division of Hand's brigade, and Brigadier General William Maxwell's New Jersey brigade stayed on the left.[13] Clinton's New York brigade brought up the rear. In the center of these formations were 1,200 packhorses and 800 head of beef cattle.

The ambush was discovered from the top of a tall tree by a scout who detected camouflage and warriors in war paint crouching in the dead leaves behind the concealed log breastwork. The alerted Americans immediately formed up to make a frontal assault on the barricade. The skirmishers were met with heavy musket fire from the Indians behind the concealed stockade. Riflemen and light infantry troops, the special forces of the time, rushed forward to skirmish with the defenders in front of the defense and at the same time tried to surround the enemy to prevent them from retreating. Cannon were brought up and for two hours the artillery sprayed grapeshot, shells and spikes at the stockade.

With shells bursting behind them, many warriors thought they were surrounded and fled. Butler regrouped those who remained and with his rangers retreated back up a hill behind the stockade. A patriot thrust along the river on the defender's right flank caused the Indian line to break. Braves and their Redcoat supporters ran off or escaped on pack horses. Most, however, were able to fall back up the steep hill to join Butler and have the advantage of fighting from high ground. The Americans would be forced to struggle up the steep incline through dense foliage to press their attack against concealed warriors.

The New York and New Hampshire troops then moved around the left flank and prepared to charge up the hill. The New Hampshire men blundered into a swamp and took heavy losses until the Yorkers broke through to them. The two brigades pressed on up the sharp half- mile incline and faced withering barrages of gunfire from the screaming, well armed Indian warriors who fought from tree to tree.

American officers gave the order to fix bayonets and hold fire until the men reached the crest of the hill. Not accustomed to the onslaught of a bayonet charge, the Indian lines began to falter. Warriors and rangers fell back through the heavy woods to the top of the hill. When the patriot soldiers reached the summit they fired a full volley that broke the Indian defense. The action at this point was best described by Nathaniel Davis a New Hampshire soldier:

> *"The enemy commenced a fire from behind every tree and at the same time commenced a war whoop. We were ordered not to fire until we had obtained permission from our officers, but to form a line of battle and march forward as soon as possible. We did in good order and at the same time the Indians kept up an incessant fire upon us from behind trees, firing and retreating back to another tree, loading and firing again and still keeping up the war whoop. They continued this mode of warfare until we had driven them half way up the hill when we were ordered to charge bayonets and rush on. We then in our turn gave our war whoop in the American style which completely silenced the unearthly voice of their stentorian throats."*

The braves fled on baggage horses. They left their dead behind, along with packs, blankets, tomahawks and spears. The fierce encounter at Newtown had lasted six hours. Americans had won the battlefield but they had failed to close the trap. Most of the enemy force escaped north along the river and survived to fight again. Patrols chased them for two miles and killed eight more braves. Colonel John Butler reported 10 men killed and nine men wounded but at least 20 bodies were found by the victors. The Americans lost 12 men and had 39 men wounded during the fray.

The triumphant American troops then burned all 20 houses in Newtown's and destroyed 150 acres of ripe corn, beans potatoes and squash. For the next two days they obliterated everything that could not be eaten or carried away. American soldiers had become hardened to Indian- style warfare and adopted the ways of the warriors. The frenzied men scalped all Indian bodies that were found. Two New Jersey officers skinned corpses to make boots.

The day at Newtown had not been costly for the patriots in terms of casualties. Even Sullivan, who had feared that the operation would be a disaster, boasted of his victory and reported that he and Clinton had already destroyed 14Indian towns. As he wrote, his men were "industriously employed in destroying Newtown," a job that would take an entire day.

Sullivan made several key decisions after the battle. He decided that the artillery slowed his forces and sent his heavier guns back, keeping only three small cannon. After finding an abundance of food in the towns he required his men to live off enemy produce and livestock.

Invading the Indian Heartland

After the fighting stopped, detachments of Continental troops rushed north into the darkness hoping to catch up with the enemy at the villages of Catherine's Town and Mintour Falls.[14] They found that the fleeing Indians had paused there briefly to rest but had not attempted to regroup. Cooking fires were still warm but the towns were abandoned.

At this point Generals Sullivan and Clinton reassessed their strategy. From the light showing of warriors at Newtown they surmised that the route ahead might be trouble-free and decided to push forward. Their first encampment was at Elmira, New York situated in beautiful level and fertile country. Following their normal practice they burned the houses of the village and cut down all the crops in the surrounding countryside.

After slogging through a nearly impenetrable swap they reached abandoned Catherine's Town where enemy campfires were still burning. From there they began the 40 mile trek up the east shore of Lake Seneca and continued continuing to destroy houses, cornfields and even an Indian burial ground. They reached the present day town of Hector, about halfway up the lake, on September 4.

Here the invaders learned that the Indian nations were planning to make another stand. It would be at Canadesega, the capitol of the Seneca tribe and the largest town that the expedition had so far encountered. The Americans were amazed to find that it too was deserted except for one inhabitant. It was a three year old, ragged and hungry white boy who could only report, "*my mammy is gone.*" An artillery captain took over his care: smothered with attention by hundreds of homesick soldiers he became the unofficial mascot of the expedition.

Before leaving, a stockade fort, a blockhouse and 60 closely spaced cabins were burned down. Expansive fruit orchards, corn and vegetable fields were ruined. The lighthearted soldiers impaled pumpkins, squash and melons with their bayonets. General Sullivan admonished the troops for looking ridiculous.

The American leaders paused here to again access the feasibility of continuing to move so deeply into perilous Indian country. The home base at Tioga was 100 miles away. They were so far out that they began to fear being surrounded and cut off. With the troops in high spirits and a bountiful food supply from the ripening harvests found in abundance along the way, the decision was made to press on.

After reaching the top of Lake Seneca the Continental troops turned west toward their final objective, the capitol of the Indian Nations at Geneseo (Genesee, New York). This was the source of most of the bountiful harvests that sustained the raiders of the American frontier settlements.

As the American Army moved toward Geneseo, a scouting party of 26 volunteers, led by Lieutenant Thomas Boyd, was sent out to explore the unfamiliar area ahead for signs of opposition.[15] Along the trail they spotted five Indians who disappeared into the woods. Boyd's guide suspected a trap and told him not to follow. Boyd ignored the warning and blundered into the concealed Indian camp. A fierce hand to hand skirmish ensued. The tomahawk wielding braves scalped 13 of Boyd's men and captured him and Sergeant Thomas Parker.

The two were taken to Cuylerville, near Geneseo, where Brant interrogated them. Brant assured Boyd of his safety after they identified themselves as freemasons. Brant left the captives with Chief Little Beard an angry extremist who tortured and executed Boyd and Parker in a most grotesque way. Boyd was tied to a tree by his own intestines and forced to run around the tree until he fell dead. The tree, a large oak reported to be 240 years old, still stands in a commemorative park. It is known as the "Torture Tree." A poignantly worded marker nearby reads: *This wayside shrine marks the place whereon Sept. 14, 1779, two young soldiers of the Revolution, Lieut. Thomas Boyd and Sergeant Michael Parker met death undaunted in the line of duty after lingering They marked with their blood the western limit in the State of New York of the great struggle for America.*

After learning that a British force might be on the way to reinforce them the Indians decided again to make a last ditch attempt to obstruct the assault on their capitol. At the present day town of Avon, 15 miles from the capitol city, the Indians led by Butler, Brant and Old Smoke assembled a war party of 400 braves. They were greatly outnumbered and knew that the only chance to stop the Americans would be another ambuscade.

Crouched down in a narrow ravine the warriors were primed to stun the unsuspecting advancing columns. This was the force that Boyd's scouting party had accidently met. The sounds of gunfire from this melee alerted the main assault force to the danger ahead and the Indians lost the element of surprise. The tragic sacrifice of Boyd's patrol had spared the American Army from entrapment and annihilation by the vengeful Iroquois.

After fording the Genessee River the Americans moved on until they arrived at the picturesque capitol of the Indian Nations. It was situated between the river's west bank and the present day town of Cuylerville. The villages of Geneseo were pleasantly located in an idyllic setting on a seven mile grassy plain along the meandering river. The weary Americans gazed with amazement and admiration at this fertile plain extensively covered with ripening crops. Some compared it to the Garden of Eden.

When they reached the main village, they found 128 well-built, multifamily houses filled with abundant amounts of husked corn. As usual the inhabitants had run away only moments before and left their cooking fires burning. The euphoria of the jubilant troops soon turned to horror when they found dogs devouring the severed and mutilated heads of Lieutenant Boyd and Sergeant Parker. In an enraged frenzy the soldiers destroyed every article of food they could find. Corn was burnt or thrown into the river. Houses were burned to the ground and cattle and horses were killed. Nothing was left but bare land and timber. The entire winter food supply of the Iroquois was destroyed.

At Geneseo Sullivan announced that the objectives of the expedition had been achieved and the army would be heading back to Tioga. Rationing was relaxed and everyone enjoyed a feast of roast beef and potatoes. On September 15, 1779 the occupying troops burned and destroyed any remaining crops and fruit trees that could be found in the valley and started back, retracing the 130 mile route to Tioga.

The Indian chiefs had learned while torturing Boyd's party that the American forces would stop at this point and decided that is was futile to offer further resistance. Facing the winter and starvation from the devastation of their crops, 5,000 vanquished Indians headed 100 miles west to the stronghold at Fort Niagara to seek provisions and shelter from the Loyalist allies.

The timing of the Sullivan-Clinton expedition was well planned. The summer and early fall was harvest time and it was too late in the season for the Indians to replant. The winter of 1779-1780 was the coldest in the century and the people of the Iroquois Nations left with little food froze or starved to death or subsisted on roots gathered in the woods

Those Indians who did not survive the winter continued to make raids on the frontier settlers but on a lesser scale than before the expedition. When the British surrendered at Yorktown in 1781, small bands of Iroquois were still inflicting carnage on the frontiers of New York, Ohio and Pennsylvania. The destruction of their homeland now provided full justification for Native Americans to seek revenge in the years that followed. An American officer commented "the nests are destroyed but the birds are still on the wing."

Native Americans were confused when The Treaty of Paris ended the war in 1783 and brought peace. British ambassadors simply made no mention of the Iroquois Nations in the settlement. Indian rights and land boundaries remained undefined. The Indians felt betrayed and abandoned when their parental friends sailed away taking many white and black loyalists with them. The loss of their strong ally left them helpless to resist the onslaught of a half million white Americans pressing to surge westward.

Following the war Americans began settling the newly vacant areas in relative safety and eventually isolating the remaining pockets of impoverished and demoralized Iroquois into villages and towns. Much of the Iroquois land would be surrendered by the controversial Treaty of Fort Stanwix in 1784.[16] This agreement ceded huge tracts of land in New York, Pennsylvania and the Ohio territory to the new nation. In the years that followed, the land of the Six Nations would be completely absorbed by other inequitable treaties with the State of New York and most of the native population would migrate to Canada, Oklahoma, and Wisconsin.

When the triumphant patriots arrived back at Fort Sullivan in Tioga they found time to celebrate their conquest. They were greeted by a 13 gun salute and a regimental band. Two days of partying were climaxed by a lively dance of friendly Onieda warriors. Rations of beef and flour were abundantly given out and included a gill (one quarter of a pint) of whiskey for each soldier and a half pint of rum for each officer.

On October 9, 1779 orders came from General Washington to Sullivan to march his brigade to West Point, New York while Clinton's New York Brigade trudged east over 150 miles of mountainous country to their winter quarters at Jockey Hollow, Morristown New Jersey. Here the rigors of the Indian campaign would seem minor compared with trying to survive the longest and most severe winter of the revolution and the entire eighteenth century.

General Sullivan reported to Congress on his accomplishments. He boasted to Congress, *"The number of towns destroyed by this army amounted to 40, beside scattered houses. The quantity of corn destroyed, at a moderate computation, must have amounted to 160,000 bushels, with a vast quantity of vegetables of every kind. Every creek and river has been traced, and the whole country explored in search of Indian settlements, and I am well persuaded that.... there is not a single town left in the country of the Indian Nations."*

Sullivan received an unexpected cool reception from Washington and other military leaders. He was faulted for not sending progress reports back during the campaign and never reporting the strength of his regiments. His extreme caution and constant demands for overwhelming numbers of men and shares of the army's meager supplies and weapons had been excessive and had caused delays. The entire mission was regarded by many as overkill. While he had succeeded in destroying villages and foods supplies he did not capture any populated villages or take hostages as directed. He had failed to block the enemy's escape at Newtown and showed lack of resourcefulness by not pressing on for the final 75 miles to Fort Niagara for ma final decisive victory. Sullivan was appalled by this criticism. He claimed bad health and resigned from the army a few weeks after his return.

The Sullivan-Clinton campaign of total destruction has been compared to the better-known scorched earth march to the sea of General William Tecumseh Sherman in the Civil War, 85 years later. While the objectives were alike, the men of the Continental Army faced far greater challenges in 1779. They penetrated far into an uncharted enemy country subject to constant threats of ambush by a savage enemy. Any faltering would result in their slaughter by an adversary who did not comprehend the concept of surrender. They had to move through endless forests and cross rivers and mountain ranges and their supply lines were stretched out hundreds of miles.

Many of the objectives of the Sullivan- Clinton Campaign were fulfilled. The dreaded Senecas and Cayugas were vanquished. Their villages were burned, the bountiful cornfields and gardens destroyed and their orchards were cut down. After peace was signed, Americans had the right to demand property in these conquered western lands. Large parcels were given by Congress and the states to Revolutionary War veterans as bounty land for their service. Many of these men had been on the campaign against the Iroquois and had passed through this bountiful and picturesque frontier country. Now they returned in peace to western New York and Pennsylvania to settle, build homes, barns schools and communities. Many of their descendants still live here today. [17]

Casualties on both sides were surprising light during this campaign but the battle would have a profound effect on the United States history. The migration into Indian lands doubled the size of the new nation in just one generation and millions of settlers would head west during the next 100 years. The founding fathers must have had a hidden agenda for the invasion. They knew that to achieve the manifest destiny they would have to possess Native American lands.

The Sullivan –Clinton Campaign and the battle of Newtown have been hailed as incredible military feats. But, many have mourned the devastation of the Native American civilization and view it as a time of despair. The powerful Iroquois Nations that had existed for over a quarter of a millennium were ruined. This league that had conquered and ruled the tribes of a quarter of the continent and was mightier than any other confederation of Native American in history would never exist again in North America.

An American officer writing home to his fiancé during the campaign lamented, *[I write with] great loneliness which is creeping into my soul with every mile and every hour that separates me from you. I really feel guilty as I applied the torch to huts that were homes of content until we ravagers came spreading desolation everywhere…Our mission here is to destroy but it may not transpire that we pillagers are carelessly sowing the seeds of empire.*[18]

In 1790, Cornplanter one of the great Indian military leaders was introduced to George Washington. He told the new president, *"When your army entered the country of the Six Nations we called you Caunotaucarious, Town Destroyer, and to this day when your name is heard our women look behind them and turn pale, and our children cling close to the necks of their mothers"*

Exploring the Route of the Sullivan-Clinton Campaign

Autumn is the best time to follow the footsteps of the Continental Army during the Sullivan-Clinton campaign and to visit the places where their Native American adversaries lived and fought. The first blush of color on the verdant foliage and frosty mornings have a chill that portends the arrival of the bitter upper New York State winter. The momentous events of 1779 occurred during this season.

General James Clinton's New York Brigade began their trek in Canajoharie, New York on the Mohawk River. They headed south in early June to follow the Susquehanna River from Lake Oswego to Tioga on the Pennsylvania border. Here they joined up with the Sullivan's larger column that had left Easton, Pennsylvania on June 16. The plan was for the combined brigades to head north toward the Finger Lakes and into the uncharted heartland of the Iroquois.

Following the Clinton or Sullivan route is about a 1,000 mile round trip. Original orderly books, muster rolls, officer's journals and other contemporary records provide a vivid account of the progress of Clinton's column and trace the march of the New York Brigade on a daily basis for almost the entire 20 week campaign.

We start our tour in Albany to follow Clinton's New Yorkers. Anyone with an interest in original records of New York history should visit the archives at the Cultural Education Center at the state capital. This is a first rate facility with an extensive collection of original records, knowledgeable staff and state of the art equipment for viewing microfilm.

Traveling west from Albany along picturesque Mohawk River, you soon become aware of New York's greatest 19th century engineering accomplishment, the Erie Canal. All of its 400 miles were built by the muscle power of men and horses. The Erie Canal was opened in 1825. Sections of the Mohawk were later "canalized" by superimposing a uniform channel with dams and locks. At Little Falls, New York you can visit a lock which is one of the highest lifts in the world. General James Clinton, leading the New York Brigade through here in 1779, could never have imagined that his second son De Witt would become the future governor of the state and the driving force behind the canal project

Many of the valley's first settlers were German refugees from the Palatine area of Germany and Revolutionary War veterans who migrated to the western frontier to claim their bounty land. These hard-working pioneers were attracted to the rich farmland along the banks of the broad river. For the next 100 years their villages served as departure places for settlers heading west.

This area abounds with reminders of the campaign. Fort Klock on the Mohawk at St. Johnsville, 50 miles from Albany, is a little altered example of an 18th century fortified stone house. It was used as a place of refuge from Indian raiders and Tories throughout the War for Independence. The riverbank directly below the small fort served earlier as a docking place for bateaux, the flat bottomed boats that supplied the site when it served as an early fur trading post. Its two-foot thick walls are loop holed so that muskets could be fired through them from inside. Fort Klock houses an interesting museum of artifacts, found on site, and mid 18th century household items that enabled the occupants to be completely self- sufficient.

Fort Plain is on the opposite side of the Mohawk River. Nothing remains of the log structure that once stood here on a high hill overlooking the river. It served as headquarters for the defense of the entire Mohawk Valley during the Revolutionary War. This historic marker is evidence of the Indian Campaign:

1779 Clinton March

Col. Lewis Dubois with the 5th New York Regiment and Artillery

left Fort Plain for Otsego Lake June 25, 1779.

The New York troops struggled south for 20 miles, dragging cannons, flatboats and supply wagons over hills and through the trackless wilderness to the village of Springfield at the head of Lake Oswego. This rustic little crossroads town where the patriot troops massed to prepare to sail down the lake has changed little since that time. Today, a few intriguing antique shops are nestled in colonial clapboard houses along its short main street. Bearded young men in traditional Amish garb framed a new house nearby.

Most of the troops marched south along the eight- mile- long Lake Oswego. The boats were loaded with supplies and artillery. This pristine mountain lake is over a mile wide in most places. There is no evidence of the march of New York soldiers along the lake. They must have traveled along the west bank which is direct and level and the path of present Route 80. This is a scenic ride that passes by lakeside summer cottages and quiet small towns that seem to have changed little over the past 200 years.

Cooperstown is located at the end of the lake. The New York Brigade paused here waiting for Sullivan to mass his army at Tioga. It must have been an enjoyable six weeks resting in the pleasant July weather. Today this charming town has many points of interest. The plethora of museums, gift shops, restaurants and other tourist attractions, including the Baseball Hall of Fame signals that it is best avoided by historians in the summer season. The New York soldiers camped on the shore of the crystal clear lake on a grassy plain. It's easy to imagine them fishing, hunting and swimming at this site during their enjoyable summer interlude. The land at their campsite gradually ascends from the lake a few hundred yards to a prominent Indian burial mound.

Lake Oswego narrows to about 50 yards here at its southern terminus. This is where General Clinton built a dam to raise the water level of the lake. When the dam was broken, his boats could ride the surge to float out into the Susquehanna River. No remnants of the wooden barrier remain. A monument standing in the water marks the length of the structure's span. A marker at this site reads:

Clinton's Dam- Opened August 9, 1779, 2000 men and 200 bateaux went down the Susquehanna.

Clinton's men ended their pleasant sojourn at Cooperstown and set out on the 130 mile, 14 day trip down the river to Tioga. The Susquehanna is one of America's greatest waterways. It flows 400 miles over the mountains of Pennsylvania to enter the northern end of Chesapeake Bay in Maryland. The river begins at the southern end of Lake Oswego where it is a narrow and shallow creek. It has many rapids and sand bars and is only about 25 yards wide in most places. It does not widen until it reaches Oneonta, New York, about 20 miles south of Cooperstown.

Without James Clinton's brilliant feat of building then breaking the dam, the constant hauling of loaded boats over shallows and exhausting portages would have made this trip impossible. Drive down the west bank of the river and follow the daily entries from the brigade's original orderly books to make this fascinating a ride. The road and passes through Unadilla, Otsego, Sidney, Afton and Owego. New York Troops camped each night in these small towns. There are no historical markers during this entire run down the river. Campsite locations, identified in the old records with the name of the owner's farm, have been lost in history.

The Susquehanna River takes a turn to the west at Binghamton, New York and continues for 50 miles to a junction with the Chemung River at Tioga, (now Athens, Pennsylvania), just over the state border. Here, Clinton's New York troops finally joined with the larger part of the invading army under Sullivan. Tioga was renamed Camp Sullivan in 1779 by the army on its return from the campaign. Nothing remains of the fort here, but its perimeter is well defined by descriptive markers and monuments.

Today, a bridge spans the Chemung River at this point. In the past, a portage of about a hundred yards was required between the rivers. A plaque attached to a large boulder marks the burial place of several soldiers killed at a skirmish in the nearby village of Chemung. The site of Camp Sullivan was identified by Solomon Talada, a soldier who returned to Athens to live after the war. His statement was verified by Indian skeletons discovered on the site before 1839.

The few museums found in towns along the way focus on Indian lore rather than the Revolutionary War history. It should be remembered that the rich culture of Native Americans existed in this region for thousands of years while American troops passed through here in a few days and destroyed these places.

Along the Chemung River, on Route 17, about five miles southeast of Elmira, lies Newtown Battlefield Reservation. This State Park stands on the summit of a high rise that has been named Sullivan Hill. A tall granite obelisk commemorates the battle and an observation deck with descriptive signs overlooks the valley. Curiously, the actual site of the battle is about two miles away from this commemorative park and the view is obscured by trees.

On the road up to the park there is a small general store, "The Outpost," owned by Rosamund Piatt. She proudly displayed a guest book that had been signed, over the years, by visitors to the store. Among the more interesting entries were notes left by descendants of General Sullivan, Indian chiefs and veterans of the battle.

Rosamund is an enthusiastic amateur historian. She has an extensive trove of old maps and other written accounts of the Battle of Newtown. Her collection of hundreds of artifacts, mostly of Indian origin, was found in nearby fields and along the riverbank. It includes arrow and spear heads and stone tools. This display would be the envy of any major museum.

To reach the actual Newtown battle site, turn off Route 17 at Lowman. Entering this small hamlet you find the site of the southern boundary of the Indian-Tory defenses. Both English and American flags fly above a small park here.[18]

Newtown Battlefield August 29, 1779, is marked on a brass marker on a large boulder. A nearby sign reads: The position of the line of rude breastworks where British and Indians disputed the advance of Sullivan's Army. A few yards down the road is another boulder that marks the position of the American Light Infantry troops who charged the camouflaged barricade in a frontal assault.

While many historians consider Newtown to be a pivotal battle of the entire Revolutionary War, oddly the site of the ridge where the heavy fighting occurred is still on private property and impossible to find without directions from local residents. Off the main street in Lowman is an unpaved road that winds a few hundred yards up a steep hill to the battle site. Daunting signs often appear with such messages as *Stop- Private Property- Trespassing Strictly Forbidden!*

There are a few modest homes along the unpaved, one lane drive. Mailboxes all bare the name Gilsen. At the crest of the hill is an open area that was once a plowed field. Cross it to the rear slope of the hill to see where the American soldiers charged up the hill through the dense woods, with bayonets fixed, into the vigorous gunfire from screaming Indian warriors.

This battle site property is the ancestral land of the Gilsen family who has steadfastly refused to sell this hallowed ground to the state. In 2004, the 225th anniversary of the battle, they allowed a reenactment of the event on its actual site which was attended by hundreds of people. Some years ago, a bayonet was turned up by the Gilsens while they were plowing the fields on the crest of the hill.

A small graveyard lies nearby. Stones mark the graves of soldiers and Indians who were killed in the battle. A local resident pointed out where the events of the battle took place. His vivid description of the struggle at Newtown provided a concise account of the fierce hand- to- hand fighting on that fateful day in 1779. Earlier that day he had unearthed an old brass buckle using his metal detector. It was buried over a foot deep and he believed it was an artifact from the fighting. This visit to the forgotten Newtown Battlefield at Lowman is a fascinating and emotionally moving experience.

Route 17 turns north a few miles past Elmira, at the town of Horseheads. This village received its peculiar name when the Indians captured several emaciated horses from the advancing Continental Army. They slaughtered the animals and impaled their heads on posts to frighten the invaders.

The road continues north for 15 miles along Catherine Creek the source of a nearly impenetrable swamp. The troops slogged through this quagmire while pursuing retreating warriors to Montour Falls, at the south end of Lake Seneca. The town was named by the Loyalists in honor of the Indian Queen, Esther Montour. She was a tall, handsome, half-white, Seneca clan mother. In 1777 her son was killed during the raid on Wyoming. To avenge his death she clubbed 15 bound American prisoners to death.

The 35 mile drive along the west shore of this charming Finger Lake is enchanting. Along the lake, at the town of Hector, a historic marker reminds us of the campaign: General Hand camped here with the Light Infantry on September 4, 1779. Hector was one of the many Indian villages devastated by the Americans. The entire army stopped here: perhaps Hand's advanced guard of light infantry is recognized because they were the first to arrive.

At the northern end of the lake, the American expedition turned west into the larger villages of Canadesaga (now Geneva, New York) and Canadaigua, which still carries its Indian name. Here Sullivan paused to decide whether or not to continue on the perilous last leg of the invasion, the 50 mile trek to Geneseo, the principal stronghold and capitol of the Indian Nations. Farm stands along the way displayed a dazzling array of pumpkins, apples, gourds and many kinds of fresh vegetables. I was reminded that it was where that the jovial soldiers cavorted with this produce impaled on their bayonets.

The Genesee Valley, New York's richest agricultural region, derives its name from the Seneca word for "beautiful vale." The Genesee River meanders through this lush, two mile wide expanse of rich farmland. The weary and hungry soldiers had been in the field for three months. They must have rejoiced when they came upon this paradise of lush grassland covered with abundant food crops and orchards. The reason why the Iroquois Nations located the center of their civilization in this idyllic valley is apparent.

The largest of the Indian towns in the valley was Chenussio, now Geneseo. The town was called Genesee at one time. Today, it's a quaint hamlet set amid farmland on a grassy bow of the river. The sites of the ambush and loss of the ill-fated scouting party, led by the brash 22 year old Lieutenant Thomas Boyd are nearby. The scene of the capture and death of most of Boyd's 30 man patrol can be found on Route 20A.

Groveland Ambuscade Park is about two miles away. On a stone obelisk an engraving reads, Scene of the massacre, after a desperate and heroic struggle of Lieut. Thomas Boyd's scouting party by an ambuscade of British and Indians under Butler and Brant September 13, 1779. The opposite side lists the names of the men who perished on the spot.

The site where the prisoners Boyd and Parker were taken to be killed and mutilated is on Rt. 20 near Cuylerville. The Boyd- Parker Memorial Park and the "Torture Tree" are here. This is the same giant oak under which the men were killed. A plaque mounted on a boulder a few yards away bares this poignant message: This wayside shrine marks the place where on Sept. 14, 1779, two young soldiers of the Revolution, Lieut. Thomas Boyd and Sergeant Michael Parker met death undaunted in the line of duty after lingering torture. They marked with their blood the western limit in the State of New York of the great struggle for American freedom.

Following in the footsteps of the Continental Army as it trudged into the hostile Indian territory of upper New York State in 1779 is a fascinating journey back in time. Surprisingly, the country remains much the same since the days when the soldiers were here. Most of the land is still covered with endless virgin forests. Today's highways follow the exact routes of Clinton's and Sullivan's troops and the pathways of Native Americans who preceded them. The many Indian place names are constant reminders of the days of the mighty Iroquois Nations.

The Sullivan-Clinton Campaign is not as well known as other major events in the War for Independence. Reading some of the original accounts of the expedition will greatly enhance the fascination of this trip. Most residents who you can meet at historic sites along the way, were all able to relate in detail the historical events that took place where they lived. This trip was a delightful respite, away from the relentless bustle of New York's metropolitan area, to places where a more traditional and genuine America still exists.

Chapter Nine

Cruel Mutinies But a Kind Winter–Pompton and the Preakness Valley, New Jersey, 1780-1783

A Brutal Mutiny and a Benign Winter

In July 1780, the main body of the Continental Army moved into an area known as the Preakness Valley also called Pompton and Totowa. Today it encompasses Wayne Township, Pompton Plains, Totowa and Pequannock, New Jersey. Many significant events occurred here during the Revolutionary War, yet, except for a few local residents, this place in our "Crossroads State" has been overlooked in history and evidence of the War here is often unmarked and unrecorded.[1]

Located on the long range of mountains that extend north across the New York state border the place was a land of fertile valleys and hills rich in minerals. There is iron ore and an abundance of lead, lime, sandstone and slate. Dutch farmers were the first European immigrants to settle in Pompton as early as 1694. They purchased large tracts of land from the Indians and began building, farming and mining the rich land. Located at the meeting of the three flowing mountain streams, the Pequannock, Wanaque and the Ramapo Rivers, the area was named "Pompton" from the Indian word meaning "Meeting Waters".[2]

General Washington had many problems at Pompton. The army was losing many men due to the expiration of enlistments and supplies were difficult to procure with worthless continental currency. He used the stately Dey Mansion in Wayne as his headquarters during the month of July 1780 and returned again in October and November of that year.

At the Dey House Washington received some of the best and worst news of the war. He heard of the momentous decision of France to join the American cause. The depressing report of the defection of Benedict Arnold reached him here and the tragic mutiny of the New Jersey line occurred nearby in today's town of Bloomingdale in January of 1781.

The most illustrious leaders of the war lived here in private homes during the 1780 encampment. Alexander Hamilton, the Marquis de Lafayette, and Generals Anthony Wayne, Lord Stirling and Nathaniel Greene all camped here with their regiments. In 1781, the entire Continental Army and all of the French forces under Rochambeau joined forces at Pompton to march south to the final critical allied victory at Yorktown.

Finally, during the winter of 1781-1782 the New York Brigade at full strength with about 2,000 men camped here on the bank of the Pompton River. This was their first stop on the return from the Yorktown victory. Here they were visited by General Washington and his wife Martha and inspected by Baron Von Steuben. Today, the site of this campground is unmarked and unknown except to a few local historians.

Headquarters for the Continental Army

In June 1780, action in the war shifted to the southern states. The Hessian brigades of the British Army withdrew from New Jersey after being beaten back at Connecticut Farms, now Union and Springfield New Jersey. After the 800 foot long pontoon bridge to Staten Island from Elizabeth was dismantled, Washington believed that they had no immediate plans to return and moved the entire Continental Army toward the Hudson River. He set up the headquarters of the main army in Pompton, New Jersey between Morristown, New Jersey and West Point New York.

Located at an important crossroads for commerce and communications roads intersected here that led south to Paterson, Paramus, Acquackanonck (Passaic), Newark and Morristown, New Jersey and north to Ringwood, Suffern, Haverstraw and West Point, New York. From Pompton the American Army could quickly move 20 miles to the Hudson River if the British invaded north from New York City. The rich farmland of the area offered abundant sources of food as well as proximity to iron forges for shot and cannonball.[3]

The valley was also in a position to protect the southern entrance to Smith's Clove. The Clove was a long valley extending 23 miles from New Jersey through the Hudson Highlands to West Point. It was the main highway and line of communication for the Continental Army during the entire eight years of the war. Present day Interstate 87 follows its path. Washington valued the security of the Clove and considered control of the route to be equal in strategic importance to the Hudson River.

On July 4, 1780, Washington arrived in the Preakness Valley and dispersed his brigades over the Preakness Valley. He set up headquarters in the luxurious Georgian mansion of Colonel Theunis Dey in lower Preakness. Dey was a colonel in the Bergen County Militia. The Dey home would serve as the headquarters of the Continental Army from July 1 until July 29 and again from October 8 to November 27, 1780. [4]

The main body of the army arrived three days earlier and camped along the Totowa Heights near the Great Falls. The encampment covered the center of the high ground to the rear of the present Laurel Grove Cemetery in Paterson. The Marquis de Lafayette had his headquarters at the house of Samuel Van Saun at Lower Preakness. Major General Stirling was quartered nearby at the home of George Doremus. A detailed map shows the campsites of all the American Army units at Totowa and Preakness, New Jersey and its vicinity in October and November 1780.

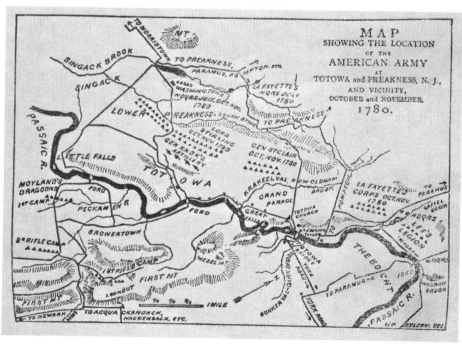

Although Pompton was not regarded as a long term encampment the troops tried to make themselves as comfortable as possible despite few materials and limited time. Tents or huts were set on floors of broad, flat stones and crude chimneys of stone and clay erected on the exterior. In 1857, when Totowa farmers began plowing up the land at the base of the mountain they found these stone floors along with cannon balls and other artifacts of military occupancy.[5]

Food and clothing were scarce but rum and wine taken from the British a month before at the Battle of Springfield were plentiful. All soldiers were issued a gill of rum (four ounces) each day. Officers amused themselves by giving receptions and visiting the nearby Paterson Falls which was regarded as a great natural wonder.

Good News and a Treacherous Visitor

This first visit of the American Army to Pompton was interrupted by momentous events. On July 20, a dispatch rider rushed up to the Dey mansion and gave General Washington this message. "Yesterday afternoon, the long expected fleet of our illustrious ally appeared off Newport." The French Fleet had arrived in Rhode Island with 6,000 troops.

He immediately replied, "As a citizen of the United States and as soldier in the cause of liberty, I thankfully acknowledge the new mark of friendship (from Louis XVI)… and I feel a most grateful sensibility for the flattering confidence he has been pleased to honor me with on this occasion. …."[6] This was the most decisive moment in the war and fortunately the Pompton location provided quick access to the French allies and a perfect springboard for a joint attack on New York. This event was never to happen since French General Rochambeau persuaded Washington that trapping the British Army on the Yorktown Peninsula was a more sensible strategy.

That same week Brigadier General Anthony Wayne convinced Washington that it would be advantageous to raid the territory between the Hackensack and Hudson rivers. So many loyalists lived in the area that it was known as "The English Neighborhood." This rich farmland teemed with livestock which supplied the British Army in Manhattan.

The objectives of the raid were to procure these supplies to feed the American Army at Pompton and to capture a blockhouse on the Palisades. This defense, directly opposite 80th street in New York, was the headquarters of a band of marauding Tories that were pillaging the farms of Bergen County Patriots. Wayne's hidden agenda was to draw the British across the river and attack them by surprise.

Washington was only willing to commit Wayne's Pennsylvania Brigades and a regiment of dragoons for the raid. He correctly perceived that with only 4,000 men the Continental Army would be no match for the 12,000 well trained and well equipped British troops in the city. [7]

The raid was a disaster for the Americans. Wayne's force of 1,800 men was held off at the blockhouse by only 84 Tory defenders, and he lost 50 men. The British sensing an entrapment did not cross the Hudson River. The humiliated Wayne returned to Pompton with only some captured livestock.

On July 28, General Benedict Arnold arrived in camp. This visit enabled the traitorous American officer to gather intelligence on the strength of the American forces which he reported to British Commander Sir Henry Clinton in New York City. At Pompton, Arnold persuaded Washington to appoint him commander of West Point. He defected two months later after delivering the plan of the defenses of that fortress to the enemy.

On July 29, the British Army in New York City moved north to attack the recently arrived French Army in Rhode Island. Washington promptly moved east toward Paramus, crossed the river at Dobbs Ferry and prepared to attack the upper part of the city. This threat forced the British to withdraw back to protect the city that had served as their northern headquarters since 1776.

The Dey Mansion as it appears today

Washington returned to the Dey mansion on October 8, 1780 and the troops reoccupied the encampment site of the previous summer for the next two months. On November 27, as the fifth winter of the war approached the American Army marched out of the Pompton area. Washington dispersed his northern brigades to the Hudson Highlands and Morristown but left two brigades in New Jersey. The troops were spread out in this manner to avoid the problems of the previous year when the entire army massed at Jockey Hollow, Morristown, where there was a limited area to forage for food and supplies.

Only detachments of the New Jersey and Pennsylvania Brigades remained in New Jersey. With the American Army and supply base gone from Morristown the British had little reason to invade the interior of the state. The New Jersey Brigade was left at Pompton and nearby Chatham. The Pennsylvania regiments camped 15 miles away at Jockey Hollow and occupied the site of the previous winter encampment.

The Mutiny of the New Jersey Line

A seven day mutiny of the 200 soldiers of the New Jersey Brigade was brought to a dreadful end in Pompton. Two of the leaders were convicted at a brief courts martial. Forced to kneel in the snow they were immediately shot to death by their distressed companions who were ordered to act as their firing squad.[8]

The mutinies started in Jockey Hollow with the Pennsylvania Regiments who faced another cold winter. Angry over the familiar problems of vague enlistment terms, not enough food or clothing and no pay, they rebelled on New Year's Day, 1781. They killed an officer and wounded two others and started off for Philadelphia to take their case directly to Congress. The Pennsylvanians were persuaded to return and were granted several concessions. Much to the chagrin of General Washington's some were awarded back pay and grievances about clothing and food shortages were settled. Of the 1,500 mutineers 1,300 claimed that they had served over three years and were given honorable discharges based only on their word that they had not enlisted for the duration. The mutiny of the Pennsylvania Brigade was the largest in the history of the United States armed forces.

Encouraged by these gains the New Jersey Brigade rose up in revolt only three weeks later. They had not been paid in over a year and lacked warm clothing. Most suffered from frostbite and scurvy. As in most of the Continental Army many men who had enlisted for "three years or the duration of the war" complained that these terms implied "whichever comes first." They soon learned that would not be going home but were compelled to continue serving for the duration of the war. Neglected by both military authority and the Continental Congress the men felt that they could not endure another winter.

The New Jersey mutiny occurred at Federal Hill in what today is the town of Bloomingdale. The site is on a rocky promontory that overlooks the junctions of the Newark-Pompton Turnpike and Paterson –Hamburg Turnpike, important routes of commerce and communication during the entire war. The location is on Union Avenue only a half mile west of Exit 55, Route I 287.

In January 1781, the 160 New Jersey troops who remained at Federal Hill had little to do except to nurse their grievances. Some of the restless officers insisted that receive back pay and petitioned the New Jersey legislature. The lawmakers graciously complied with their request and used all the money in the New Jersey treasury to be to pay them off.

After appeasing the officers, Commissioners Reverend James Caldwell and Colonel Frederick Frelinghuysen were appointed to investigate the claims of the soldiers. Unfortunately, enlisted men were not informed of this effort. They rebelled on Saturday evening, January 20.

The mutineers choose Sergeant Major George Grant a deserter from the British army as their leader. A few defiant men declared that unless their demands were met they would join the enemy. Most, however, let it be known that they would not become traitors and would resist any attempt by Tories to persuade them to change sides.

The mutineers seized muster rolls and two cannon. Then they marched 20 miles to the town of Chatham where an additional 300 New Jersey troops were camped. The mutineers found few of these men willing to join them. To American officers it appeared that the rebellious soldiers were on their way to Elizabethtown to join the British forces in New York City.

On Monday, January 22, the commissioners met the men and assured them that their grievances would be heard. Colonel Elias Dayton, commander of the New Jersey Line and Colonel Israel Shreve, highly respected officers assured the men of these promises, but insisted that they return to their duty before any discussions could begin. The men agreed and after promising to put themselves under the command of their officers they were all given a general pardon.

On Thursday, January 25, on the way back to Pompton insubordination and disorderly behavior erupted again. This second uprising was led by Sergeant Gilmore and Private Tuttle. Officers were threatened and orders were not obeyed. An officer with a bayonet held to his chest defended himself by knocking down his assailant. By Friday the last of men straggled back from Chatham and all was quiet at Federal Hill during the night.

Washington, headquartered 50 miles away in New Windsor, New York with most of the army feared that insurrections could become wide-spread and cause America to lose the war. He immediately moved his headquarters to Ringwood, New Jersey 30 miles closer to Pompton. He then sent General Robert Howe with

1000 reliable New England troops on a six day march through deep snow to Federal Hill. When they arrived they surrounded the New Jersey huts and trained three cannon on the camp. Howe then ordered the insurgents to parade in ranks without weapons. Some obeyed but others tried to escape and were blocked.

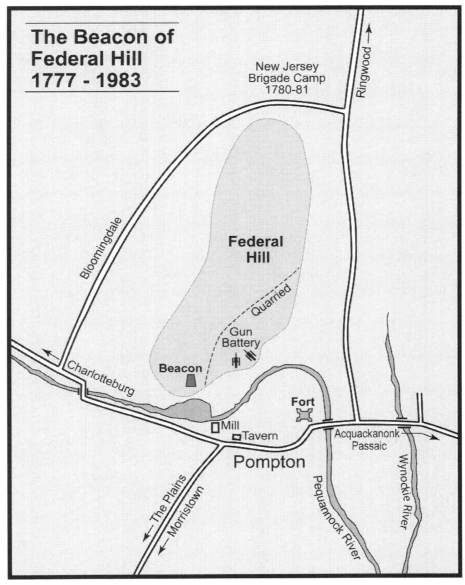

General Howe ordered that three of the guiltiest ring leaders to be tried by courts martial. After a brief hearing they were convicted and sentenced to death.

New Jersey officers insisted that Grant's life be spared since had been forced to take command and had tried to dissuade the men. The guiltiest of their fellow mutineers were selected to be the firing squad.

The starving, barefoot Jersey soldiers were paraded on the snow to witness this punishment. When two had been executed, Grant was pardoned. A reprieve at the last moment was a common occurrence since the condemned soldier would live to fight again and the shock effect on the spectators was achieved. Army Surgeon James Thatcher provided an eyewitness account of the tragic event:

"The first that suffered was a sergeant [Gilmore], an old offender: he was led a few yards distance and placed on his knees; six of the executioners, at the signal given by an officer, fired, three aiming at the head and three at the breast, the other six reserving their fire in order to dispatch the victim, should the first fire fail; it so happened in this instance ; the remaining six then fired, and life was instantly extinguished. The second criminal [Tuttle] was, by the first fire, sent into eternity in an instant. The third [Grant], being less criminal, by the recommendation of his officers, to his unspeakable joy, received a pardon. This tragic scene produced a dreadful shock, and a salutary effect on the minds of the guilty soldiers. Never were men more completely humbled and penitent; tears of sorrow and of joy rushed from their eyes, and each one appeared to congratulate himself that his forfeited life had been spared."

William Nelson, in his classic work on Passaic County, *Paterson and its Environs (Silk City)*, is one of few sources to provide a detailed account of these events. He reported in 1920, "In a thick wood, on the bleak and desolate summit of a rocky knob of the Ramapo Mountains, overlooking the Pompton Lakes Station on the New York, Susquehanna & Western Railroad, the hearty traveler can find two rude piles of weather-beaten field-stones. These are pointed out as marking the lonely, dishonored graves of the two Jersey mutineers."

The graves have not been found since their location was reported by Nelson. Edward J. Lenik one of New Jersey's best known archeologists has searched for the site and suggests that it may not be there at all. Eye witnesses reported the men were buried where they fell. He believes that it is unlikely that the bodies of the mutineers were dragged to the mountain top to be buried in the solidly frozen ground.

Washington ordered the chastened New Jersey Brigade to Morristown a week after the executions where they were quartered in the huts formerly occupied by the Pennsylvanians. They remained here until July 8, 1781 and then marched for Kingsbridge, now Bronx, New York to join the main army. Later that year they marched to the battle of Yorktown under the command of the Marquis de Lafayette where they admirably redeemed themselves. The New Jersey light Infantry took part in the assault and capture of Redoubt Number 10 at Yorktown. The fall of this strong point in the British lines resulted in the final decisive victory of the war.

Command and control continued to be a vexing problem for the American Army as the war continued for over two more years. Defiance rose due to lack of pay and continued service despite the end of hostilities. But there were no large scale mutinies in the Continental Army after the tragic example at Federal Hill. While Washington always sympathized with his unfortunate soldiers he demanded unswerving discipline and loyalty.

Encampment of the New York Line- Winter 1781-1782.

The triumphant 2nd New York Regiment arrived in Pompton on December 11, 1781 after an exhausting 600 mile march from Yorktown, Virginia. They had shown unusual valor during the furious siege that raged around the British stronghold on the tip of the York Peninsula. It was the final decisive battle of the American Revolution.

As British cannon balls rained down on their positions at night The New Yorkers dug trenches close to the front lines. At the climax of the struggle they stood in the thick of the action less than 100 yards from the British Redoubt Number 10. This vital British defense bastion was captured in hand to hand fighting by The New York Light Infantry commanded by Colonel Alexander Hamilton. The fall of the redoubt as well as an adjoining one, captured by the French is regarded as the turning point of the battle. Many people regard this action as the real end of the entire war.[9]

Yorktown fell on October 17, 1781, two days after an intense Franco-American bombardment. Colonel Philip Van Courtlandt's proud 2nd New York Regiment assembled on the field of surrender and witnessed the capitulation of the forces of General Lord Cornwallis. A total mof 7,000 Redcoats and Hessian soldiers laid down their arms and became prisoners. But the war dragged on for the next two years and into its sixth winter.

Despite their fatigue, the morale of the combat weary New York troops soared from the euphoria of the glorious victory at Yorktown. They left the devastated town for Fredericksburg, Virginia on November 3, with 460 prisoners. After turning their captives over to the Virginia Militia they began a grueling 39 day march back to New Jersey for the winter.

It began to snow when they crossed the Delaware River. The "Yorkers" were buffeted by blizzards as they passed through Trenton, Princeton, Bound Brook and Morristown on their way to Pompton. Many of the New York soldiers were returning to this place. They had camped there on the way to Yorktown only three months before.

Surgeon James Thatcher of the Light Infantry Corps, trudged north with the New York troops and described the long march back from Virginia, "On account of the inclemency of the season we have suffered exceedingly from cold, wet and fatigue during our long march but we return in triumph to rejoice in our respective regiments, and enjoy a constant exchange of congratulations with our friends on the glorious and brilliant success of our expedition which closes the campaign."[10]

The encampment of Van Cortlandt's 2nd New York with 2,000 men in the winter of 1781-1782 has been lost in history and few details survive. Their visit is overshadowed by the larger encampments during the previous winter that is described above.

The snow was eight inches deep when The New York Brigade arrived at Pompton on December 11, 1781. The first order of business for the weary soldiers was to build huts for the winter along a gently sloping bank of the Pompton River. The Continental Army had camped on the site and nearby areas during the previous year.

After two weeks of huddling in flimsy snow bound tents the huts neared completion. The first signs of the encroaching winter portended another bitter cold season. Anticipating the worst, the New York huts at Pompton were constructed more substantially than those at Jockey Hollow. Built of heavy logs with roofs of plank or timbers, each had a fireplace and housed eight men. After the deadly winters at Jockey Hollow and Valley Forge, the seasoned Continentals became proficient in building shelters that were more substantial and could be erected in 24 hours. As with previous large encampments, the incessant plundering of civilians for food and the tearing down of their fences for firewood served to diminish the image of the army at Pompton. [11]

In December, most senior officers left the camp for the comforts of their homes as they had done in previous winters. Even Reverend John Gano, the New York Brigade's Chaplain, went home on furlough. He decided that it would be too cold to hold regular church services in the chilling weather.

Several enlisted men also granted furloughs during this period and headed home to the Hudson River Valley, 30 miles away. Others are shown as "on command," out on patrols in the Preakness valley or at the blockhouse above Suffern, which guarded the entrance to Smith's Clove.

Unlike previous winters, the January weather, turned mild, and spirits rose when a supply of new uniforms arrived at the camp although food was still in short supply. The New York troops settled into the warm huts and began to enjoy a degree of comfort which they had not known in years.

Orderly books show that at Pompton many available amenities enhanced the quality of life for the soldiers during that winter. Women camp followers washed clothes for two shillings and even provided their own soap. Barbers, tailors and shoemakers sold their services for modest fees.

In the early spring, as the weather warmed officers began returning from furlough. The pious Reverend Gano was greeted by a soldier who said, *"we have been in want of everything during the winter, clothing, provisions and money, but hardest of all for us was that we did not have the word of God to comfort us."* The conscience stricken clergyman was distraught until he learned that the incorrigible joker was taunting him for having departed for the winter.[12]

On March 30, 1782, George and Martha Washington arrived at Pompton from their winter quarters at Newburgh, New York, 30 miles north. They spent the weekend with the New York Regiment. They stayed in a modest inn, known as the "Yellow Tavern." near the Cantonment that Colonel Van Cortlandt used as his headquarters. The couple departed on Monday morning with an armed escort for their protection. Washington's coach traveled up Smith's Clove through Suffern, Ringwood and Tuxedo, New York, following the Clove Road which is the route of the present Interstate 87 Thruway. They then passed through New Windsor and arrived back at Newburgh by evening.[13]

During the early spring the men of the New York Brigade drilled tirelessly on the flat fields near Pompton to prepare for a general inspection by General Baron Von Steuben. Nine months had passed since he had reviewed the New York troops before the march to Yorktown. The formidable German martinet arrived for the inspection at Pompton on April 5, 1782. He gave the Brigade high praise for its professionalism and efficiency in parade ground maneuvers.

At this time in the war the American armed forces had reached a peak of readiness and proficiency equal to that of Europe's finest armies. Even the French officers admired Von Stueben and openly complemented him for the success of his training and the aptitude of the American troops.

While at Pompton in early August 1782, Washington found time to provide recognition to the soldiers who had made such great sacrifices over the past seven years.[14] He awarded chevrons to those who had served with bravery, fidelity and good conduct. Those chevrons were to be worn on the sleeves of the men's uniforms. One hash mark was given out for each three years of service.

On August 21, 1782 the New York Regiment broke camp at Pompton and marched 25 miles to Haverstraw. They crossed over the Hudson River at Kings Ferry to Verplanck's Point, near Peekskill, New York where they joined the main army for the planned assault on New York City. This was the last military occupation of Pompton during the Revolutionary War.

Washington and the main army massed north of New York City at the end of the summer of 1782. While peace negotiations were taking place a threatening English Army of 12,000 still remained in the city. It was the last stronghold of the British Army in America. Both sides prepared for a final Franco- American assault in the spring. This battle was likely to determine the outcome of the war.

Today, the campsite where the New Yorkers bivouacked in1781 and 1782 is a beautifully landscaped, commemorative park, on the west side of Route 202 (Terhune Road) in Wayne, New Jersey. The road winds along the bank of the Ramapo River, in an area of gracious homes in a wooded setting. This bucolic place belies its proximity to the bustling New York metropolitan area that surrounds it.

Located at the southern edge of the Ramapo Mountains, the park gently descends about 100 yards to the shore of Pompton Lake. At the time of the Revolution the Ramapo River was narrow and only 25 yards across. In 1836, the river was dammed at this point to form the present day mile long Pompton Lake. The ground of the 1781-1782 encampment slopes down to this remarkably pristine body of water.

Those trying to identify the place as a Revolutionary War landmark will find it difficult to locate. The park was the site of the home of the world famous author,

Albert Payson Terhune, who achieved fame with his many books which about dogs which were written between 1900 and 1940.

On ten acres his father had bought in 1860, Terhune built a large Victorian estate house. He named the home and its surrounding acreage, Sunnybank. Much of the land was lost to developers in the 1960s and the house was demolished in 1969. Reference is made in a descriptive pamphlet issued by Wayne's Department of Parks. It refers, in error, to Van Cortlandt's Regiment's being there in 1777-1778.[15]

Terhune found artifacts belonging to an American Revolutionary officer, who was buried with a British officer's sword, Hessian shackles and rusted cannonballs. Nelson reported that on the wooded hillside at the estate remains of huts were unearthed, together with bullets, flints, gunlocks and a sword of British workmanship.

Armed forces occupancy of the Preakness Valley ended with the departure of the 2nd New York Regiment in August, 1782. The location of the valley on the southern approach to Smith's Clove, the main north-south corridor from New Jersey to West Point, ensured that it would continue as a conduit for other military events in the final months of the war.

In June, 1782, Pennsylvania troops mutinied over lack of pay and threatened Congress. The legislature was forced to move from Philadelphia to Princeton. Washington sent a detachment of 1,500 men for their protection from the New Winsor Cantonment near Newburg, New York. This was the final movement of a large body of troops through the Pompton area.

In the summer of that year, Washington passed through here on his way from New Windsor to Philadelphia to confer with Rochambeau. The Generals met to plan how to contain the 12,000 British troops remaining in New York City. If peace discussions in Paris broke down this force might become aggressive and the war could still be lost.

After the peace treaty with Great Britain was signed in April 1783, troops released from New Windsor marched through Pompton to their homes in the southern states. They remained under the command of their officers. Congress feared the hungry soldiers would pillage civilian homes and create havoc throughout the new nation

George and Martha Washington left the Headquarters in Newburgh after the signing of the peace treaty in September 1783 and passed through Pompton on the way to Rocky Hill, New Jersey. The 51 year- old- General gave his farewell address to the army there on November 12.

Off to Yorktown

During 1780 and 1781, British forces were operating on two fronts. At that time the main arena for operations in the war shifted to the southern states. British General Cornwallis captured Savannah, Georgia and followed up with victories at Charleston and Camden, South Carolina. The outnumbered American forces under Generals Nathanial Greene and the Marquis de Lafayette avoided a final decisive battle but weakened the enemy by attrition and forced the Redcoats inland to stretch out their supply lines. This Patriot strategy paid off by inflicting heavy casualties on the invaders with victories at Cowpens, Guilford Courthouse and Kings Mountain in the Carolinas.

As the year 1781 drew on, Sir Henry Clinton, the top English commander, headquartered in New York City, ordered Cornwallis to establish a permanent camp for the winter at a port in the mid Atlantic states. A location at a protected harbor would serve as a fortified naval position and a shelter for the British fleet. Cornwallis selected Yorktown a small port at the tip of the York Peninsula in Virginia. He arrived there during the summer with the southern Army of 8,300 men.

Yorktown seemed to be an ideal location, protected and supplied by the British Fleet and reinforced by sea from New York. If threatened, an army could easily be evacuated by the fleet. The selection of Yorktown as a base was the biggest blunder in the entire eight years of the Revolutionary War. Cornwallis had overlooked the possibility that his army could be entrapped there.

The main forces of both armies in the north had been stalemated for two years around New York City. Here Washington's smaller force of 9,000 was massed above New York City along the Hudson River. Fourteen thousand British troops confronted them in Manhattan. The Redcoats had held this area for six years, since early 1776. During this time they had become well entrenched with a perimeter of defenses north of the city and in Long Island where they were strongly supported by the sympathetic loyalist population. The formidable English fleet could protect from incursion from the sea.

The stakes for both sides at this time could not have been higher. A successful American assault against the mightiest British bastion in America could win the war for the new nation. If defeated, however, the loss of Continental Army would end a futile six year struggle against the world's greatest super power. Losses would be appalling and the dream of independence would be over. For the cautious Sir Henry Clinton, a final defeat for his northern army would end England's massive effort to control its rebellious colony. The adversaries were reluctant to face off.

The dilemma for the Americans began to end when a French Expeditionary Force arrived in Rhode Island a year earlier with 7,800 men and the powerful French Fleet under the command of Count de Grasse. The French joined the Continental Army at Dobbs Ferry, New York in July 1781. Washington now had incredible resources at his disposal. The allied army was now in position to assault the British fortifications at Kingsbridge across the Harlem River from Manhattan and on Long Island. The long awaited siege of New York could begin.

After conferring with Comte de Rochambeau the Commander of the French Land forces Washington settled on another approach. This plan was so daring and fraught with so many risks and uncertainties that it seemed ridiculous. Washington was at first was reluctant to abandon this long carefully planned strategy of an assault on the city from the north, but the availability of the French fleet opened other options. Why not try to trap the southern British Army at Yorktown, rather than sustaining appalling losses and risking defeat by attacking from the north?

The success of a Virginia campaign depended on a series of uncontrollable events that had to occur with precise timing. The allied army would have to travel up to 600 miles in seven weeks to reach the battlefield. When they arrived, there was no certainty that the British would still be there. The French Fleet had to arrive to block the British warships from evacuating or reinforcing Cornwallis. There was no certainty that the French would appear on the coast at the right time. Lafayette, with the southern American army, had to reach the Yorktown from the Carolinas to increase the American forces.

If Sir Henry Clinton had discovered that the allied armies had left New York with only a small force at West Point he could invade north up the Hudson River to Canada and split the states. Separating New England from the other states would effectively end the war. A feint was necessary to convince Clinton that the attack would be through Staten Island.

Even more incredible was the fact that the entire venture depended on a surprise attack. The Franco-American army of 16,500 would have to move south secretly over nine states in its race against time. If the British side learned early that the allied troops were leaving New York the British fleet would sail south to evacuate or strengthen the beleaguered Cornwallis.

To maintain this ruse through New Jersey, landing craft were hauled south, roads were improved and bread ovens built in Chatham. An amphibious attack seemed imminent as Washington moved into position opposite Staten Island. Sir Henry Clinton, noting all of this activity, was convinced that the Allied army would attack there. Secrecy had to be complete so that deserters or Tories in New Jersey would not alert the enemy. Even high-ranking American and French officers were not informed of their final destination until the armies had reached Princeton.

The deception was completely successful and all of the difficult obstacles were miraculously overcome. The victory at Yorktown has come down in history as the successful end of the American Revolution although the peace treaty would not be signed until two years later.

To get to Yorktown the allied army first crossed the Hudson River 15 miles north of Dobbs Ferry at Kings Ferry. It took seven days for the combined forces to cross over the river with supply wagons, cannon and horses. The haggard soldiers of the Continental Army came first with bare feet and clad in the remnants of tattered uniforms or ragged civilian clothes. After three days, the French began arriving. In sharp contrast, they were well disciplined and fully equipped infantry with immaculate white uniforms with blue, pink or green facing.[16]

The allied armies began their epic march to Virginia from Haverstraw, New York where they were massed on the west side of the river along present Route 9W. The road served as a staging area before starting out on August 22 for the long trip south. The main body of the Continental Army moved south through Paramus, Acquackanock (Passaic) and Springfield. The five days that the armies spent moving through New Jersey have been obscured in New Jersey history by the battles at Monmouth, Trenton and Princeton and the Jockey Hollow encampment.[17]

The French Army accompanied by the 2nd New York Regiment and Lamb's Artillery Regiment left one day later and took a more westerly route. General Washington rode with Lamb's Artillery. The 2nd New York guarded 40 bateaux (invasion landing craft) pulled by oxen. They stopped for the first night at Suffern, New York.

An interesting eyewitness account comes from an American who passed through the town. "In that area males are very welcome since we did not meet many of them, where one entered into a house there the first thing they did ask whether one did not want to stay with them they would hide you until the French were gone, one also encountered everywhere Hessian soldiers who had deserted."

Leaving Suffern, New York the western column marched 20 miles to Pompton following present day route 202. Cromot du Bourg, a French officer reported,

"We went from Suffern to Pompton, the road is superb. This is an open and well cultivated country, inhabited by Dutch people who are almost all quite rich. We arrived in good season and the camps being set and the troops arrived, I thought I could do no better than to go to Totawa to see a cataract (the Paterson falls) which is considered to be one of the most curious sights in this part of the country."

American soldiers left few descriptions of the march through New Jersey. For them the terrain, towns and people were familiar and much like the places they lived. Many detailed accounts come from French officers and men. They viewed New Jersey as an exciting wonderland filled with surprises. The French divisions left Suffern for Pompton along present day Route 202.

Baron Ludwig Von Closen a French officer states in his diary, "The Jerseys where we are now abound in all kinds of produce. The inhabitants have kept it neat and have retained their gentle and peaceful customs, and have been very friendly towards the army. It is a land of milk and honey, with game, fish, vegetables poultry etc."[18]

The columns passed through Oakland, New Jersey, crossed the Pompton River and set up camp in Wayne Township on the Newark Pompton Turnpike, north of the Pompton Meeting House and the Reformed church of Pompton Plains. Washington stayed that night nearby at the Schuyler-Colfax House in Wayne. All of these historic buildings have survived the years and are splendidly preserved and well maintained. The next day the French trudged 12 miles south through Pompton Plains, Lincoln Park, Montville, Lake Hiawatha and Hanover Township to Whippany. The location of their campsite in Whippany was on Whippany Road, on what is today Lucent Technologies Park.

Rochambeau's Divisions arose early the following day and tramped 15 miles from Whippany through Morristown and Basking Ridge to Bullion's Tavern (Liberty Corner). The campsite there was just one day away from Bound Brook where they joined the Continental Army. The French Army with 7,000 soldiers with 2,000 horses and 700 draft oxen swarmed down the main streets of hamlets that had fewer than 50 houses and 200 inhabitants as they hurried south through New Jersey.

Young noblemen mounted on splendid steeds with plumed silver helmets commanded the French columns. A unit of 600 Huzzars wore tall black hats and sky-blue jackets adorned with gold loops and braid and bright yellow breeches. The farm families lining the dirt roads along the route were dumbfounded by this spectacle and fascinated by the splendid parade with bands playing and superbly clad soldiers speaking an exotic foreign language. They cheered wildly and offered the soldiers freshly baked bread. [19]

From Bound Brook and Princeton the Franco-American task force departed for Yorktown on the last major battle for both sides on the Continent of North America and one of the most brilliant military campaigns in the history of the world.

THE SCENE TODAY

Spread over about five square miles encompassing several contiguous, residential New Jersey towns, many of the visages of the time remain today at the locations of these revolutionary era events in the Preakness Valley.

Eighteenth century buildings abound and are remarkably well preserved and maintained. Built over by residential development regimental campgrounds can be located on a first-rate map drawn by Washington's Cartographer Robert Erskine Surveyor-General in 1780. This remarkable document depicts campsites, waterways, main roads and even topography.

Physical features such as Great Notch, a gap through the hills, and Two Bridges marking the junction of the Pompton and Ramapo Rivers were well know to the Continental Army. Route 202, the road used by the French columns in 1781 follows exactly the same path. Four rivers: Passaic, Pompton, Pequannock and Ramapo flow through the valley. Historic sites can often be found in relation to these waterways. Existing streets bear original place names. Rifle Camp Road is where 300 men under Major James Barr camped. Cannon Ball Road passes near the Pompton forge.

The main body of the army was camped along what is now Totowa Road. The left wing stretched out from the Laurel Grove Cemetery to Goffle Brook Park in the town of Hawthorne. The "Artillery Park" of General Knox was located on Totowa Road at the crest of the hill that descends to the Dey Mansion. The right wing, occupied by the New Jersey Brigade, extended to Two Bridges. Alarm towers built on the surrounding ridges had barrels of pitch ready to ignite and a canon to sound an alert.

Federal Hill, in the Town of Bloomingdale, rises conspicuously above the Pompton Valley. The Pequannock River meanders along its base. A beacon and a gun battery were placed at the summit to alert Patriots if the Redcoat Army advanced west. In the winter of 1781 this was the scene of the mutiny of the New Jersey troops.

A marker near the hill reads: "Federal Hill Historic Site-The site of the Revolutionary war era Pompton Mutiny which occurred in the cold harsh winter of 1781. It was in the eastern valley overlooking Bloomingdale that an encampment of weary troops mutinied, consequently their two ringleaders were arrested, tried, and executed in the vicinity of what is now known as Union Avenue."

Climbers have frequently visited Federal Hill since it was being described by Nelson in 1920. Curiously, since that time, there is no mention of the graves of the two mutineers. A small WWI ammunitions storage vault and the remains of a German Bund Camp built before WWII. Today, Federal Hill, privately held, has never received designation as a state or federal historic site. The 500 acre wooded tract is environmentally sensitive and is under threat of development.

The ruins of the forge at Pompton still stand above what is today the Hamburg Turnpike in Pompton Lakes. A survey, dated 1726, showed an iron works there used to supply war materials to troops during the French and Indian War. The forge produced and tools, nails and horseshoes for the local inhabitants. A dam was built with a water raceway to the forge. Located against the side of the hill the furnace built of sandstone was fueled by wood from trees on the site.

In 1777, the forge was busily filling orders from General Henry Knox for 7,000 cannonballs weighting from four to 18 pounds and ten tons of grape shot. Heavy demand for ammunition kept the Pompton furnace busy until late in the 1780s. There were several changes in the ownership of the Pompton Lakes Ironworks. The final owner was the Ludlum Steel and Spring Company which operated the forge until 1907. In the 1980s, the remains of the furnace were reinforced with planks to prevent its collapse by roadway blasting in the vicinity.

Eighteenth century homes of Dutch colonists housed the generals of the Continental Army during the encampments. Some of these are house museums and contain interesting artifacts and period furnishings while private owners occupy others.

The most prominent of the early homes is the Dey Mansion. It served as George Washington's headquarters during the two 1780 encampments. This superb example of Georgian architecture was constructed between 1740 and 1750 and is considered the jewel of the early homes in the Preakness Valley. [20]

It was the home of Colonel Teunis Dey who commanded the Bergen County Militia. He offered the easterly side of his large home to Washington. During the General's stay, many key military leaders including Hamilton, Lafayette, Wayne,

Lord Stirling and Benedict Arnold were frequent visitors . Washington's "Life Guard" (personal bodyguards) slept in the rafters. The Commander-in Chief occupied four rooms which included his office.

Purchased by Passaic County from a private owner in 1934, and then restored the brick and stone mansion is now open to the public. The two- acre site includes a formal garden, picnic area, blacksmith shop and a plantation building. The Dey Mansion serves as the meeting place for several Revolutionary War organizations including the New Jersey regiment, Heard's Brigade, a reenactment group. Tours are offered on most days and original artwork, furniture, period antiques and other 18th century items are displayed.

The Yellow Tavern served for many years as an overnight stop for stage coaches. It stood in a grove of trees at the intersection of Hamburg Turnpike and Wanaque Avenue in what today is known as Federal Square. Colonel Van Cortlandt used the building as his headquarters during the encampment of the 2nd New York Regiment in 1782. General Washington and Mrs. Washington visited him in March and stayed four days before returning to Newburgh. It was torn down in the 1890s

A pioneer settler in the area, Arent Schuyler built the Schulyler-Colfax House in 1696. It is the oldest home in Wayne Township. Its front door is on the Hamburg –Paterson Turnpike and the Ramapo river runs behind it. Washington stayed here I from July 1to July 7, 1777 and returned several years later for the baptism of a Schuyler child A family cemetery is located on the north side of the house. It's one of the few colonial homesteads on the east coast of that age that has continually remained in the original family's ownership for eight generations. It was purchased by the town from Jane Colfax in 1993 and now serves as a museum. [21]

Built around 1740, the Mead-Van Duyne house that served as Wayne's headquarters is on Berdan Avenue is owned by Wayne Township and was moved seven miles from its original site on the path of Route 23. Two massive fireplaces flank this cut stone Dutch colonial house which is listed on the National Historic Register. It stands near the Van Riper-Hopper House of 1786 a restored house –museum which includes an archeological laboratory containing thousands of artifacts from local sites. [22]

The Doremus House built in 1760 stands on Route 202 in Totowa. Washington stayed here after the battle of Springfield in June 1780. It was the headquarters of Lord Stirling during the 1780 encampments. At that time there was a hospital in the rear of which all evidence has disappeared. The French army camped in the orchard on the way to Yorktown.[23]

The Demarest House is a 1760 Dutch homestead and was used for several years as a parsonage for the Dutch Reformed Church. Completely dismantled in 1850 it was rebuilt using the same materials in an unsuccessful attempt to rid it of ghosts. Local residents still report seeing strange blue and green lights in the upper windows. It is privately owned.

The Van Saum House is an old Dutch house was built in1769. It served as the Headquarters of the Marquis de Lafayette during July, 1780 encampments. An active spring on the property maintains a constant temperature of 34 degrees year round. It must have refreshed many a soldier and horse. The home is privately owned.[24]

The Pompton-Preakness Valley was the hub of continuous action during the entire duration of the Revolutionary War. Major encampments, the passage of armies and a tragic mutiny all occurred here during the eight year period. It was a picturesque agricultural valley where prosperous famers of Dutch ancestry lived serenely. They were trustworthy people who provided sustenance and respite for weary soldiers recovering from the terrible winter at Jockey Hollow and the long march back from Yorktown. While their lives were impacted by the presence of thousands of soldiers in their midst, their patriotism and hospitality never waned. From this place Washington could keep a watchful eye on the most important British stronghold in New York City. It was here that he received remarkable news that our French allies had arrived. This event would lead to victory for the cause of independence.

Chapter Ten

Forgotten Huts and Bad Memories
Washington's Last Winter,
New Windsor, New York, 1782-1783

At Long Last- the Final Campground

New Windsor is located in the Hudson Highlands, 60 miles above New York City and six miles inland from the river town of Newburgh, New York. Like Valley Forge and Jockey Hollow in New Jersey it was an advantageous location for the Continental Army to spend the last winter of the war. This was still a fragile time for independence. It was a time of anxiety between the last great battle and the final peace. Event there would have a profound influence on the future of the new nation.

After struggling for eight years and coming close to victory and peace, events occurred here that brought the new nation perilously close to losing the war. Threats of mutiny developed on a massive scale at New Windsor. A rebellion by the Army could still defeat the cause of independence or result in the new nation ruled in future years by the military rather than civil authority.

Here George Washington was confronted by the greatest challenge of the entire war, dealing with his own men. The war was not over but the Continental Army wanted to go home. Restless and frustrated American soldiers perceived that their job was over after the decisive victory at Yorktown a year before. However, while peace talks were progressing in Paris strong British forces in New York City and Charlestown were prepared to strike again.

At New Windsor the soldiers continued to be poorly fed and clothed and had not been paid in over a year. The monotony of life during the long winter gave soldiers the time to brood about what would happen to them when peace arrived. Morale of the Army's leadership was worse. The disgruntled officer corps was preparing an insurrection if their demands for pay, promotion and pensions were not approved by a congress that was close to bankruptcy. The civilian population had also lost its sense of urgency after Yorktown and sustaining a peacetime army was for them a low priority.[1]

The British through their loyalist spy network were well aware of the pending disaster. Sir Guy Carleton, the British commander in New York City was certain that the American troops would revolt. He began preparing to absorb them and planned to offer generous bounties to all defecting officers and soldiers. He even prepared a gracious welcome for General Washington.[2]

Settling in for the Last Winter

In October 1782, the Continental Army left Verplanck's Point near Peekskill, New York for New Windsor. They moved north for 15 miles along the east bank of the Hudson River to the Highlands. This short march was miserable due to continuous heavy rains. The army camped that night in the woods without cover. In the morning, they crossed the river at the town of Garrison opposite West Point. The weary troops marched the last few miles over Butter Hill Mountain into a cantonment area at New Windsor.[3] They remained here six months until the end of the war.

Seven thousand troops followed by 280 women and 220 children arrived at New Windsor. Over the next two months, the soldiers worked tirelessly to build 700 huts and transform 1,600 acres of forest and meadows into a livable base camp. The huts in the earlier camps at Valley Forge and Jockey Hollow had been constructed to last only for one winter. New Windsor was built to endure and because of its permanent nature was called a "cantonment."

Surrounded by forests the place could provide building materials and firewood. It was at the junction of main roads and near the Army supply depots at Newburgh and Fishkill, New York. Ridges that form a barrier from the Hudson Highlands north to Massachusetts provide natural protection at the site. From New Windsor the American forces could support West Point and other river fortifications and keep a watchful eye on the British Army that posed a threat from New York City. They could also move south down Smith's Clove a protected valley leading directly to New Jersey. Today it is the path followed by Interstate 87.

The New Windsor Cantonment after the war ended in 1783 was forgotten except for the bitter memories of the nearby civilian population. As in all previous large encampments, hungry soldiers stole livestock and tore down civilian buildings and fences for building materials and firewood. The army devastated woodlands, drained meadows and left piles of refuse. The location of the cantonment was known it became a distant memory and did not receive any public recognition for over sixty years.

Many soldiers that arrived here had been at this place before. In 1775, the first year of the war troops gathered at this place on their way north to invade Canada. In 1777, the battered survivors of the battle of the Twin Forts located 15 miles south had stumbled into the site to regroup under the wounded General James Clinton. [4] The New York Brigade had also camped on the site several times on the way to confront the Indians along the Mohawk River and the frontier in western part of New York State.

Washington set up his headquarters in the Jonathan Hasbrouck house in Newburgh six miles away where he had spent two previous winters. Ranking officers including Major General Horatio Gates, the Commandant of the Cantonment and Major General Henry Knox, Artillery Commander were also quartered in nearby private homes. To keep the troops supplied, under control and ready for a surprise attack, regiments and brigades were placed in the camp in the same positions that they would be in battle.

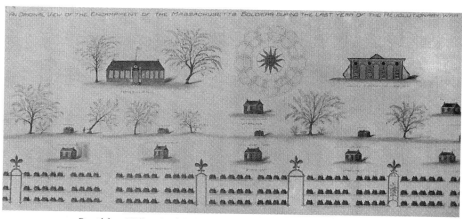

Detail from William Tarbell's sketch of the New Windsor Cantonment showing the huts of the 7th Massachusetts Regiment.

Most of what we know about the physical layout of the Cantonment comes from a large sketch drawn at the time by Private William Tarbell of the 7th Massachusetts Regiment. It has miraculously survived the years passed down through his descendants. The large drawing measures 2 X 6 ½ feet and shows hundreds of huts. Tarbell memorialized his own hut with his initials. Private Tarbell's drawing also shows eight guardhouses. These were built to keep the enemy out, but in practice were used to look out for soldiers and prevent them from wandering out at night to plunder neighborhood farms.

Headquarters activities and most of the huts were centered about Temple Hill. At the center of this raised ground a large all- purpose building was built of logs. It was 110 feet long and 30 feet wide and served as administrative offices, an indoor church and a place for general meetings of officers and was often used as a meeting hall for the Masonic Fraternity.[5] It was named the "The Temple of Virtue" but after uproarious parties took place it was referred to simply as "The Temple". The Temple is prominently displayed in Tarbell's drawing and was the largest structure built by the Continental Army during the Revolutionary War.

West of Temple Hill the troops began constructing an earthwork causeway across a swamp and flooded area. The morass separated less fortunate soldiers from the well nourished Massachusetts Brigade with new uniforms who were quartered near the hill. New York, New Jersey and New Hampshire Regiments with tattered uniforms and gaunt appearance were shunted off to this remote place a mile away where they would be out of the sight of visiting dignitaries. It was also necessary to spread the men out for reasons of sanitation and availability of firewood. The causeway was a 400 yard long embankment constructed of long bundles of branches covered with earth. It was washed out a number of times during the winter but remnants of the structure can still be seen today. The inaccessible site of the western huts lies unmarked and forgotten adjacent to the New York Thruway, Interstate 87.

Each company built two huts of heavy timber with roofs and doors of split-oak slabs. Each hut housed 16 men. These dwellings measured fourteen feet wide and sixteen feet long with a fireplace at each end and one window and were built in two long lines on the slope of a hill. Officers occupied barracks near a central parade ground on Temple Hill. A hospital and a bakery were nearby.[6]

A cemetery has never been found at the Cantonment. Graves may have been purposely concealed so that spies could not count the losses. The dead may have been buried at local cemeteries or at the head of the parade ground near the temple. No remains have ever been discovered at the camp.

New Windsor Cantonment, "Temple of Virtue" - In 1782, General Washington ordered the troops to construct a large building that would serve as a chapel for Sunday services. The resulting Temple of Virtue, as it was known was 110 feet by 30 feet. It was used also for courtsmartial hearings, commissary and quartermaster activities and officers' functions. The original Temple Building was damaged by lightning in June 1783, and was sold. Today's structure is a representation built in 1964-1965.

The Army's Rebellion Threatens the New Nation

At New Windsor the American troops had better housing and were better fed and clothed than at any other time during the war, but conditions were still difficult. Peace negotiations had begun but they proceeded very slowly. Would the insolvent Congress send the soldiers away without resolving the issues of back pay, pensions and land bounties? As the weeks passed and talk of peace was heard more frequently soldiers were becoming increasingly vexed by the question of veterans' benefits.

In October, Washington pleaded with Congress about the lack of funding for the army and the promotions for officers held back to save expenses. He also reported on the punishing manual labor of building huts and the cutting and hauling of firewood.

Marauding, disgruntled soldiers began getting out of control. Desertions increased and civilian property ruthlessly plundered. Only generals and commanding officers were authorized to issue passes to leave the Cantonment. Roll call was taken four times each day, and those found to be absent were singled out for punishment by having their names was read out at the regimental parades. A special patrol formed from each brigade went about capturing foraging men.

In April, Washington personally ordered that apprehended prisoners be punished immediately, on the spot, by up to 100 lashes. Anyone found with stolen property in their possession was "to be tried for their life" by general courts martial. That same week, three men were caught out of the camp at night. They had killed an ox that belonged to a neighboring farmer and were each given 100 lashes.

The men were kept occupied with the hard physical labor of completing the causeway and Temple and the endless need for firewood. Whenever groups of men gathered to talk it was mostly about news of the momentous negotiations at the peace table in Paris. Without the threat of combat, boredom and unrest increased and punishments were casually given out for very minor offenses. An order from a Massachusetts regiment read, *"Any soldier that should be detected at playing at that unsoldierlike game of pitch penny, chopping wood, or throwing any filth or dirty water --- may depend on having the sentence of a court martial carried into execution."*

The tedious day to day routine was occasionally relieved by the need for patrols at the front. To keep the British confined to New York City the front lines stretched for twelve miles, from Kings Ferry east across Westchester County. Soldiers must have welcomed these two week tours of duty to relieve the boredom.

As it became more evident that the end of the war was approaching, tension continued to mount throughout the army about veterans' benefits. As regiments merged officers were declared redundant and forced to retire. They left the army penniless and sold personal property to pay their way home. After listing their grievances, a delegation of officers from the Cantonment went to the Continental Congress in Philadelphia with a petition listing their grievances.[7]

General Mc Dougall, the top ranking officer in the delegation, warned Congress "a mutiny would ensue if no pay was immediately advanced." By March, no action had been taken by the empathetic but helpless Congress. An uprising by the Continental Army led by its officers seemed inevitable and could result in the setting up of martial law in the country to collect back pay. An unauthorized meeting by the officers was called for March 15 at the Temple to reach an agreement for an insurrection. Washington cancelled this meeting but called for a general meeting of all officers.

Frustrated by his failed attempts to obtain any help from Congress, Washington then faced the most perilous time of the Revolution. Appalled by the conduct of the angry and disloyal officers, he officially declined to attend the meeting at the Temple. But to the surprise of everyone he appeared as the meeting began. Many believed he had come to allow himself to be made the military dictator of the fledgling nation.

General Gates, the presiding officer, offered Washington the courtesy of first addressing the mutinous crowd and was stunned when he accepted. Those who had always shown the Commander In Chief respect and deference were now a sea of angry faces. A short speech was his most critical address of the entire war. An eyewitness recalled the event,

> *"When the General took his station at the pulpit in the Temple, he took out a written address from his coat pocket, and his spectacles, with the other hand, from his waistcoat pocket, and then addressed the officers in the following manner: 'Gentlemen you will permit me to put on my spectacles, for I have not only grown gray, but almost blind in the service of my country.' This little address, with the mode and manner of delivering it drew tears from the officers."* [8]

His dramatic message was so effective that after the meeting the insurgent officers wept and unanimously passed a resolution that ensured the army would continue to support Congress and the country. Heading off this uprising was a greater victory for Washington than any he had gained on the battlefield.

The near-mutiny at New Windsor did not seem to extend to the lower ranks. With spring approaching, soldiers planted gardens and cleaned up the filth and rubbish from the winter while anxiously awaiting signals from their rebellious leadership. Despite warnings about gambling they pitched buttons their spare time. Buttons had been substituted for pennies in the impoverished cantonment.

Peace at Last

On March 18, 1783 the news of a possible peace treaty finally arrived from abroad. Washington still fearing that the enemy might strike waited a month to make this news official. For the first time the army could begin to relax their rigorous preparations and training for a spring offensive. On April 15, Congress signed a provisional treaty of peace. The next day, the first official communication sent from the British in New York City was brought to the Cantonment. The message stated that General Guy Carleton acknowledged that articles of peace had been signed in Paris and that he planned to release all American prisoners.

The Commander in Chief issued a proclamation from the Temple on April 19 ordering a cessation of all hostilities and a cease-fire. It was eight years to the day since the first shots of the war had been fired at Lexington and Concord. A proclamation was read and an extra ration of liquor was issued to each man to drink to "perpetual peace, independence and happiness for the United States of America. The thousands soldiers who had enlisted for the duration of the war must have felt especially proud when Washington acknowledged their contribution: *"Those gallant and persevering men who resolved to defend the right of their invaded country so long as the war should continue. For these are the men who ought to be considered as the pride and boast of the American Army."* The announcement was followed by three thunderous huzzas for the "War Men" from the ranks. Chaplain John Gano gave "thanks to almighty God for his mercies" and the choir sang a hymn, accompanied by a regimental band.[9]

A celebration continued through the night accompanied by fireworks, cannon and musket fire. A huge bonfire at the Temple illuminated the mass of celebrants. Local farmers were perhaps the most jubilant of all. The plundering occupants of the Cantonment soon would be leaving and their livestock and fields, now being readied for spring planting, would be safe once more.

After thwarting the attempted mutiny and achieving a cease fire, Washington's problems were not over. While there was a cessation of hostilities, a final peace treaty still had not been signed. The "War Men," who had enlisted for the duration, did not know the difference between a ceasefire and a final declaration of peace. For them, the war was over, and they were eager to get paid off and head for home. Many had expected their release three years before but had faithfully continued to serve. If the "War Men" left, the Continental Army would lose over half its strength.

Added to the apprehension was the fact that 6,000 British prisoners were to be released and would soon rejoin their units. There still was the possibility that without final agreement the strong British force in New York City could abrogate the provisional peace. The cause of independence for the defenseless new nation remained in jeopardy.

Evidence of unrest at the Cantonment is shown by the increase of desertions, drunkenness and the disobedience of orders. The sale of liquor was restricted, and extra guards had to be posted to keep the restless soldiers from roaming out of the camp at night. Little else aside from getting back pay and being released was discussed whenever the men gathered. The accomplishments of the battle-hardened veterans over the past eight years were already fading from public consciousness. The soldiers of the Continental Army were treated with suspicion and regarded as an economic burden during the final days of the war.

The Patriot forces had to be kept intact until the British sailed for home and a formal peace treaty was agreed to. Congress still could not raise the money for the three months back pay that had been promised to the departing troops. In an attempt to appease the disgruntled veterans, they voted to allow them to keep their muskets. This gesture did not cost anything and might buy some short-term goodwill. However, Congress soon regretted this decision when it realized that large groups of armed men suddenly turned loose without funds might terrorize the civilian population.

As a precaution, that regiments would march back to their home states together under the direction of their officers before their release. At the Cantonment men were treated as virtual captives and fed a constant diet of often inedible salted meat and fish. A few promissory notes for overdue pay were offered to the soldiers. Speculators, at great discounts, immediately bought these from the men who needed clothing and money for food on the way home.

Finally, in May, fearful of a riot in the ranks at the Cantonment, Congress passed a resolution furloughing the "War Men." Furloughing meant that soldiers could go home, but had to return if required. In a scheme to save Congress decreed that these furloughed men would be taken off the payroll. With the furlough, came the promise of a discharge with a final treaty of peace. The "War Men" at the Cantonment were officially given the news that their army service would be over on June 8, 1783.

Forgotten Huts

The question of how to pay off the army still was not resolved. Washington was deeply aware of the sensitivity of this issue for his troubled soldiers. Privates were entitled to six and two-thirds dollars each month in devalued Continental currency an amount that would barely cover the cost of a good dinner during most of the war. Regular pay had been discontinued five years before in the summer of 1777.

When released from service, soldiers received a furlough document signed by General Washington showing the number of years they had served. Washington still feared the strong British force in New York City despite the cessation of hostilities and peace negotiations. He was not willing to release the Continental troops unconditionally without the ability to recall them before a final peace treaty. The document read: *The within certificate shall not avail the bearer, as a discharge, until the ratification of the definitive treaty of peace: previous to which time, and until the proclamation of thereof shall be made, he is considered as being on furlough. George Washington.*[10]

To avoid an opportunity for a crisis to develop, the troops were allowed to depart without ceremony or fanfare. Men assembled on the parade ground in front of the Temple for their last time together. Each soldier carried his musket, a few small personal items and a food ration that would last only for a few days. To the familiar sound of fifes and drums, the veterans of the Continental Army left the New Windsor Cantonment on their final march home. Their women and children, many of whom had followed the army for several years, followed each unit. Major Christopher Richmond described the scene in a letter to General Horatio Gates on June 15, 1783, *"The Men for the war have been sent off agreeable to the directions of Congress…without thanks they have been sent-without a farthing of money in the pockets of either officer or soldier- and without provision to help them on their way home- tis shocking, I can say no more about it."*[11]

Over the next two weeks a mass evacuation of the Cantonment occurred. About two-thirds of the army, 4,500 men, left the place. A few days later, Colonel Van Cortlandt of the 2nd New York Regiment returned to New Windsor and sadly observed, *" I found on my return to the cantonment that almost all were gone, as only a few were left and they wanted assistance some unwell and others without means of removal."*[12] Disabled soldiers were probably left behind in the care of a few surgeons. Some New York troops and a regiment of Canadians also remained. They feared a hostile reception when they reached their homes which were still in British occupied territory.

Washington persisted in his efforts to obtain pay for the departing soldiers. He pleaded not only to Congress but also to the governors of each state. Many public officials resented his efforts and regarded his actions as interference and an unsolicited intrusion of advice had already forgotten the contributions of the army. Most men sold their muskets for food on the way home. Congress and state officials, still apprehensive about possible insurrections, insisted that the veterans march home under the control of their officers.

Most of the discontented troops departed peacefully with only one exception. Three hundred troops of the Pennsylvania Line, led by their sergeants, mutinied in Philadelphia. They surrounded the building where Congress was in session and demanded payment of back wages. Washington was distressed by this alarming incident, but soon learned that most of the mutineers were new recruits and not his faithful, veteran "War Men." The rioters dispersed before other troops arrived to suppress the rebellion. Washington reassured the country that the rest of his army had served with fidelity, bravery and patriotism and, *"with perfect good order would retire to their homes, without settlement of their accounts or a farthing of money in their pockets."*

Some of the veterans had to march hundreds of miles to their homes in the southern states and New England. Men bid a last farewell to comrades as they dropped out of the line of march near their homes. Men had served for years together through ordeals that few others have had to face. They may have wept as the familiar sound of the fifes and drums faded in the distance and they remembered their many friends who did not return.

The last troops left New Windsor in the summer of 1783 and the Treaty of Paris officially declared the end of the Revolutionary War on September 3, 1783. Getting rid of the army caused rejoicing among the residents of the area. For many years they had seethed with resentment and remembered ravenous soldiers pilfering livestock and tearing down fences for firewood as well as the forced quartering of officers who were crowded into their modest homes. Payment was eventually made for some of the damage and rent for quarters occupied by the officers, however, the compensation in the form of certificates or paper money was considered hardly worth the trouble of collecting.

The site of the Cantonment forgotten in the decades after the war languished in sleepy irreverence for over 60 years until Samuel W. Eager visited the site in 1846. He was the first historian to record the entire history of Orange County and appreciated the importance of the place. Eager solicited oral history from older people who could recall the events of 1782 and 1783 and the impact on their lives caused by the presence of 7,000 troops in their neighborhood. An aged war veteran was the only person who could positively identify the land where the Temple had stood reported that it was on the farm of Jabez Atwood. The Atwood house was still standing there at the time.[13]

Although recollections of local residents still focused on their annoyance with the voracious soldiers, Eager was able to uncover vital forgotten facts from the eyewitness accounts. These living witnesses proved that Washington's famous address to the rebellious officers was delivered in the Temple and that this structure was actually on the grounds of the Cantonment.

The next visitor was Benjamin J. Lossing in 1851. Lossing was an ambitious historian who traveled throughout the northeast to visit hundreds of places connected to the Revolutionary War. He described each place and the people he met along the way. He then drew sketches of both people and sites. His remarkable book is a treasury of oral history from the diminishing number of people who remembered the war years. Lossing

Lossing's description of the Cantonment 68 years after the army had abandoned it contains a sketch of the entire campground viewed from the west. A meadow and the site of the remote western huts appear in the foreground. Also shown is a drawing of the Temple based on a description provided by Robert Burnet, who was an officer at the Cantonment during 1782. Lossing was also able to identify the foundations of the building, trace the line of the causeway and locate the remains of several huts.

After this visit the Cantonment did not receive attention again until 1883. That year 5,000 people gathered to commemorate the one hundred year anniversary of the end of the war. A fieldstone obelisk was erected and a soldiers' cemetery was claimed to have been located east of the Temple.

Few graves have been found. The relatively low number of deaths at New Windsor, as well as Jockey Hollow, can be attributed to lessons learned at Valley Forge. Shelter, water supply and sanitation were all improved after that hard early winter.

Local historian Russell Headley was next to describe the site of the neglected place in 1896:

> "*The long period that has elapsed with the absence of all care, has sufficed to destroy all of the interesting features of bygone days; but it is still possible to find traces of the Army's occupation and fix accurately the locations of the different divisions. The present causeway by the willows was constructed...by the soldiers while the parade ground carefully formed of flat stone still exists, hidden away in a dense thicket...*
>
> *A few walls of the soldier's dwellings still remain standing in the tangled wildwood and clumps of briars; but the indifference of so many years has borne full fruit, and most of the habitations are leveled with the ground and their sills lie mouldering in the woods.*"

The National Temple Hill Association founded in 1932, had objectives of preserving the site and building a replica of the Temple. The group soon located the remains of one of the original huts. Nathaniel Sacket, a local merchant moved it to nearby Mountainville where it became part of a house purchased it in 1783. The structure was disassembled and moved back to the Cantonment grounds in 1934 and forms the walls of one of the replica huts. A document dated September 2, 1783, at the museum shows that the temple and 137 huts sold at auction for a total of 252 pounds. The equivalent sum of $631 is also noted.

In 1954 construction began on the reproduction of the Temple based on Lossing's description of the building. The stone obelisk erected in 1883 still stands near the Temple. The restored area opened in 1965 and became a New York State Historic Site two years later. A museum and visitor's center houses a small but interesting collection of artifacts found on the grounds. Musket parts found here prove that the Army used a combination of French and British weapons. A three pounder, brass cannon, muzzle-loaded artillery, muskets and other Revolutionary War memorabilia are on display. The highlight of the museum is the original drawing made by William Tarbell in 1782-1783.

A National Purple Heart of Honor wing was added in 2006, dedicated to preserving the stories of Purple Heart recipients through exhibits and taped interviews. While Washington initiated the award in Pompton, New Jersey, it was formally instituted here on August 7, 1782. The Cantonment covered 1,600 acres. The restored area represents only the small central entry area. It was here where the well-fed Massachusetts brigade in fresh new uniforms was on display.

The ruins of the causeway that crosses the swamp to the remote site of the New Jersey, New Hampshire and New York huts disappears mysteriously into a heavily wooded area that is not accessible to visitors. Mike McGurdy, Director of the staff at the Cantonment, explained to me on my first visit there in 2003, that when the army arrived in 1782 it was dryer and more habitable because of a drought. When I told him of my intention to visit the place he explained that since its discovery in the 1920s it had been rarely seen by the public. The location was not publicized to discourage artifact collectors with metal detectors. Convinced that I was a serious historian with a respect for historic preservation he suggested I return during a dry period. He then drew a map to the area west of the swamp and along elevated Interstate 87.

I returned a few months later and started my trek to the abandoned western hut site from Temple Hill. The terrain slopes down from there to a large park on the other side of Route 300. In the park are stone remnants of the outlines of the foundations of the Massachusetts huts and a more recent commemorative bell tower. There are two replica huts at the bottom of the slope. In the rear of these structures are the ruins of the causeway which lead into the dense foliage.

I followed McGurdy's hand drawn sketch and Weed's 1930 map based on the original drawn by Simeon DeWitt cartographer for the army in 1783. Weed shows that the western hut foundations were there in 1930. The maps showed that the campground lies between the swamp and Revolutionary Road, now Route 300, and Interstate 87 which had been cut through in 1947.

I tried to follow the remnants of the causeway, but soon was ankle deep in the mud of the impassible swamp. I met with the same problem that the army had found there over two centuries before. After walking west about a half mile, and passing through an industrial park I entered a trackless wilderness that in the wet weather could not be penetrated. After hiking several hundred yards through tall marsh grass and thick woods I heard the sound of traffic and realized that I was getting nearer to Interstate 87. Finally I reached a stone wall running parallel and below the elevated highway.

My search was over. Strewn along the wall in several places were a number of obvious hut foundations. Two parallel walls ran in front of the structures marking off a thoroughfare about 25 feet wide. I found a weather beaten, half buried sign, laying face down. It read, "State Historic Site, No Digging." A park staff member, the last visitor to the inaccessible and forgotten place, likely placed it there many years ago by The traffic speeding by on the Interstate, only 50 feet away was completely oblivious to the proximity of this hallowed historic place where the tattered soldiers bided time awaiting word of peace. It was from here that they marched home for the final time.

I attempted to return by taking a shortcut directly back to Temple Hill. Although it had not rained in weeks I was stopped again by swamp mud and pools of open water.

Today the New Windsor Cantonment is a delightful state park. Easily found off the Interstate 87 (New York Thruway), Exit 17 a few miles from Newburgh, New York. The grounds are open from mid-April through October. Military reenactments take place on the parade ground. A staff of knowledgeable docents in period dress and uniforms demonstrate musket firing, military medicine and surgery, blacksmithing and camp life.

In April 2010, I was invited by the Brigade of the American Revolution to be the speaker at a weekend of military battle reenactments, firing demonstrations and period activities. The talk focused on my book, "The War Man," the true story of a soldier who was at the Cantonment and served during the entire war. I delivered my talk in the Temple and had the honor to speak from the exact spot where General Washington addressed his rebellious officers in 1783.

APPENDIX I.

Continental Army Rank Insignia - Revolutionary War

When the war began in 1775, there were not enough uniforms in the Continental Army to distinguish the officers from the enlisted men. The Continental Congress tried to standardize a uniform of brown, but lacked authority and lacked the funds required. Officers wore remnants of old military dress; with no thought given to similarity of color. The enlisted men wore their work or hunting clothes. Many had no coat or shoes and wore handkerchiefs for hats.

When Gen. George Washington took command of the Army at Cambridge that year, he introduced badges so that rank would be indentified at sight. Generals and their aides wore sashes. Field grade and company officers wore cockades in their hats and non-commissioned officers were identified by epalettes.

General Washington standardized uniforms and insignia by issuing General Orders from his New Jersey headquarters in Morristown, New Jersey on June 18, 1780. At the time the Continental Army expected to join forces with French troops soon and he wanted the Americans to have an acceptable appearance. All, except generals, were to wear the color uniform of their regiment or corps. "All officers as will warrant as commissioned, to wear a cockade and side arms, either a sword or a genteel bayonet." Officer's epaulettes were silver for infantry and cavalry and gold for artillery. General Orders specified the following insignia for officers:

Commander in Chief- Three silver stars on a gold epaulette.

Major General- Two silver stars on a gold epaulette with black and white feathers in hat

Brigadier general-One silver star on a gold epaulette and white feather in hat.

Colonel- Two epaulettes, one on each shoulder.

Lieutenant Colonel- Two epaulettes, one on each shoulder.

Major-Two epaulettes, one on each shoulder.

Captain- one epaulette on right shoulder.

Subaltern (Lieutenants and Ensigns) - one epaulette on left shoulder.

General Orders issued from Newburgh New York on May 14, 1782 specified the following insignia for Non-commissioned officers:

Sergeant- red epaulette on right shoulder.

Corporal- green epaulette on right shoulder

APPENDIX II.

Pay of the Continental Army and Exchange Rates

This monthly payments schedule was issued by the Continental Congress on May 27, 1778. While pay was computed in Continental dollars, payment was often made in pounds of an equivalent amount that were paid out in specie (gold and silver coins or pieces of eight.) Odd amounts were provided in shillings, equivalent to 20 to a pound. Inflation, rampant throughout the war, made pay rates confusing to calculate. A conversion rate of about 2.5 dollars per pound was often used by many Continental Army Regiments from 1777 to 1782. There were few paydays during the entire war. In December, 1776 Congress provided that militia joining forces with the regular army be paid equally.

	Pay per mo.	Subsistence per mo.
Colonel-	$75	$50
Lieutenant Colonel-	$60	$40
Major	$50	$30
Captain	$40	$20
Lieutenant	$26 2/3	$10
Ensign	$20	$10
Sergeant-	$10	--
Drummers and fifers	$7 1/3	--
Corporal	$7 1/3	--
Private-	$6 2/3	

Appendix III.

Company Muster Roll, 1st New Jersey Regiment, Jockey Hollow,

January 21, 1780

Appendix IV.

Orderly Book, Sullivan-Clinton Campaign, Tioga, New York,
August 16, 1779

Appendix V.

Return of Sick and Wounded in Military Hospitals, March 1, 1780.

A General Return of the Sick and Wounded in the Military Hospitals belonging to the Army commanded by his Excellency General George Washington, from Feb. 2 to March 1. 1780.

Places where military hospitals Are open	Admitted during the Month	Discharged during the Month	Deserted during the Month	Dead during the Month	Remaining in hospital March 1.					
					Convalesant	Wounded	Sick of Acute Diseases	Sick of Chronic diseases	Venereal	Total
Yellow Springs	21	10	-	1	5	4	-	45	1	55
Philadelphia	12	69	-	-	8	-	-	1	-	9
Danbury	-	-	-	-	17	6	3	4	-	30
Trenton	1	2	-	-	3	1	6	1	1	12
Pluckemin	32	32	3	2	12	1	8	40	29	90
Baskinridge	15	10	-	3	5	2	14	10	2	33
Fishkill	-	-	-	-	30	2	6	47	10	95
Albany	4	3	3	1	6	8	13	44	15	86
Camp (Morristown)	-	-	-	-	128	9	123	246	57	563
	85	127	6	7	214	33	172	439	115	973

Total From the Eastern Hospitals under the care of Dr. Turner at Danbury and Boston-no returns to the Director General have come for several months for several months.

W. Brown

Appendix VI.

Depreciation Schedule–Continental Bills of Credit (Dollars), 1777-1780

Depreciation Schedule –Continental Bills of Credit specified by the New York Congress in 1781. Number of Continental bills required to equal $100 in specie (coined money) on the dates shown.

1777

Sept. 1,	100
Oct. 1,	109
Nov. 1,	121
Dec. 1,	133

1778

Jan. 1,	146
Feb. 1,	160
Mar. 1,	175
Apr. 1,	203
May 1,	230
June 1,	265
July 1,	303
Aug. 1,	348
Sept. 1,	400
Oct. 1,	464
Nov. 1,	545
Dec. 1,	634

1779

Jan. 1,	742
Feb. 1,	1868
Mar. 1,	1000
Apr. 1,	1104
May 1,	1219
June 1,	1344
July 1,	1346
Aug. 1,	1631
Sept. 1,	1800
Oct. 1,	2032
Nov. 1,	2340
Dec. 1,	2597

1780

Jan. 1,	2932
Feb. 1,	3333
Mar. 1,	4000

In 1775, the Continental Congress began issuing paper money known as Continental currency, or Continentals. Continental currency was denominated in dollars from 1/6 of a dollar to $80, Continental currency depreciated badly during the war, giving rise to the famous phrase "not worth a continental". Most people believe that the American bills depreciated because people lost confidence in them since they were not backed by tangible assets, but the problem was that too many were issued. The British also waged economic warfare by counterfeiting Continentals on a large scale. By May 1781, Continentals had become so worthless that they ceased to circulate as money. Continental bills are now very rare, and are sought after by collectors.

Notes

Chapter One

1. Smith Justin H., *Our struggle for the Fourteenth Colony*, New York: G. P. Putnam and sons, 1907 pg 42.

2. The Quebec Act of June 22, 1774, Great Britain, The statutes at large ... [from 1225 to 1867] Cambridge:: Printed by Benthem for C. Bathhurst, London, 1762-1869

3. Wright Robert K., *The Continental Army*, Washington, D.C: United States Army, Center of Military History, 1983, 25.
   4. Muster Roll, Captain Robert Johnston's Company at Clarkstown, New York, August 4, 1775, National Archives.

5. Muster Roll, Captain Robert Johnston's company at Fort Ticonderoga, October 3, 1775, National Archives.

6. Philip Schuyler to George Washington, July 18, 1775, Philip Schuyler Papers, New York Public Library.

7. Dupuy, Earnest and Dupuy, Trevor, *The Compact History of the Revolutionary War*, Portland, Or: Hawthrone Books Inc, 1963, 68.

8. Philip Schuyler Papers, New York Public Library.

9. *"Journal of Major Henry Livingston of the 3rd New York Continental Line"* Pennsylvania Magazine of history and biography, 1898. 9-33

   Livingston's Journal provides a vivid day-by-day account the actions of the New York troops from the time they departed from Albany in September until they reached Montreal after the fighting at Fort St. Johns.

10. Major Thomas Hobby and Captain Matthew Mead were with the Waterbury 5th Connecticut Regiment. Both were wounded in the first attack on Fort St. Johns on September 6, 1775.

11. The Royal Savage was captured by the American force when Fort St. Johns fell but afterward ran aground during the battle of Valcour island on October 1776. She was burned to prevent her from falling into British hands.

12. Philip Schuyler to the Continental congress, September 19, 1775. Schuyler Papers, New York Public Library.

13 Colonel Charles Preston commanded the 26th Cameron Regiment and had been Montgomery's superior officer before the war. He was taken prisoner at the surrender of Fort St. Johns and held prisoner of war in Connecticut.

14. Colonel Rudolphus Ritzema commanded the 3rd New York Regiment at the Battle of Fort St.Johns and continued on to the failed siege of Quebec. He deserted during the battle of White Plains in November 1776 and joined the British Army. He then led Loyalist companies for the next month and then disappears from military service.

15. Richard Montgomery to Janet Montgomery, September 5, 1775, *Janet Montgomery Papers*, Edward Livingston Collection, Princeton University Library.

Janet Montgomery, *"Reminiscences"*, ed. John Ross Delafield, Dutchess County Society Yearbook, (1930). An unpublished manuscript of the document is at the New York Historical Society.

16. Philip Schuyler to the Continental Congress, September 29, 1775. Schuyler Papers, New York Public Library.

17. Richard Montgomery to Janet Montgomery, October 6, 1775. *Janet Montgomery Papers*, Edward Livingston Collection, Princeton University Library.

18. See these detailed accounts of the battle at Fort St. Johns for vivid and comprehensive coverage of the engagement:

"Journal of Major Henry Livingston of the 3rd New York Continental Line" Pennsylvania Magazine of history and biography, 1898. 9-33

Livingston's Journal provides the best daily account of the action and follows the New York troops from Albany in September, 1775 until they reached Montreal after the fighting at Fort St. Johns in November

Bird, Harrison, *Attack on Quebec, the American Invasion of Canada, 1775*. Oxford University Press. , 1968.

Gabriel, Michael, *Major General Richard Montgomery*. Madison, N.J: Fairleigh Dickinson University Press.2002.

Lanctot, Gustave ,*Canada and the American Revolution 1774–1783*, Harvard University Press, 1967.

Morrissey, Brendan. *Quebec 1775, The American Invasion of Canada*, Oxford, U.K: Osprey Publishing. 2003.

19. Philip Schulyer to George Washington, November 6, 1775, Schulyer Papers, New York Public Library.

20. Richard Montgomery to Robert Livingston, October 5, 1775, Robert R. Livingston Papers, New York Public Library.

21. Philip Schulyer to David Wooster, October, 19, 1775, Philip Schulyer Papers, New York Public Library.

22. *Journal of Major Henry Livingston, New York Continental Line*, Pennsylvania Magazine of History and Biography, April 1898, 22.

23. Chipman, Daniel, *Memoir of Colonel Seth Warner*, Middlebury, Vt., L.W. Clark, 1848.

24. Richard Montgomery to Philip Schulyer, December 5, 1775, Philip Schulyer Papers, New York Public Library.

25. Lefkowitz, Arthur, S., *Benedict Arnold's Army, The 1775 Invasion of Canada During the Revolutionary War*, El Dorado Hills, Ca. Savas Beatie, 2008.

26. Roberts, Kenneth R., *March to Quebec*, Rockport, Maine, Down East Books, 1980.

27. Musee du Fort St. Jean Museum, Official Site/History. Saint-Jean-sur Richelieu, Quebec, Canada.

28. Fort Lennox, National Historic Site of Canada, Isle Aux Noix, Parks, Canada, www. pc. gc. ca.

Chapter Two

1. Primary Sources:

Clinton, George, *Public Papers of George Clinton*, Albany, NY: Ed. by Hugh Hastings, State of New York, 1900.

Chastellux, Marquis de, *Travels in North America in the years 1780, 1781 and 1782,* Chapel Hill, N.C: University of North Carolina Press, 1963.

Auburey, Thomas, Travels through the Interior Parts of America, Boston and New York: Hough Mifflin Co., 1923.

Lossing, Benson, *Pictorial Field Book of the Revolution*. Vol. I. 1850. chapter xxix.

National Register of Historic Places-Nomination and Approval-Fishkill Supply Depot. To William Murtagh, Keeper of the National Register, National Park Service, Washington, D.C., August 29, 1973

Maps:

Erskine Military Map of 1778, New York Historical Society Quarter Bulletin, January 1923, 128,129.

Huey, P. R., Map Of Fishkill Site, National Register of Historic Places, 1968. modified 2006 by Byster, M.

Anne Van Wyck, Map of 1912, Van Wyck, Anne, The Descendants of Cornelius Van Wyck, New York: 1923, 67

Shows location of unmarked gravesite where possibly thousands of Continental soldiers lie within the boundary of the Fishkill Supply Depot

Secondary Sources:

Goring, Richard, *The Fishkill Supply Depot and Encampment During the Years 1776-1778*, Waterford, N.Y: New York State Office of Parks and Recreation, Division of Historic preservation, December, 1975.

Bielinski, Stephan, *The Fishkill Supply Depot*, Albany, N.Y: New York State Education Departments, State Museum, 1971.

2. Fishkill Historical Society, www.fishkillhistoricalsociety.org

3. Town of Fishkill, Town History- Historic Sights, Willa, Skinner, Town Historian, 2004.

   Boatner, Mark M., Landmarks of the Revolution, 235.

4. New York Congress. E. M. Rutterbur, ed. Catalog of manuscripts and Relics in Washington's headquarters Museum, Newburgh N. Y: Newburgh: Journal printing House 1890, 98.

5. Koke, Richard J. and Carr, William H., *Twin Forts of the Popolopen, Forts Clinton and Montgomery, New York, 1775-1777.*

6. Auburey, 153.

7. Chastellux, 86,87.

8. Deyo, Ernst K. Historical papers of the Historical Society of Newburgh Bay, 1906, XIII, 96

9. Boatner, 236.

10. MacCracken, Henry Noble. *Old Duchess Forever!* New York: Hastings House, 1956.

    Smith, James H. *History of Duchess County, New York*, Syracuse, New York: 1882. Reprinted: Interlaken, New York: Heart of the Lakes Publishing.

11. Auburey, Vol. II 153,154.

12. Brinkerhoff, Van Wyck, *Historical Sketch and Directory of the Town of Fishkill*, Fishkill landing, N.Y: Dean and Spaight, Fishkill Standard Office, 1856, 75-83.

13. Clinton Papers, 414.

14. Muster Rolls, 5th New York Regiment, June, July, August, 1778.

15. Fitzpatrick, John Clement, *The spirit of the American Revolution; New Light from some of the Original Sources of American History-The Invalid Regiment and its Colonel*, Boston and New York: Houghton Mifflin co., 1924.

16. Guide to the Van Wyck Homestead Museum, Fishkill Historic Society, P.O. Box 133, Fishkill, New York, 12524.

Defending What's Left of a Revolutionary Site" by Fernanda Santos, New York Times (Late Edition - East Coast), New York, N.Y., June 18, 2006, page 14.

17. Clinton Papers, Vol. 1. 47, 93,420.

18. Reynolds, Helen Wilkinson, *Dutch houses in the Hudson Valley Before 1776*, Dover Publications, 1965, 352.

19. Clinton Papers, Vol. 1. 359, 391.

20. John Milner Associates, Inc. 535 North Church St. West Chester, Pa. 19380.

21. Hasbrouck Frank. Ed. *The History of Dutchess County*, Poughkeepsie, N.Y: S.A. Mathieu, 1909, 319-320.

   Farrell, Mara, and Sandy, Bill, RPA *The Fishkill Supply Depot*, The Dutchess Historian, A publication of the Dutchess Historical Society, Vol. XXXVIII, Spring, 2010, 3,4.

22. Farrell and Sandy.

23. Friends of the Fishkill Supply Depot is a non-profit organization advocating the preservation, study, and proper interpretation of the Fishkill Supply Depot and Encampment. Friends of the Fishkill Supply Depot, Inc. PO Box 311 Fishkill, NY12524,> info@fishkillsupplydepot.org

Chapter Three

1. Johnston, George. *History of Cecil County, Maryland: and the early settlements around the head of Chesapeake Bay and on the Delaware River: with sketches of some of the old families of Cecil County.* Baltimore, Maryland: Regional Publishing Company, 1967.

2. The stars and stripes were officially adopted by Congress on June 14, 1777. Some New Jersey historians believe that the new flag was flown at the Battle of the Short Hills on June 26, 1777. There is no evidence to support this in the any contemporary accounts of that engagement.

3. Anderson Troyer S., *The Command of the Howe Brothers During the American Revolution*, New York and London: Oxford University press, 1936.

4. Montresor, John. *Journal of John Montresor, Collections of the New York Historical Society for the Year 1881*, New York, N.Y: 1881. 428-431.

   Montresor was appointed Chief Engineer in America and captain in late 1775. He was present at the Battle of Long Island and at the execution of Nathan Hale in 1776. In 1777 he was involved in the military campaigns in New Jersey and present at the action at the Battle of the Short Hills.

5. Montresor, 441.

6.. Johnson, 326.

7. Johnson, 318.

8. Detweiler Frederic C., *War in the Countryside, The Battle and Plunder of the Short Hills-New Jersey, June, 1777,* Plainfield, N.J: Interstate Printing Co., 1977.

9. Montresor, 442-442.

10. Andre John, *Journal of Major John Andre,* Boston, Mass: Ed. Henry Cabot Lodge. 1903

    Montresor, 412.

11. Anderson, 335.

12.. Anderson, 328.

13. Marker at site of Aiken's Tavern reads, "Quarters of General William Howe, September 3 to 8, 1777. The tavern was then owned by Matthew Aiken, who laid out this village and named it Aikentown. It was later renamed for Glasgow in Scotland. Location: DE 896, east side, near US 40, at Glasgow near Methodist Episcopal Church.

14. Eye witness account of Lieut. Henry Strike, 10th Regiment of Foot, Light Infantry, Maryland Historical Journal 1964

15. Meiners Jorm, *"The Unknown Marburger" Another Portrait of Jaeger Colonel Ludwig on Wurmb is Found*, Scotland, Pa: Journal of Johannes

Schwelm Historical Assn. 2011.

16. Bauermeister Carl Leopold, *Journal, Major Carl Leopold Bauermeister, Adjutant General of the Hessian Forces in America 1776-1784*, New Brunswick N.J: translated and annotated by Bernard Uhlendorf, Rutgers University Press, 1957.

17. Ewald Joseph, *Captain Joseph Ewald, Diary of the American War: A Hessian Journal*, New Haven: translated and edited by Joseph Tostin, Yale University Press, 1979, 77.

   Johann Ewald served with distinction through the Revolutionary War as a Captain in the Hessian jaegers. He arrived in this country with the second Hessian division before the Battle of White Plains, in 1776.

18. Burgoyne Bruce E., *Captain Heinrich Philipp von Feilitsch. Bayreuth Jaeger Company , Diary if two Ansbach Jaegers*, Westminster, Md: Heritage Books, 1998.

19 Extract from the journal of Sergeant Thomas Sullivan of H.M. Forty-Ninth Regiment of Foot, 3 September, 1777, Philadelphia, Pa: Magazine of History and Biography, Vol. 31, Historical Society of Pennsylvania, 1907, 410

20. Fitzpartrick John C., *The \Writings of George Washington from Original Manuscript Sources, 1745-1799*, Washington: U.S. Gov't Printing Office, September 3, 1777.

21. Wilson, Emerson W. *Hale Byrnes-Boyce House, the Story behind a Delaware Jewel*, Compiled by the Delaware Society for the Preservation of Antiquities, 1999, 20 pages

22. Johnston Henry P., *The Yorktown Campaign and the Surrender of Cornwallis*, 1781, New York: Harper & Brothers, 1881. 32.

   Anderson, 342.

23. The Washington–Rochambeau Revolutionary Route (W3R) is a 680-mile long series of encampments and roads used by U.S. Continental Army troops under George Washington and French troops under Jean-Baptiste de Rochambeau, during their march from Newport, Rhode Island to Yorktown, Virginia in 1781. The route was designated a National Historic Trail in 2009. Interpretive literature, signs, and exhibits

describe the key role of French diplomatic, military, and economic aid to the United States during the Revolutionary War.

24. Thatcher James, M.D., *Military Journal of the American Revolution, 1775-1783*, Boston Mass: Cottens and Barnard, 1827, 270.

25. Thatcher, 272.

26. Lee Kenneth, *The French Forces in America*, 1780-1783, Westport, Conn: Greenwood Press Inc., 1978.

27. Berdan Marshal S., *Elkton, Marry-Land*, Washington Post, February 13, 2002.

28. Historical Society of Cecil County, 135 East Main Street, Elkton, Md.

28. *Oldfields Point, Landmark of the Revolution*, Elkton Md: Cecil Whig, January 22, 1937.

29. Pencader Heritage Museum, Cooch –Dayett mill Complex, 2029 Sunset lake Road, Newark Delaware, www. Pencader Heritage.org

30. Cooch, Francis A., *Little Known History of Newark, Delaware and its Environs*. Newark , Del: The Press of Kells, 1936

Edward W. Cooch, Sr., *History of Iron Hill, The Folks of Welsh Tract*. Pencader Heritage Association[undated].

31. Brown, Robin, *Study Shows Cooch's Bridge Fight Was More Than Minor Skirmish*, Wilmington Del: News Journal, September 9, 2008.

Chapter Four

1. Several detailed eyewitness accounts of the battle have survived. I have relied on these primary sources and documents to describe the combat action. Curiously, the same incidents are often that occurred during intense fighting were related by witnesses on both sides and version differ widely depending on which side is telling the story. The most comprehensive reports and maps are from British and Hessian officers.

Andre, John. *John Andre's Journal, 1777-1778*. Boston, Mass: Bibliophile Society, 1904.

An interesting and well written work by one of the war's most well-known figures.

Muenchhausen, Friedrich Von. *At General Howe's side 1776-1778.* Monmouth Beach, N. J: Kipping and Smith eds. 1974. 19.

First hand accounts of Howe's Aide at the Short Hills.

Howe, William, *The Narrative of lieutenant General Sir William Howe in a Committee of the House of Commons on the 29th of April 1779 relative to his conduct during his late command of the Kings Troops of North America.* London, England: H. Baldwin, 1780.

Montresor, John. *Journal of John Montresor, Collections of the New York Historical Society for the Year 1881,* New York, N.Y: 1881.

Robertson, Archibald, *Archibald Robertson: His Diaries and Sketches in America, 1762-1780,* New York: ed. Harry Miller Lydenberg, Collections of New York Public Library, Arno Press, 1971, 139.

Archibald Robertson, was a lieutenant in the Royal Engineers. He served in America from 1775 to 1780 and during his service he faithfully kept a diary and drew numerous scenes in his sketchbooks.

Tustin, Joseph P. (trans, ed) (1979). *Johann Ewald, Diary of the American War: a Hessian Journal.* New Haven, CT: Yale University Press. 69

Buttner, Johann Carl, *The Adventures of Johann Carl Buttner In the American Revolution,* NewYork: Cremenz, 1828, Reprint by Chas, Fred Heartman. 44.

Buttner was a new recruit in Von Ottendorffs' Corps of Pennsylvania-Dutch Volunteers. He was captured in the fighting at the Short Hills and personally interrogated by Cornwallis. He agreed to enlist in the Hessian Grenadiers in exchange for his freedom. His narrative is unusually candid and compelling.

2. Detwiller, Frederic C. *War in the Countryside: The Battle and Plunder of the Short Hills New Jersey, June, 1977,* Plainfield, N.J: Interstate Printing Corporation, 1977. 14.

This 49 page work is the most comprehensive narration and interpretation of the battle that I have found. It has copious references notes, original maps and illustrations. Detwiller is an architectural historian who grew up in Scotch Plains amid the lore of the conflict. This effort was his contribution to the bicentennial events in the state.

3. Major Robert Erskind was commissioned as the official surveyor for the American Army in 1777. a "rock" connected to Middlebrook by a trail along the crest of the first ridge of the Watchung mountains is plainly visible on two of his maps.

4. "The Stars and Stripes" was officially adopted by Congress on June 14, 1777 and while the action at the Short Hills provided the first opportunity for the flag to be flown in combat there is no evidence of its appearance there. More likely that is was first displayed10 weeks later on September 3, in Delaware at the Battle of Cooch's Bridge.

5. New Jersey Archives, State Library, Trenton, N.J. The extensive plundering of the countryside by both British and American troops before and after the battle led to a large number of damage claims from civilians. An exact description of the property and often the dates when the damages occurred appears in these inventories. Several are dated the week of the battle. An examination of these records provides a representative picture of the contents of the farmhouses and shops and craftsmen's tool of the era.

6. Davis, T. E. *The Battle of Bound Brook,* Bound brook, N.J: The Washington Campground Association,1981.

7. Vermeule, Cornelius, *Revolutionary Campground at Plainfield, an address delivered before the Continental Chapter, Daughters of the American Revolution,* Plainfield N.J: January 9, 1923.

This remarkable work, by a descendant of the Vermeule, family provides a complete account of activities at the farm that was turned into a fort in 1776 in today's North Plainfield,   Details of regimental and troop movements in the area focuses on the New Jersey militia units. The Vermeule Mansion built in 1803 now stands on the site three miles from the Short Hills on an eight acre Green Acres Park

8. John Adams to Abigail Adams, June 18,1777, *Letters of Delegates to Congress,1774-1779,*Washington: Library of Congress 1976-1996, vol. 7. 207.

9. The Ferguson Rifle was the first breech loading rifle used by an organized

military force. It fired six to ten rounds per minute which was an exceptionally high rate of fire for its day. Only two hundred of the weapons were made by four British firms. It was designed by Major Patrick Ferguson and issued to his rifle corps in 1776. His unit served with Howe's Army in North America. While far ahead of its time the superior fire power of the gun was not appreciated. Tactics of the time favored manpower over firepower and were better suited to the standard muzzleloader. Rifle units were singled out as priority targets and took high casualties especially among officers. The rifles were difficult and expensive to produce and easily broke down in combat. After limited use at Brandywine later in the year their use was discontinued.

10. Colonel Armand-Tuffin arrived from France in 1776 and began recruiting volunteers for the Continental army and paid most of them from his own pocket. Washington appointed him Colonel then General in June 1778. He was at the battles of New York, Monmouth, Short Hills, Brandywine, Whitemarsh and the Siege of Yorktown.

11. Major-General John Vaughan served in the British Army from 1776 until 1779. He led the grenadiers at the Battle of Long Island, and was wounded in the thigh; he commanded a column in the Battle of Short Hills a column during the successful assault on Fort Clinton and Fort Montgomery in October, 1777. In 1779 he returned to England but was immediately appointed Commander-in-Chief in the Leeward Islands.

12. Rawson, Marion Nicholl, *Under the Blue Hills: Scotch Plains New Jersey,* The Historical Society of Scotch Plains and Fanwood in cooperation with the Scotch Plains American Revolution Bicentennial Commission,1974.

13. Howe, William, *Narrative before the House of Commons. 29 April.' 1779*, 15.

14. *Plan d l' Affair de Westfield & du Camp de Raway, 1777 Geography and Map Division Library of Congress.*

This unsigned map has been ascribed to Lieutenant Friedrich von Wangenehim of the Hessian Jaeger Corps a unit that was active in the battle. The map covers about 15 square miles and shows the roads on which the British forces marched, troop positions, locations of British and American officers, topographical features and British campsites after the battle.

15. Ricord, F. W., *History of Union County, New Jersey*. Bowie, Md: Heritage Books, 2007.

16. Muenchhausen, 20.17.

McGuire, Thomas J (2006), *The Philadelphia Campaign, Vol. I: Brandywine and the Fall of Philadelphia*. Mechanicsburg, PA: Stackpole Books. 54-56.

Chapter Five

1. Koke, Richard J. and Carr, William H., *Twin Forts of the Popolopen, Forts Clinton and Montgomery, New York, 1775-1777,* Bear Mountain Trailside Museum, Bear Mountain, N.Y: Published by the Commissioners of the Palisades Interstate Park an the American Scenic and Historic Preservation Society, July 1937.

This extraordinary work is the most comprehensive document written to date on the history of the Twin Forts. It covers selection of the site and design and construction of the forts. A vivid account of events leading to the battle is provided with a detailed description of the battle and subsequent abandonment and rediscovery of the site. Materials are drawn from primary sources and period and period maps of the fortifications are included.

2. Charles I. Fisher, ed., *The Most Advantageous Situation in the Highlands: An Archeological Study of Fort Montgomery State Historic Site,* The New York State Museum, Survey Project No. 2, Albany, 2004.

Sparling, Reed, *Rescuing Hallowed Ground*, Hudson River Valley Review, Marist College, Poughkepsie N.Y. August 2002. 23-27.

A concise account of the restoration and archeological efforts at Fort Montgomery and manyinteresting details of the battle from primary sources.

3. Koke and Carr,5

Journals of the New York Provincial Congress, 1,179-180

4. Koke and Carr, 17.

5. Diamant, Lincoln N., *Chaining the Hudson,* New York: Carol Publishing Co.,1989.

   A similar chain was stretched across the Hudson at West Point in 1778.

6. McDougall, Alexander, *General McDougall's Diary-Extracts,* Report into the loss of Forts Clinton and Montgomery, April 5,1778, Vol. III.

7. Colonel Lewis Dubois was born in 1728 at New Paltz, New York. Appointed captain in 1775 in Col. James Clinton's Regiment, served in Canadian Campaign. Appointed colonel of the 5th New York Regiment in Nov. 1776. Commander at Fort Montgomery in 1777. Led the 5th Regiment on the Clinton- Sullivan Campaign of 1779. Resigned in 1779, died Ulster County 1802.   From Address of E.M. Ruttenber, Esq. Newburgh N.Y. Historical Society.

8. Mayers, Robert A., *The War Man*, Yardley, Pa: Westholme Publishing, 2009, 61.

9. Muster Rolls for the New York 5th Regiment July, August, November and December 1777. National Archives

10. My description of the details of the battle is based on the testimony of the people who participated in or witnessed this fierce combat:

    General Alexander McDougall's Report into the loss of Forts Clinton and Montgomery, Fishkill., April 5,1778

    Sir Henry Clinton, *Clerical copy of report on the Battle of Fort Montgomery, New York, October 9,1777,* manuscript (11 pages), Guilder Lehrman Collection, New York Historical Society.

    Clinton George, General and Governor Clinton's explanation of the battle, Court of Inquiry into the loss of Forts Clinton and Montgomery, February 1778.

    Barber John W. and Howe, Henry, *Historical Collections of the State of New York, Account by "a gentleman" who was at Fort Montgomery when it was taken, Written three days after the battle. Orange County, New York*: S. Tuttle 194 Chatham Square, N.Y. 1841, 422

Revolutionary War Pensions, National Archives. Many personal details provided by the soldiers at the battle are revealed by examining their pension applications filed in 1818 and 1821. Note, for example, the document of Private Benjamin Lattimore 2nd Company, 5th New York Regiment, an African American soldier who was captured at the battle and escaped.

Leggett, Abraham, *The Narrative of Major Abraham Leggett*, New York: Charles H. Bushnell, 1865.

Pawling Henry, *The Journal of Henry Pawling*, Olde Ulster Historical and Genealogical Magazine, Huguenot Historic Society, New Paltz, N.Y. January 1906, 335-366. Lieutenant Pawling was captured at Fort Montgomery. His diary describes treatment of the captured Americans and their captivity on a prison ships.

11. Slater Elizabeth, *Doodletown: Hiking through History in a Vanished Hamlet on the Hudson,* Palisades Interstate Park Commission Press.

    A comprehensive history of this ghost town beginning with its first settlement in1762. It focuses mostly on history after the Revolutionary War. 1996.

12. Fort Montgomery Visitors Center, 690 Route 9W P.O. Box 213, Fort Montgomery, NY 10922.

13. Colonel Mongo Campbell, 1728- 1777 served as Captain with the 46 Regiment of Foot Royal Highland Regiment. Killed in Battle at Fort Montgomery. Little is known about him. Most prominent British officers were on the Philadelphia campaign at that time.

14. Ephraim Fenno, 2nd Lieut Knox's Artillery Regt. Continental Army in 1776, Captain Colonel Lamb's 2nd Continental Artillery in 1777. Taken prisoner at Fort Montgomery October 6, 1777. He continued to serve in Corps of Artillery, 1783-1784. Historic Register of Officers of the Continental Army, Washington, D.C. Francis Bernard Heitman, The Rare Book Publishing Co.,Inc., 1914

15. John Vaughan, General, born 1738. Accompanied Cornwallis to America in 1775. Participated in the Battle of Long Island and Fort Montgomery. and was later assigned to the Carribean area in 1779. Died in the West Indies in 1791

16. Beverly Robinson was a wealthy and politically prominent New York Loyalist who entered the British military service. He was commissioned a colonel and personally raised a regiment known as the Loyal American Regiment. He also commanded acorps called the Guides and Pioneers. Robinson was heavily involved in the treason of Benedict Arnold and it is generally believed that he was acquainted with the traitor's purpose before it was known to Sir Henry Clinton. He accompanied John André to Dobb's Ferry to meet Arnold before the two conspired to plan the fall of West Point.

17. Johnson, James M. PhD. *A Warm Reception in the Hudson Highlands*, Sea History, Autumn 2001. The action of the fleets in the river below is superbly described by Johnson a retired colonel, US Army, Director of the Military History Department at West Point Military Academy and later Executive Director of the Hudson River Valley National Heritage Area. Colonel Johnson is this historic area's most prominent historian and an active participant in the 5th New York Regimental Re-enactors.

18. Leggett, Abraham, Journal.

19. General Alexander McDougall's Report into the loss of Forts Clinton and Montgomery.

20. Conley, Jan Sheldon, *The Battle of Fort Montgomery- A Short History*, Purple Mountain Press, Ltd, Fleischmans, N.Y. 2002. 22.

    This concise account of the battle was written by a descendant of David Rose, a militia man, who lived less than a mile away from the Forts. It describes his experiences at the time of the battle, provides a chronology of events and early attempts at archeology of the site.

21. Pawling Henry, Jounal

22. Koke andParr, 59

23. Lossing, Benson, J., *The Pictorial Field Book of the Revolution, Harper and Bros. N.Y. 1860.*

24. Reginal Pelham Bolton and Edward Hagman Hall,

    Pioneer archeologists who conducted the first systematic exploration of the Fort Montgomery battle site in 1916-1918.

25. Lenik-- Lenik, Edward, *A Tour of Fort Montgomery Historic Site,* Transcribed and edited by Dr. Carol Siri Johnson, May 2000 www. fortmontgomery.org, 1-18. This work describes all major features of the site with historic and archeological commentary and color pictures.

26. Fischer, *The Most Advantageous Situation in the Highlands.*

27. Fort Montgomery Battle site Association, Formed 1997 it has been a strong advocate for the preservation and enhancement of the site with the State of New York. P.O. Box 376, Fort Montgomery, N.Y.10922.

Chapter Six

Primary Sources

There are excellent research opportunities in primary source military documents and well researched secondary sources for Jockey Hollow during the winter of 1779-1780. These materials were reviewed in the preparation of this narrative on the camp:

Thatcher, James, M.D. Surgeon Continental Army, *A Military Journal during the American Revolutionary War, from 1775 to 1783.* New York: Arno Press, 1969

Fitzpatrick, John C. *Writings of George Washington from Original Manuscript Sources, 1745-1799,* 39 vols. (Washington D.C. U.S. Printing Office [1931-44]

Military .Records covering Jockey Hollow during the winter of 1779-1780:

Jedidaih Swan's Orderly Book

General Orders, Headquarters Morristown, Regimental and Brigade Orders. Period reviewed, Dec 7, 1779 to May 31, 1780

Orderly Books of the Fourth and Second New York Regiments, 1776-1783, Talmadge, Samuel, Albany: University of the State of New York, 1932.

Shelly, Fred,ed. Ebenezer Hazzard's Diary, New Jersey During the revolution, New Jersey Histpory, XC, Autumn, 1978, 169-180.

Secondary Sources

A History and Guide, Morristown National Historic Park, Division of Publications, National Park Service, U.S. Dept. of the Interior, Washington, D.C. 1983, Guidebook to JH.

Websites Morristown National Historic park: www.cr.mps.gov/history/outline.

 www.preservationnj.org, www.nps. gov/morr

Cunningham, John T., *The Uncertain Revolution*, Cormorant Publishing, West Creek N.J. 2007. This superb description of the winters at Morristown by an esteemed New Jersey Historian also covers other significant military and political events of the Revolution and an account of the development of Morristown into the country's first National Historic Park in 1933.

Otten, William L., *Colonel J. F. Hamtramck*, William l. Otten, Jr., Port Aransas, TX. 1997, 231-238.

Mayers, Robert A. *The War Man-The True Story of a Citizen Soldier Who Fought from Quebec to Yorktown*, Yardley Pa. Westholme Publishing, 2009, 123-142.

2. Smith, Samuel Stelle, Winter at Morristown, 1779-1780,Monmouth Beach, N.J. Philip Freneau press, 1979.

3. A History and Guide, Morristown National Historic Park.

   Thatcher, 180-198.

4.Buchanan, John, The Road to Valley Forge-How Washington Built the Army that Won the revolution, Hoboken, N.J: John Wiley and Sons, Inc. 2004.

5. The Washington Association of New Jersey founded in 1784 is one of the oldest preservation organizations in the nation. It' s mission is to preserve and maintain the Jacob Ford mansion, Known as Washington's headquarters in Morristown N.J.

6. Tallmadge, Orderly Book, 4th New York Regiment. Headquarters, Morristown, Dec. 21, 1779 205

7. Talmadge, Orderly Book, 4th New York Regiment Headquarters,

Morristown, Dec. 7, 1779, 191.

8. Martin, Joseph Plum and Sheer George, *Private Yankee Doodle*, Boston Little Brown, 1962.

For another account by a soldier at Jockey Hollow see:

Greenman, Jeremiah, *Diary of a Common Soldier in the American revolution 1775-1783*, de Kalb, Ill: Northern Illinois University press, 19178.

9. Mayers, 126, 127.

Thatcher, 188,189.

10. Talmadge, Samuel, Orderly Books. Descriptions of court martial hearings and punishments are described in all orderly books of the Regiments at Jockey Hollow almost on a daily basis

Mayers, 136, 137.

Thatcher, 195-197

11. Major Christopher Richardson to Major General Horatio Gates, June 15, 1783, Horatio Gates Papers, New York Public Library.

12. Carp E. Wayne, *To Starve the Army at Pleasure*, University of North Carolina Press, Chapel Hill, N.C: 1990.

Chapter Seven

The definitive work on the battle of Monmouth is William Stryker's book published in 1927. While it is well done in most respects, the description on the battle is confusing. The account is riddled with patriot fervor that typified the writing of that time and results in it being that he is unobjective and dated. A new comprehensive work on Monmouth interpreting the event in the light of the recent archeology is overdue on this pivotal event in American history.

Joseph Bilby and Katherine Bilby Jenkin's 2010 work, *Monmouth Courthouse*, published by Westholme in 2010, is an admirable and well written account. It frames the battle in the broader history of Monmouth

County and its analysis of the commanders and weapons of both armies makes it a fascinating read.

These works, along with the review of the primary source reports of Washington's letter to the Continental Congress and Sir Henry Clinton's report to Parliament on the battle as well as the court-martial proceeding of Charles Lee are essential reading for the best comprehension of the events of the campaign and battle.

1. Stryker, William S. *The Battle of Monmouth,* Port Washington N.Y., London: Kenekat Press, 1927.

   Sivilich, Daniel M., Stone, Gary W., *The Archeology of Molly Pitcher, The Royal Highlanders and Colonel Cilley's Light Artillery,* 16 pages, Library, Monmouth Battlefield Visitors Center Collection.

   Stone, Garry Wheeler, Sivilich Daniel M., Lender Mark Edward. *A Deadly Minuet: The Advance of the New England "Picked Men" against the Royal Highlanders at the Battle of Monmouth",* The Brigade Dispatch, 1996.

   Peebles, John, The Diary of a Scottish Grenadier, Edited by Ira D. Gruber, Army Records Society (Great Britain), Stackpole Books, 1998.

2. *Jones, Thomas, History of New York During the Revolutionary War,* N. Y: Trows Printing and Bookbinding Co.,1879, Vol. 1, 236-237.

3. *Parliamentary Register or History of the Proceedings and Debates of the House of Commons,* Vol. XI, 465.

4. Sparks, Jared, *Writings of George Washington,* Boston: American Stationers Co. 1837, Vol. V, 323.

5. *Journals of the Continental Congress, January 1, 1778,* Washington, D.C: Library of Congress, US Printing Office, 1904-1937, Vol. IV, 347-354.

6. Sparks, Jared, For Washington's opinion of the concessions see Letter to John Bannister, Delegate to Congress from Virginia, Vol. I, 321.

7. Moore, George H., *The Treason of Charles Lee; Major General, Second in command of the American Army of the Revolution,* N. Y: Charles Scribner, 1858.

8. Lowell, *The Hessians and Other Auxilliaries of Great Britain in the Revolutionary War,* 47.

9. *Journal of Captain John Montresor,* Pennsylvania magazine of History, Vol VI, 189.

10. Stryker, 52.

11. The New Jersey Gazette, July 1 1778. Burlington and Trenton, N.J: Library of Congress.

12. Clarke, Alured, *Lieutenant Colonel Clarke's Order Book,* British Seventh Regiment of Foot, June 21, 1778.

13. Ewald, Johann, Diary, 84.

14. Stryker, 84.

15. Woodward, E. M., *History of Burlington County,* Philadelphia, Pa: Everts and Peck, 1883.

16. See these sources for accounts of the British march

Ward, 574, Andre 77,78. Green, F. V. 143. Dawson Vol. 1. 415,416.

17. General Clarles Lee's Court-martial Transcript- *General Court Martial, Headquarters, Brunswick, July 4, 1778,* Lord Stirling, President.

18. Washington's to Henry Laurens, President of the Continental Congress, Englishtown, July 1, 1788.

19. Sir Henry Clinton to Lord George Germaine, Colonial Secretary of George III, New York: July 5, 1778.

20. Sivilich, Daniel M., Analyzing Musket balls to Interpret a Revolutionary War Site, Historical Archaeology, 1996,30(2):101-109.

Chapter Eight

1. The Sullivan-Clinton Campaign and the conquest of the Iroquois Nations has been well documented with biographies, diaries and histories prepared by participants in the events. In this narrative I have relied on these

primary sources and other original records.

Orderly Books of the Fourth New York Regiment, 1778-1780, Albany, N.Y: University of the State of new York, 1932. (referred to as Tallmadge.)

Samuel Talmadge was a staff officer in the New York Brigade during the campaign and provided details of the activities of Clinton's troops almost on a daily basis. This account is a treasure trove of information on troop movement, locations, discipline and other details of military life.

Orderly Book of Lieutenant Henry Dodge of the 5th New York Regiment, MSSL1994.1.447195 pages, Society of Cincinnati Library, Washington D.C.

Dodge was with Clinton's Brigade from August 9 to November 11, 1779 and described activities at camps along the Susquehanna, River, Tioga, Oswego, Canajoharie, Easton, West Point and other places.

Muster Rolls, Regimental Records by Company Units, National Archives.

These original records were headcounts for each company taken on a monthly or bimonthly basis. They show the name, rank, enlistment information and status of all officers and men and note those killed or missing, those on duty elsewhere, deserters and the sick.

Rogers, Wiliam Rev., *Journal of a brigade Chaplain in the Expedition Against the Six Nations,* Rhode Island Historical Tracts No.7, Sidney S. Rider, 1879. Complete text on line: Ancestry.com.

Barr, John, *John Barr's Diary,* Extracted from Orderly Books of the Fourth New York Regiment, 1778-1780, The Second New York Regiment, 1780-1783 by Samuel Tallmadge Prepared for publication by Almon W. Lauber, PhD., of the Division of Archives and History, Albany, The University of the State of New York, 1932.

This work provides interesting personal experiences, weather reports and insights into the daily lives of soldiers.

Sproule, Moses, The Western Campaign of 1779: *The Diary of Quartermaster Sergeant Moses Sproule.,* R. W. G. Vail, ed., New York Historical Society Quarterly, 41, 1957.

Journal of Major General John Sullivan Against the Six Nations of

Indians, 1779, Auburn, N.Y.: Knapp, Peck and Thompson, New York Genealogical and Biographical society, 1887. Harburn, Todd E., *The Sullivan Clinton Campaign and the Battle of Newtown from Two Original Accounts,* (British 60th Royal American Regiment), Burning Issues Newsletter, Volume 12, Issue 1. March 2004.

Shoharie, N.Y: Burning of the Valley Military Assn. The Burning Issues Newslettler 225th Preview, 2003.

Secondary Sources that I found well researched and unique in their depiction of the Sullivan-Clinton Campaign:

Williams Glenn F., *The Year of the Hangman,* Yardley, Pa.: Westholme Publishing, 2005.

Mintz Max., *Seeds of Empire, The American Revolutionary Conquest of the Iroquois,* New York,: New York University Press, 1999.

Otten, William L. Jr., *Colonel J.F. Hamtramck, His Life and Times, Volume One, 1756-1783,* Port Aransas TX.: published by William L. Otten, Jr. 1997.

Davis, Nathan, *History of the Expedition Against the Indian Nations,* Pliny H. White, US Center of Military History-The Continental Army, New Hampshire,1868.

2. Hagan, William T., *Longhouse Diplomacy and Frontier Warfare*, Albany, N.Y: New York State Education Department, 57

3. Stone, W.L., *The life of Joseph Brandt-Thayendanega: Including the Border Wars of the American Revolution, New York:* A.V. Blake, 1838.

4. Hagan, 9.

5. Hagan, 35.

6. Mintz, 14.

7. Yesteryears, Quarterly Magazine of New York State History, Volume 19, No. 75, Spring 1976.

8. Cherry Valley is a town in Otsego County, New York, northeast of the city of Oneonta.

9. *Account of the Tory and Indian Attack on the Wyoming Settlement,* Poughkeepsie, N.Y: New York Gazette, July 20, 1778.

Raphael, Ray, *A Peoples History of the American Revolution*, Harper Perennial 2002, 202-205

Battle and Massacre of Wyoming, Historical Address at the Wyoming Monument July 3, 1878 by Steuben Jenkins Wilkes-Barre, Pa.

10. *The Battle of Minnisink-Colonel John Hathorn's Official Report*, Wisconsin Historical Society, Draper Manuscript Collection, Vol. 20F, 35.

11. George Washington to Major General John Sullivan, headquarters, Middlebrook, May28, 1779 Fitzpatrick Vol. 15, 171-173.

12. Adamiak, Stanley J., *The 1779 Sullivan Campaign, A Little Known Offensive Strategic to the War, Breaks the Indian Nation's Power,* A research paper, Pennsylvania State University, www.earlyamerica.com/review,1998,Sullivan.html

13. Poor was a ship-builder from Exeter, N.H. He was appointed colonel in the 3rd New Hampshire Regiment in 1775 and was at the battles of Saratoga and Monmouth. He became brigadier general in 1777and was mortally wounded in a duel in 1781.

14. Catherine's Town was an Iroquois town named for the Seneca leader Catherine Montour. It was located at the south end of Seneca Lake, near present-day Watkins Glen . The towns of Catharine, Montour, and Montour Falls are all named for Catherine Montour

15. Sproule, Footnote 61, 29

16. "The Documentary History of the State of New York", by E.B. O'Callaghan, M.D.; Albany NY: Weed, Parsons & Co., 1850 , Vol. text of treaty of 1768 379–381.

The Treaty of Fort Stanwix between North American Indians and the British Empire was signed in 1768 at Fort Stanwix, located in present-day Rome, New York. It was negotiated between Sir William Johnson and representatives of the Six Nations (the Iroquois).

17.Williams, 290.

18. Mintz, 183.

Stember Sol, *The Bicentennial Guide to the American Revolution, Volume I,* New York: Dutton and Co. Inc., 1974 142- 161.

An interesting personal visit in 1974 along the path of the expedition that describes the places as they appeared that year.

Chapter Nine

1. William Nelson and Charles A. Shriner, *Paterson and its Environs,* New York: Lewis Historical Publishing Co. 1920. This coverage of events at the Pompton Preakness Valley during the revolution provided the most thorough account I found in researching this area.

   The Location of the American Army at Totowa and Preakness, N.J. and Vicinity, October and November 1780., filed as a copy, Karpinski Collection, Map Division, New York Public Library.

2. History of Wayne Township, Wayne Township Historical Commission, 475 Valley Rd. Wayne, N.J.

3. Brubaker, Robert M., *A Wondrously Beautiful Valley, A Commemorative History of Wayne N.J.,* Wayne Township Bicentennial Committee, 1976.

   Berce, William, Under the Sign of the Eagle, Wayne Township Historical Com., Louis Borgetts, 1964.

   An Online Guide to Discovering the Role of New Jersey in the Revolutionary War and the Nation's Founding. Wayne New Jersey Revolutionary War Sites • Wayne New Jersey Historic Sites.

4. Nelson and Shriner, 242,243.

   Berce, 1-41.

5. Nelson and Shriner, 245.

6. Washington, George, Head Qrs., New Jersey, July 16, 1780. *The Writings of George Washington from Original Manuscript Sources,* University of Virginia.

7. Bason-Wildes, Harvey Emerson, *Anthony Wayne: Trouble Shooter of the American Revolution,* New York: Harcourt Brace and Co., 1941.

Stille, Charles J., *Major General Anthony Wayne and the Pennsylvania Line,* Philadelphia Pa: Lippencott Co., 1893, Vol. I, 219

8. Cappazucca, John, Federal Hill : *An Extroadinary Environmentally Sensitive and Historically Significant Area,* Executive Summary, prepared for the Passaic River Coalition and the Borough of Bloomingdale, August 1,2001.

Nelson and Shriner, 438-441, 261,263.

Thatcher, James, MD, Military Journal, Oct. 31, 1781. 302. 252,253.

Hester, Tom, *Mutiny! Ringleaders Condemned and Shot, January 27, 1781,* Bloomingdale,N.J: The Star Ledger, August 26,2001.

Zalinski, Annita, *The Pompton/ Federal Hill Mutiny,* Passaic County Historic Society Newsletter, March 2003.

9. Muster Rolls of New York Brigade at Pompton-January to June 1782.

Talmadge, Samuel, Orderly Books of the Fourth and Second New York Regiments, 768-771, 778.

10. Thatcher, October 31, 1781, 302.

11. Castellux, Francois Jean, *Travels in North America, In the Years 1780,1781, 1783,* New York, 1828,

12. Van Corlandt, 59.

13. Nelson and Shriner, 268.

14. Tallmadge, General Orders Aug. 7, 1782, Headquarters Newburgh, New York.

15. Nelson and Shriner, 267.

Sunnybank, Former Estate of Author Albert Payson Terhune, Pamphlet, (undated) Wayne Township Historical Site, Wayne, N.J.

16. French Army (Route Number 5) from Suffern to Pompton on the site of Major Bauman's, Vol I 128, 151-189. Washington-Rochambeau

Revolutionary Route. www.W3R.us.org

17. Van Cortlandt, Philip, *Revolutionary War Memoirs and Selected Correspondence of Philip Van Cortlandt*, Tarrytown N.Y:Sleepy Hollow restorations, 1976, 59.

18. The Journal of Baron Von Closen, *Evelyn M. Acomb, The William and Mary Quarterly, Third Series, Vol. 10, No. 2 (Apr., 1953), 196-236*

19. Nelson and Shriner, *265.*

20. Di Ionno, Mark, *A Guide to New Jersey's Revolutionary War Trail*, New Brunswick, N. J: Rutgers University Press, 2006. 120.

Berce, 236.

Nelson,and Shriner, 237.

21. Berce, 236.

Di Ionno, 121.

22. Township of Wayne, 475 Valley Road, Wayne, N.J. 07470.

23.-Revolutionary War Sites in Montvale N.J., New Jersey Register of Historic Places.

24. Berce, 236.

Di Ionno, 122.

Chapter Ten

1.These primary and well prepared secondary accounts were reviewed for this narrative:

Dempsey, Janet, *Washington's Last Cantonment "A High Time for a Peace,"*

Library Research Associates Inc., 1990.

This remarkably thorough account of the 12 months the Continental Army spent at the New Windsor Cantonment was prepared under the auspices of the National Temple Hill Association. Alan C. Aimone,

Military History Librarian at West Point, directed the research. Frequent and effective use of quotes from original sources makes this an excellent reference source on the period.

Castellux, Marquis de, *Travels In North America 1780, 1781,and 1782*, New York Times and Arno Press, 1968.Vol 1:126.

Corning, Elwood A., *Washington at Temple Hill*, Lanmere Publishing Co., Newburgh, N.Y. 1932. This work focuses on the personal activities of Washington during the cantonment and the other times he used Newburgh as his headquarters. A detailed description of the Falls house and other historic homes in the area is provided.

The Winter Cantonment of the American Army and its Vicinity for 1783. A military Map by Simeon DeWitt, Geographer to the Army, made for George Washington. This map is of great value since it provides the layout of huts, roads, mills, churches and historic houses in the Cantonment area. Collection of New York Historic Society.

2. Nagy, John A. *Invisible Ink-Spycraft of the American Revolution*, Yardley Pa: Westholme Publishing, 2009

3.Abbatt, William, *Memoirs of major General William Heath* ed., William Heath Diaries and Papers, Massachusetts, Historical Society, 1901.

Thatcher, James, MD, Military Journal, Oct. 30, 1782. 323.

4. Corning, Elwood A. *Washington At Temple Hill*, (Stirring Scenes at the falls House,) Newburgh N.Y: Lanmere Publishing,

5. Most of the officers of the army were Masons and Masonic designs and symbols may have appeared in the temple, but the building is set on a north- south basis while Masonic temples are oriented east-west. There was a proper lodge at West Point and officers may have traveled there to attend meetings.

6. Pickering, Timothy, Quartermaster General, *Timothy Pickering Papers, 1731-1927*, (Regulations for Hutting), Boston, Mass: Massachusetts Historical Society MSN-708, 31.

Diary of Ebenezer Elmer, New Jersey Line, November 7, 1782, Proceedings, new jersey Historical Society, III,1848, 101.

7.Paterson, Thomas Egleston, *The Life of John Paterson, Major General in the Revolutionary Army,* G. P. Putnam's Sons, N.Y. 1898.

A delegation of officers left New Windsor for Philadelphia on Dec 3, 1782, led by General McDougall, to present Congress with a list of grievances. The document addressed pay and officers' pensions and was signed by 14 officers.

8.Shaw, Samuel, *Journals of Samuel Shaw*, Wm. Crosly and H.P. Nicols, Boston 1817.

An eyewitness account of Washington's address of March 15, 1783.

9."A Chaplain of the Revolution: Memoirs of the Rev. John Gano." Historical Magazine, 5 (November 1861), pp. 330–335

10.Fitzpatrick, Washington papers, 26: 464-465.General Orders, Newburgh, June 2, 1783,

11.Major Christopher Richardson to Major General Horatio Gates, June 15, 1783

12.Eager, Samuel W. History of Orange County,Newburgh, N.Y: S.T. Calahan, 1846.

13.Headley, Russell, History of Orange County New York, Middletown New York: Vandusen and Elms, 1908.

Index

About the Author

As the descendant of patriot soldier Corporal John Allison, the revolution is personal to Bob Mayers. He is an active member of ten historical societies and is a frequent speaker and contributor to their publications. His service as a combat officer in both the Navy and the Marine Corps provides him with a deeper perspective of the many battles depicted in his work. He is a graduate of Rutgers University and served as an adjunct professor at Seton Hall University.

The work of Bob Mayers has been featured in *History Channel Magazine*, *Garden State Legacy* and Comcast TV programs. His writing can be enjoyed by average readers and not just hard core history or genealogy fans. His readers often comment that they regret that during their school days that they tuned out history as distant and dull. Visit him at www.revolutionarydetective.com